MUGGERS MOBSTERS & ME

by

Stephen D Smith

Nev nited

First Published in Great Britain in 2003 by

Neville-Douglas Publishing Ltd
Clumber Lodge, Hemingfield Road,
Wombwell, Barnsley S73 0LY

©Stephen D Smith 2003

A CIP record for this book is available
from the British Library

ISBN 1 901853 07 1 Paperback

Website: www.stephendsmith-author.co.uk

Typeset by Mac Style Ltd, Scarborough, N. Yorkshire
Printed in Great Britain

CONTENTS

FOR JENNIFER AND REBECCA

ACKNOWLEDGEMENTS

The Author wishes to acknowledge the following:

Dr K D Bardhan; Jeremy Beadle; Barbara Bramall; James Brandon; Graham 'Bodger' Broom; Ernesto Booth; The Ernest Booth Trio; ColourBooks Ltd; Keith Copley; Neil Crossland; Doctors and Staff of Rotherham District General Hospital; Dave Eastwood; Sue Econicoff; Jon Ford: Lewis 'The Mad Scotsman' Frame; Tom 'The Hemingfield Fussilier' Furniss; Christopher 'Goody' Good; Michael Jarvis; The Estate of Tim Johnson Deceased; Peter Large; David 'Bader' Lidster; Andrew Lovell; Donaldo Morton; Jeni Morton; Neville-Douglas Publishing Ltd; Tim 'Tenbelly' Norburn; Kevin O'Donovan; Sean 'Pagey' Page; Lionel Parker; Trevor Purdy: Rotherham Magistrates Court; Michael Smallwood: Jennifer M Smith; Rebecca Eve Smith; Jeff Taylor; Max Tuouy; Stagewear Unlimited; Martin Ward; Steven Wilford; Wilford Smith Solicitors; the memory of Ethel, Neville and Douglas Smith and Albert.

FOREWORD

This is a book of Yorkshire tales recounted by Stephen Smith. Being one of Yorkshire's leading solicitors you won't be too surprised to find most of them involve the law – both sides.

Being a nancy southerner, when reading these stories I hope you will forgive me for saying that things don't happen like this round our way.

Like most parts of the country we do have our fair share of robbers, swindlers and gangsters, except down here we call them professional city businessmen. Up north you call them by their more descriptive, accurate, personalised names such as Eightbelly, Pigpen, Knuckles and Skullcracker.

Talking of names I particularly enjoyed Stephen's story about the racing pigeon called Arse, named by Jack, one of whose sons was called Venn – "It should have been Ken But I 'ad flu when I registered him." (Plonkers Plaintiffs & Pleas).

Stephen is a naturally gifted storyteller but he possesses the even rarer talent to be able to place the tale in print so it reads as he speaks – a real treat as anyone who has heard Stephen spin a yarn will happily agree.

As a student of crime, I have read many superb writers chronicle the bloody legacies of chilling horrors, the sneaky cunning of master criminals and the single-minded dedication of the hunters.

These are things Stephen ignores!

What he does with wit, compassion and irony, is to capture the absurdities of northern criminal lore that make his books such perfect companions.

As a keen supporter of fair play and justice I know Stephen as a fantastic defender of the underdog, the dispossessed and the unfortunate. Perhaps one day he'll turn his writing talents into recounting some of those stories where he has set about redressing miscarriages of justice.

For now, I'm delighted to have yet another collection of his wonderfully whimsical stories that concentrate on the funnier side of his legal life.

I heartily recommend this book to all lovers of mischief and mirth – even those who live down south!

Jeremy Beadle
Down South
October 2nd 2003

PREFACE

It seems a long time since we released 'Boozers Ballcocks & Bail', the first in the comedy series. 'Boozers' has proved to be one of the best things I ever did and I've been thrilled to hear from so many people who appreciated it. It's due to them and their kindness that I've gone back to the drawing board to produce 'Muggers'. At the time of writing this Preface 'Boozers' has been re-printed four times so consequently I am delighted to say there are at least sixty copies out there doing the rounds!

One appreciative reader was kind enough to tell me that she had borrowed all my books to read on more than one occasion.

"You've not bought one then?" I asked.

"Not likely," she replied, "you don't have to buy them from the library and all your relatives can borrow it. It saves them money too."

It's no wonder I'm not famous!

I knew it would be Christmas when this book came out for the publisher said,

"It will be a cold day when we publish this".

I am lucky because I have some great pals who are such an important part of my life and I thank them for once again allowing me to tell of their adventures and mine and to those clients whose names have been changed to protect me!

May I just thank everyone who has been involved in the production of this book for their work and effort and for putting up with the constant alterations and changes to the text. I also thank my pal, Martin Ward, for his noting and correction of anomalies which occurred in the manuscript. I wish to give particular thanks to Jeremy Beadle for his kindness and for writing the Foreword.

So here is number four, whether there will ever be another depends entirely upon you and how many times the library lends it out. Whichever – thank you very much.

Stephen D Smith
Yorkshire, 2003

INTRODUCTION

"Is that Steve Smith?"

"Yes, it's me and may I say Merry Christmas to you Albert."

"Ay. Listen…"

"I am listening."

"These coppers 'ave got me locked up 'ere in the police station at Rotherham."

I resisted the temptation to say, "Oh, really? I thought you were phoning from the British Embassy in Guatemala," but then I realised just how upset Albert would be, under arrest on Christmas Day. I also remembered that I was a solicitor who had taken a solemn oath not to whinge and whine when being interrupted or inconvenienced on days off by clients, some of whom really didn't deserve it. Then I also remembered that Albert's family were my best clients and had bought me a watch, which I threw away in the River Don because I thought Albert had pinched it. Pricked by conscience I decided the only proper thing to do was to help him as best I could.

"Well Albert, you'd better tell me all about it but as a matter of interest, how did you know I would be at home?"

"I'm septic."

"You're what?"

"I'm septic."

"I think you mean psychic don't you?"

"No, septic."

"Oh well, I suppose you were right first time – go on tell me what has happened."

I heard Albert take a deep breath and then he began.

"Well," he said, "you know me…"

"Yes, I do," I replied, "I most certainly do."

"Well," said Albert, "You'll never believe this…."

And do you know he was right!

Chapter One

LOCKED UP FOR CHRISTMAS

Poor old Albert, the erstwhile son of Jack and Madge Heptonstall, professional small-time criminals of Canklow, Rotherham, South Yorkshire, had found himself locked up in Rotherham police station on Christmas Day and he wasn't pleased. He hadn't done anything wrong and yet the police had had the audacity to arrest him on a charge of burglary with intent.

I was his solicitor and had acted for the family for a number of years; in fact I had built my practice upon their patronage.

Fortunately I had not been drinking alcohol and consequently was fit to drive and heed the call to offer my humble services to a person in need. In short, I couldn't get out of it so I disregarded my family's pleadings (in fact there were none as they were all asleep) and prepared to set off on the ten mile journey to the nick, wearing a brand new jumper and shirt, with Father Christmas socks. For obvious reasons I changed from the new joke slippers I had been given, which made a noise resembling someone breaking wind when you put your right foot to the floor. My frost-covered car had changed colour from gold to silver only to turn back to gold again when the engine had warmed up.

It was surprising how many people were out and about on Christmas Day, hurrying here and there, carrying decorated Christmas bags of all shapes and sizes. It was even more surprising that they were speaking to strangers and wishing each other the compliments of the season, but how nice it would be, I thought, if that attitude prevailed all year.

I drove past the local Elephant and Castle public house at Hemingfield run by my friend Brad, an ex-professional footballer whose "knees had gone" but who was famous in the area for his beer cellar. The sound of Slade's *Merry Christmas Everybody* was booming out through an ever-welcoming door, heavily laden with holly and a sprig of mistletoe, which had been trapped between the door and the frame by some irreverent traveller on the way in. Despite its welcoming glow I was in no mood for frivolity, my Christmas evening having been spoiled by this visit to the Rotherham cells. "IT'S CHRISTMAS," screeched out Noddy Holder for the millionth time that week.

The next pub en route was The Artist, where some clown had spray-painted the letter "F" before the first letter of the name on the sign. A very obese lady leaned against the door jamb underneath the pub name inhaling deeply on a "roll-up" cigarette with intermittent bursts of bad language aimed at an equally obese man by the other door jamb, who appeared to be vomiting into a flower tub. I looked at the sign again and realised that she was standing in the right place.

As I arrived at the large island on the outskirts of town, a party of Christmas revellers in fancy dress laughed their way onto the central island where they played "ring a ring of roses" around one of the beacons. They were an unusual mix of cowboys and indians who were joined by a balding Hitler and another remarkably obese lady dressed as an angel who kept referring to a Knight of the Round Table as a "twat". It was a pretty remarkable thing for an angel to say but then I think she was related to the lady I had seen earlier holding up the side of the building at "The Fartist", three miles before.

I got to the police station and trudged lethargically up the five steps or so to the door, to be greeted by an ageing and nicotine-stained picture of Father Christmas in a circle stuck onto the window. Someone had scratched his head off. I looked beyond my decapitated friend and pushed open the door to see an elderly gentleman, who was stretched out along the plastic-backed seats, snoring loudly accompanied by the eerie sound of the wind whistling through a partly opened door nearby. The civilian receptionist greeted me.

"Good evening and Merry Christmas Mr Smith," she said with a false smile.

I replied in an equally false tone, "Good evening and a Merry Christmas to you too," although our circumstances decreed that there would be no merriment at all.

"What brings you to the Rotherham police station?" she asked.

"I've come to emulsion the ceilings," I said sarcastically.

"Oh, you are a one!" said the receptionist, giggling uncontrollably.

"Oh Mary, come on home, all is forgiven," mumbled the drunk as he turned over to make himself more comfortable.

"Who's your friend?" I asked as he broke wind.

"Oh, he's had one too many."

"Get away," I replied. "I could do with a pint of what he's had."

"Yes. He's been there for an hour or so and he's just sleeping it off. We can't be bothered to nick him because the cells are full and Sergeant Whitehouse has had enough."

When Sergeant Whitehouse had had enough he had certainly had enough.

Sergeant Geoffrey Whitehouse wasn't the most pleasant of gentlemen. He had lived most of his life in the Regional Crime Squad before his elevation to sergeantdom in the custody area of the local "nick". He revelled in the title of "the unhappiest man in the world" and his customers referred to him non-affectionately as Sergeant Shitehouse.

"This is the third bleeding Christmas I've had to work," said the Sergeant as he banged down his pen on the custody office counter.

I saw no point in saying that I felt the same way because he wouldn't have listened and I doubt very much if he would have cared.

"Now Mr Smith, what delight brings you to the cells on a crisp and somewhat murky Christmas night?"

"Duty calls sergeant, for the third Christmas in a row," I replied sarcastically.

The sergeant sneered before dismissing what I had said as complete folly, without substance or humour.

"I've got Albert Heptonstall in the cells."

"Oh yes," said the sergeant, "and you've also got Frank Tooling."

"Frank Tooling, who's he when he's at home?" I enquired despondently realising that my quick visit to the cells was being extended by the minute.

The sergeant took up the custody record of the redoubtable Mr Tooling and read it out.

"Frank Tooling – they caught him up the Christmas tree in town and he wouldn't come down, saying if the police wouldn't leave him alone he would jump off and plunge to his death. Despite the officer's attempts to shake him off and grant his wish he eventually climbed down of his own volition, whereupon he was arrested for being drunk and disorderly and brought to the police station – and, he's staying."

Sergeant Whitehouse had spoken and it meant that the aforesaid Mr Tooling was not getting bail. He would be spending Christmas night in the cells and would be put before a special court on Boxing Day morning and guess who was covering that court for my firm?

I turned to move towards the cell area only to be disturbed by the Sergeant again.

"You've not done yet!"

"Don't tell me there's somebody else?" I enquired disappointedly.

"Too right," said the sergeant, smiling for the first time that day. "I'm delighted to tell you you've got Zippy Jones locked up."

The very mention of the name, especially on Christmas Day, struck horror into my already tortured soul. Zippy, or Ian Malcolm Jones to use his full name, had gained considerable notoriety in legal and police circles as a persistent offender but he took exception to being locked up. In a most unusual and bizarre manner, Zippy was given to acts of self-mutilation when he was locked up but he was a self-mutilator with a difference. There is no easy way to tell this story and whilst it is true, I appreciate it probably sounds more like fantasy than anything else but then who could make up the story that follows?

Zippy was given to acts of the most dreadful and spine-tingling type of self-abuse. He was a man who was a stranger to fear, with a wanton disregard for his own health and welfare. I had dealt with them all over the years; the wrist-cutters, the drug-takers, the overdose merchants and the drinkers of rare quality, but none quite like Zippy. His party trick was inserting old nails and zips (hence the pseudonym) forcibly down the end of his penis. On one occasion he had actually inserted a piece of broken glass, with horrendous results. Zippy was going through a very bad patch and ended up being locked up on more occasions than I care to mention. He spread his patronage amongst two or three firms of solicitors, most of whom winced at the thought of visiting him in the cells for fear of witnessing one of his remarkable feats.

It was Christmas Day and it was my turn, and the thought of spoiling my Christmas night gave Sergeant Whitehouse great pleasure. Zippy had been arrested for a burglary at the butcher's shop, which was made more remarkable by the fact that he was in a wheelchair at the time having broken his leg shortly before. It had not stopped Zippy being involved with a co-accused whom he had refused to name.

The Sergeant gave me a brief rundown of the evidence in the case, which was that on Christmas Eve night an alarm had gone off at the local butcher's shop. Two men were seen to leave the shop, one of whom was in a wheelchair carrying a large number of joints of pre-packaged meat. A turkey was hanging unceremoniously from one of the handles of the wheelchair, balanced at the other side by a large pork pie in a string bag. The police were called to the scene and they found Zippy wheeling furiously from the town centre along Westgate in the direction of a suburb of Rotherham called Canklow. He was unable to outrun a Ford Granada marked police vehicle, so it wasn't long before he was arrested and he, his wheelchair, a number of joints of beef, a turkey and a large pork pie were taken into custody. His co-accused managed to escape and so the police were anxious to find him but Zippy was having "none of it", which in police parlance meant that he was not prepared to "grass" on his mate. I decided to leave Zippy until last and start my interviews with Albert, so I went to his cell and found him sitting head bowed with only a foam mattress for company. His face brightened a little as I entered but he was clearly depressed at being locked up, particularly on Christmas night.

"I've done bugger all Steve" said Albert.

"What's gone off?" I asked, "I thought you were going to Caroline's house for a Christmas tea?"

"I was," said Albert dejectedly, "but I must have got the wrong 'ouse and I couldn't remember the number, so I went round the back of this place but there was no one in. I was looking through the various windows to see if I could see anyone and I suppose it looked a bit dodgy at the time but then all of a sudden I thought I saw a light from one of the rooms so I stood on a bucket and was looking into the room when I felt this tap on my shoulder. It was one of the Feds and 'e told me I was going to try to burgle it. I told 'im I wasn't but 'e wouldn't believe me, but then 'e wouldn't believe me, would 'e?"

"Well didn't you explain what you were doing?" I asked.

"I couldn't. That would look good wun't it? There I am visiting the Chief Inspector's 'ouse and I arrive at the door with two coppers who want to check my story. That would look good, especially because these two coppers knew me. What would Caroline 'ave said? It would 'ave brought some reight disgrace to them and that would 'ave been a fantastic start, so I kept schtum."

"Well you daft bugger," I said, "There's no wonder they locked you up if you refused to say anything. They'll think that you were trying to screw the place."

"Yea, but you know I wasn't," said Albert indignantly.

"Yes, I know you weren't but you should have told them what you were doing there."

"'ow could I? I was just a bit septic."

"I think you mean you are a sceptic."

"Argh, that as well. What would she 'ave thought of me being brought there by two bobbies? They'd 'ave told 'im who I was and that would 'ave blown it."

"You realise you're going to be interviewed?" I asked sternly.

"Ay," said Albert, "I know that but I'm just going to tell them I was going to see somebody and I'd got the number wrong."

"If you do that you'll get charged. You must tell them where you were going."

"I can't," replied Albert.

"But you are going to be locked up."

"It's better to be locked up at Christmas than to face Caroline and 'er folks."

Albert was as good as his word and whilst he said he'd gone to visit somebody, he told the police he didn't want those people to be caused the embarrassment of having the police knocking on their door on Christmas night. Not surprisingly they didn't believe him and so Albert was charged with burglary with intent, contrary to Section 9(1)(a) of the Theft Act 1968.

"Marvellous," I thought. For once they've got him for something that he hasn't done."

I asked Sergeant Whitehouse about the prospects of bail.

"If he'd co-operated there would have been a chance of it, but the awkward little bugger wouldn't play ball," said the self-satisfied sergeant.

"To be frank with you, I can see your point, but I don't think he's committed an offence," I told the sergeant earnestly.

"You wouldn't, Mr Smith would you, because you are for the defence and we are for the prosecution."

"Oh no, not the good guys and bad guys shit," I thought to myself.

"You see, we are the good guys and you are for the bad guys."

I mouthed the words as he said them.

"So, in short, he's staying?" I asked.

"You've got it in one," said the sergeant ceremoniously.

Any other further elaboration or discussion was pointless, for Sergeant Whitehouse had made up his mind and there was my first client for the Boxing Day morning special court. From that moment the good sergeant became Sergeant Shitehouse to me as well.

6

Surprisingly Albert had taken it rather well, although I had the dubious duty of telephoning his father to tell him what had happened, something that I didn't particularly look forward to but then a phone call would have been such an impersonal thing so I decided I would call at his house on my way home, but first I had the other two prisoners to see. I walked to cell number two where the Honourable Frank Tooling was kicking his cell door demanding refreshment.

"If that bastard keeps kicking that door..."

The sergeant's words tailed off as he saw me looking across at him.

"...we will remonstrate with him," said the sergeant correcting himself.

"Wouldn't it be simpler to give him a cup of tea and something to eat?" I suggested, playing the peacemaker.

"What a good idea," said the sergeant patronisingly. "See if there's any sandwiches left in the back room Chalky," he said to PC White, his assistant.

The PC arrived with a plastic cup of hot coloured water pretending to be tea and a sandwich which curled more than Aladdin's slipper.

"This is all we've got," said the sergeant, "give him that and if it's not acceptable, tell him to shove it up his ..."

The sergeant's attention was distracted by the arrival of the police doctor who went into the sergeant's room at the back of the main desk.

"......... doctor, how nice to see you. We've got a couple in for you so far. Sorry to drag you out on Christmas night but there's nothing I could do, I'm afraid."

The doctor nodded and trudged to the medical room to set about starting his interviews.

I was in the doorway of the cell when I heard the Honourable Mr Tooling receive his sandwich.

"What the fuck do you think that is? It's got more curl than our lassie's 'tash."

"Tha can take it or leave it," said the PC.

"Well, I'll fucking leave it. That's never been a sandwich, some buggers 'ad it in rollers – get me summat reight or tha can shove it up thee arse."

"He won't do that," I thought to myself, "particularly not at Christmas," but then the Rotherham cell's cuisine always left a lot to be desired in those days, but quite why anyone would want to insert it into their rectum was beyond me.

I entered Frank Tooling's cell with a certain measure of reluctance. On the one hand it was Christmas night and on the other I had a client who didn't really think he should be there, but then if you had been dragged off a Christmas tree when you wanted to stay up there I suppose you couldn't expect any other reaction.

Unfortunately my expected greeting of, "Thank you for coming," or "How wonderful it is that you should give up your Christmas night just to spend time in a cell with an oik like me," or just a simple "Thank you," would have been enough but he didn't even offer me Aladdin's sandwich.

"Are tha gunna get me out of 'ere toneet or what," and "'as tha got any fags?" was the best he could do.

"I regret Mr Tooling that my answer to that must be "no" to the first question and, would you believe, "no" to the second one as well."

I further resisted the temptation to insert the sandwich into his left nostril when he replied,

"Tha's useless, tha's not even got me a smoke."

I resisted the temptation to say that I was a solicitor and not a tobacconist but I had long since learned that in dealing with people in that frame of mind, the last thing you should look for was a confrontation, even when referred to as a "gormless arse". I have to say that my patience was stretched to its maximum and so I decided to try a little repartee.

"If that's what you think, Mr Tooling, then there is little point in me sitting here wasting my time," and I tried the bell but someone had unscrewed it from the wall, damaging it beyond repair. I kicked the bottom of the cell door about four times to draw the police's attention only to hear Sergeant Whitehouse shout,

"If you kick that door again, we'll come in and kick your arse!".

I shouted that I was responsible whereupon my drunken friend retorted, "'e's talking to thee anyway," which I thought was remarkable repartee for the town drunk.

For once Sergeant Whitehouse was reasonably polite.

"I'm sorry Mr Smith, I hadn't realised it was you trying to get out."

That's alright Sergeant. I'm afraid there is nothing I can do for Mr Tooling. The general impression I get is that he has chosen to represent himself and the prospect of having Aladdin's sandwich shoved up my rear end doesn't really appeal." The sergeant appeared impressed until we were both treated to Tooling's tongue-lashing.

"Yer both tossers!" and with that the sergeant slammed the door closed.

"Hello Mr Tosser," I said to the sergeant, smiling. I wondered who the other one was.

I handed the sergeant Aladdin's sandwich and went to cell number three to see Zippy. Sergeant Whitehouse told me that he had been placed under constant surveillance because only a month or so before, on his last visit to the cells, he had shoved a rusty nail up the end of his penis. It had caused some tearing and the officer took great delight in explaining the effects in their most excruciating detail.

"I'll be alright," I said, growing in confidence.

"Well, so long as he doesn't shove one up you," said the PC.

I must admit that I'd not considered the prospect but deciding that discretion was the better part of valour I accepted the presence of a "guard".

Zippy was brought into the cell.

"I'm not talking to thee when 'e's 'ere," he said pointing irreverently at the PC whose chair was positioned in the doorway to the cell. "I'm entitled to a private consultation, that's the Judges' Rules," said Zippy firmly.

He was right, but then he should have known the rules, he'd been in the cells often enough, and so my mind worked computer-like on finding a discreet but polite way of explaining the officer's concerns in such a way as he would understand it and would not think that I was taking the mickey or taking the side of the police.

"You see Zip...I mean Ian, the police are fearful for your own safety and wouldn't wish you to attempt to injure or mutilate yourself in any rash or badly thought out whim or fancy, which might result in unpleasant physical consequences," I said, highly satisfied with the way I put my advice.

"Tha means 'e dun't want me to stick a nail in me prick," said Zippy.

"In a way, yes," I said nonchalantly.

"I know my rights and I'm going to take 'em."

"I think he has a point officer," I said. "I really do think he's entitled to a private consultation, but I promise you that if there's a hint of any difficulty I will shout."

"And," I thought, "so might he if he shoves a nail or similar object up his wedding tackle."

The officer left with some reluctance, agreeing to remain nearby, on the understanding that he would reappear if Zippy did anything silly. I was determined to get to the root of the problem so to speak...

"Why do you inflict so much misery upon yourself?" I asked him directly.

"If these bastards behave bad to me like, there's only one way to deal with them."

"Yes, but you could cause yourself very serious injury and from what I've been told, you wouldn't be adverse to doing it again."

Zippy just smiled.

I believed that this was his way of taking on the establishment. It was my opinion that his actions were an attempt to draw attention to himself with a view to getting his own way. Nevertheless, in an odd sort of way, I had to say I had a certain respect for someone who could tolerate such pain. If the police had done it to him they would have been prosecuted and sent down.

I asked Zippy the normal details and filled in my Legal Aid Board approved form, which was a sort of idiot's guide to dealing with crackpots in police stations. Zippy was not prepared to answer any questions and said he would exercise his right to silence. My presence was required to ensure that he didn't get "verballed". "Verballing" was the art of saying a defendant had admitted it when in fact he hadn't. We now have the Police and Criminal Evidence Act which imposes certain obligations upon the police during a defendant's incarceration in the police station. The tape recording procedure removes a lot of the anomalies that once existed when arguments arose as to who said what and when. It has been difficult to say who has come off best as a result. Some would say justice, whilst others would say that the system favours the accused, but it certainly removes a lot of doubt about what was said in interview.

Zippy stuck to his guns and despite a grilling by two determined detective constables, he reserved his right to silence and refused to answer. The content of the questions gave away exactly what evidence the police had and the accounts of three eyewitnesses who saw him speeding along Westgate, heavily laden with bootie on his wheelchair, spoke volumes about the strength of their case.

The police were satisfied that they had enough to charge him despite his silence and Zippy knew it too but he wasn't going to make it easy for them or for anyone else and when he was charged he shouted one word.

"BAIL!"

The police officer smiled because he knew that Zippy was already on bail for a shoplifting offence a week earlier. The basic rule in the criminal courts is "commit an offence whilst on bail and you will be locked up" but no matter how much this philosophy is preached, defendants still demand and, in some cases, expect bail.

"That's another one for Boxing Day morning court," I thought to myself and at that stage there were three of them.

I looked in on Albert once again before I left.

"I know this will be the end of it for me and Caroline. No matter which way it goes she's not going to want to know me for not turning up and even worse, for being locked up," he said despondently.

"But surely you'll tell her what's happened?" I asked.

There was a long pause before Albert replied in reflective tone.

"No point...it's done."

"But that's not fair Albert, she's got a right to know."

"Yeah but 'er father will get at 'er and make 'er pack me in. I don't want to get involved in that, it's not fair. 'e's a pretty decent bloke, even though 'e is a copper. Anyway, one thing's for sure, I've blown it well and truly."

I understood. It was a rather painful acceptance of what Albert thought were their differences in life. For my part, I thought that this relationship was a wonderful opportunity for Albert to keep on the straight and narrow, but circumstances were against him and this major setback would have long-term consequences for his rehabilitation.

I checked in at the custody desk and found Sergeant Whitehouse lecturing a rather diminutive character who had just failed the breathalyser. He was led away into a cell, crying and holding his arm from where the doctor had taken a sample of blood. Zippy Jones, who had been peering through the bars of his cell said that he looked like a child molester.

"You'll be going home now to a warm fire and a hot meal," said Sergeant Whitehouse irreverently as I put together my things.

"No, I'm going to Albert Heptonstall's home to explain to his family that he's locked up in a police station, hopefully about to be released by a sympathetic, caring, responsible and justice-seeking sergeant of consummate fairness."

"Well, that officer is not working tonight so tell them their crooked son is staying," replied the sergeant.

Just at that moment I noticed a sort of decoration or badge fixed to the lapel of his jacket. I asked him what it was only to be told quite sharply that it represented some society that worked for the benefit of people who suffer from epilepsy. He didn't say anything else so I left it at that. I later found out that his only daughter had been seriously injured in a road accident caused by a drunken driver and one of the legacies of her injuries was epilepsy. It was further evidence, as far as I was concerned, of how one's character is moulded by the events that fate places in our path, so probably there was a reason as opposed to an excuse for him being a shitehouse after all.

I made my way to the Heptonstall's residence reflecting upon what I was going to say and as I approached I saw a welcoming glow, as if a series of laser beams were shining out of each of the windows. It was dark and yet the house was brilliantly illuminated. Jack and Madge liked Christmas and their message for the world was clear, for across the windows and front door was an illuminated banner, which told us so. There was a neon lit Father Christmas, which had been screwed to the wall with his red nose flashing on and off furiously. Jack's technological genius had been such as to utilise some form of burglar device, which sent out a ray of light over a distance of about three feet. When anyone walked within range and broke the circuit, Santa would speak, wishing everyone a Happy Christmas.

Music was emanating from within and it became obvious that a great number of inebriated people were inside singing completely out of tune.

I rang the bell which played the song "Colonel Bogey" and the door was opened, very cautiously by Madge who peered out from an aperture of about four inches. When she realised who it was she opened the door and greeted me with a wide grin. The redoubtable Madge, wife of Jack, mother of Albert and others, the stabilising influence on the Heptonstall clan was world weary and old beyond her years. She must have been attractive as a young woman for there were still signs of beauty in that care-worn face.

She always wore a beautiful medallion, the most unusual I had every seen. I had noticed it often and complimented her on it. It was of enormous sentimental value to her and she treasured it above all things. It was based on the cross of the Knights of St John, highly decorative with a filigree surround and it was attached to a very ornate but beautiful twenty-two carat gold chain. Apparently it was given to Madge's grandmother by a Maltese gypsy and was handed down first to her mother and then to her. Madge showed it off with great pride, saying it was the only thing she had got which was perfectly 'legit'.

She turned her head as if to look backwards and shouted,

"It's Steve Smith, Jack."

A voice from within bade me enter. Half the residents of the street were in the front room and the smoke from at least fifty cigarettes made it reminiscent of the Grand Bazaar in Istanbul. In every corner of the room there were items of electrical machinery from videos to electric toothbrushes, reminding me again of Istanbul. There was a table in the centre of the room which was covered in a variety of lightbulbs and on a smaller table near to the kitchen was the infamous cooking pot, steaming full of whelk stew, a culinary delight which I had tasted at Jack's street party the year before.

I asked to speak to Jack alone and he took me into the kitchen, where I noticed a very large gentleman who looked more like the wrestler Giant Haystacks than Giant Haystacks himself. The only difference was that he was bigger and uglier than Giant Haystacks and looked far more hostile. He was emptying bottles of whisky, vodka and gin into a large pot.

"Our Barry's making some punch," said Jack proudly.

"Punch will be the word," I said, "if anyone drinks any of that".

"Ay, we like a good drink at Christmas. Anyway Steve, thanks for coming to our party. We didn't invite thee but tha's reight welcome."

"I'm afraid I didn't come to the party Jack and I'm sorry to tell you that I am the bearer of bad news."

Jack's amused look turned to concern.

"What's gone off?" he asked expectantly.

"It's Albert, I'm afraid, Jack. And there's no easy way to tell you. He's locked up at the police station and he's staying until the court tomorrow."

"Bleedin´ ´ell. What's ´e supposed to ´ave done?"

I found Jack's phrase of great interest for there was no acceptance of the possibility of guilt.

"I don't think he's done anything but the police seem to think that he was out burgling."

Jack was very annoyed and said so.

"Our Albert's been clean for ages and 'e's knocking about with a nice lass. 'e wouldn't be in bother."

I told Jack that I believed him and that as far as I was concerned he was innocent but bearing in mind the lad's instructions I wasn't able to tell him the full story.

"Anyway Steve," said Jack, "Come in and have a drink. Do you want some whelk stew?"

I remembered my last attempt at Jack's stew. I also declined a glass of Barry's punch but settled for a can of Guinness and we sat around the coal fire, which was burning brightly with what looked like a mixture of coal and portions of British Rail sleepers.

"Why won't they let 'im out?" asked Jack.

"Well, the custody sergeant had decided that he wasn't prepared to bail him, so he intends to put him before the court tomorrow morning," I replied.

"Who was the sergeant?"

"Sergeant Whitehouse," I replied.

"Oh, not Sergeant Shitehouse?"

"Yes, that's him."

"Then I'm not surprised. 'e don't like us and 'e certainly dunt like Albert."

"Well, there's nothing we can do tonight but I will be in court tomorrow morning and I'll apply for bail.

"Tha means tha'll turn out for our Albert on Boxing Day morning?"

"Yes, sure Jack. Your family are very important clients of mine."

"Tha'll do fer me Steve. Tha were always one of the lads. Can we take 'im owt; some snap or summat?"

I shrugged my shoulders.

"He ain't 'ad 'is Christmas dinner and I don't suppose they'll be owt much to eat there," he continued.

"Well there was mention of a sandwich," I said smiling.

"Ah, I bet it's that sandwich they offered me three months since."

"I wouldn't be surprised if it was," I said, "you've got the age about right."

Jack thought for a minute as his eyes narrowed almost concealing his bright blue eyes.

"I've a good mind to ring that copper up and tell 'im what I think."

"I can understand that Jack but I don't think it would do much good. It might relieve your frustration but at the end of the day, that's all. If I thought it would help Albert fair enough but you know me, I play a straight bat."

"Ah, tha does. I'll leave it and 'ope I don't bump into 'im this Christmas. Anyway Steve, 'ave another can of Guinness."

"That's very kind of you Jack but because it's Christmas Day I ought really to be back at home."

"Oh ah, of course. 'ave you bin out long?"

"Long enough," I said, not wanting to embarrass him with the exact details.

"Well," said Jack, "thanks for looking after our Albert on Christmas Day. I reight appreciate it and I'll not forget it either. 'ave you got time to 'ave a word with Granddad before you go? 'e thinks a lot about you yer know."

I think Jack was just being kind because I last met Granddad at the street party and he thought I was an undertaker, but he did save me from tasting the whelk stew when he pointed to his backside, shaking his head, so the least I could do was to say hello and pay my respects.

Within a minute Jack had wheeled in the old-timer. His hair was snowy white and it was obvious to see the genetic connection. He had the same shaped face, the same bright blue eyes and the preponderance of gum above a small row of teeth. The old fellow was confined to a wheelchair, his condition having deteriorated since my last visit.

"It's Mr Smith, the solicitor," shouted Jack at the top of his voice.

"He dunt look like a solicitor to me – 'e 'asn't got a tie on."

"Aye, that's because it's Christmas Day granddad and 'e's been out at the police station seeing our Albert."

"What's 'e bin to see 'im for?"

"'cos 'e's locked up," replied Jack.

"Who is?" asked granddad.

"Our Albert," said Jack.

What's 'e done now?"

"'e's not done anythin' Granddad, 'e's innocent."

"'e was innocent last time but 'e still got fined."

"Aye, but Steve's going to get 'im bail tomorrow."

"Who's going to take me dogs out?"

"I will Granddad, as soon as Mr Smith's gone," shouted Jack.

"Are you going with 'im?" he asked, pointing to me.

"No Granddad, I'm going to get off home and anyway your dogs don't like me."

"You want to get a solicitor for our Albert," said Granddad, "get that Steve Smith feller, "'e's alright."

"This is Steve Smith Granddad."

"Is it...? 'ow do Steve Smith, it's nice to see yer. Will you do me a favour and go down to the police station to see our Albert. 'e's got locked up for summat he's not done and by 'eck you've got to look old since I last saw yer."

It was pointless to argue, so I agreed that I would go down to see his grandson straightaway and with that I left the kitchen and went into the main room but as I was leaving Granddad shouted to me.

"Keep off the whelks!"

"Yes Granddad, I will," I said and I gave him the thumbs-up sign.

I looked around the assembled throng and thought if only the Devil could cast his net there it would clear up twenty-five per cent of the crime in Rotherham and district.

As I was about to leave, a very dark-haired man with a hare lip and a scar across his forehead tried to sell me a lawnmower. I assured him that I didn't have a lawn, in which case it would be useless to me. I didn't want to aggravate the situation by telling him that I didn't buy stolen property because he might have been insulted. So once again discretion being the better part of valour, I lied to him.

"Do you know anybody that wants to buy one?" he persisted.

"Not off hand," I said, pretending I was serious, "but if I do I will let you know."

"Alright," said the man, shrugging his shoulders as he walked away.

I noticed he was drinking from one of the largest glasses I'd ever seen; so much so that it needed both hands to hold it. It was one of those "yard of ale-type" containers that holds two-and-a-half-pints. He took a giant swig and then drew his left sleeve across his mouth to act as a serviette. The customary belch did not follow but a loud sniffle did.

As I waved to Madge the curly-haired man returned to me.

"Tha says tha's not got a lawn?"

"That's quite right, I haven't."

"What's tha got?"

"It's a yard actually. Yes, it's a concrete yard."

"Dus thas want it diggin' up?"

"No thanks, I'm quite happy with a concrete yard."

"Ah, but if tha dug it up tha could put soil in it's place."

"Why would I want to do that?"

"Because then tha could sow some grass seed."

"Yes, and then what?"

"Then when it growed you'd need a lawn mower."

"Yes, but I don't want a lawn mower, 'cos I've got a concrete yard."

"That's what I mean, I'll dig it up for yer."

"Yes, but what if I don't want it digging up?"

By this time I was getting rather annoyed with his persistence.

"There's no need to get shirty. I'm just trying to be 'elpful."

"That's alright, I didn't mean to be shirty but I like the concrete yard. It's mine, it's what I've always wanted. I like it as it is. I don't want anything else and whether it suits you or not, it's staying."

The man thought for a minute.

"Ay," he said, "do yer want some more concrete then? I'll put thee another layer on and smooth it out."

"No thank you, it's OK at it is"

"Some flags then?"

"No!"

"Does tha keep goldfish?"

I could not help but laugh. He was the most persistent man I had ever met but no matter what, the golden rule was never buy anything from people in circumstances like that and especially not if you didn't want it. I continued to laugh without reply.

"Does tha like cannabis?"

"NO!" I shouted as I closed the door. "I don't want any cigarettes, lingerie, pipe tobacco, false teeth, wigs or any fresh haddock either. I don't want any ceiling paint, rubbing oils, verruca cream or pile ointment."

"Does tha want two second-hand tyres?"

I closed the door firmly in his face.

"What about a vaulting pole?"

"Piss off!" I was exasperated.

I shook hands with each member of the gathered throng and went to my car. As I drove off the persistent salesman appeared at the passenger door and offered me a boomerang. I waved graciously with two fingers and drove on.

I went home to catch the end of the film "The Wizard of Oz" and switched over in time for "The Great Escape" and once again I missed the end, having fallen fast asleep in the chair. It was five minutes into Boxing Day when I woke. I was alone, everyone having gone to bed so I followed and typically couldn't get to sleep until the small hours and then, of course, when it got to half past seven I couldn't get up.

I got to the office by nine o'clock and waded my way through the Christmas post. There were bills, of course, and an unpleasant letter from the bank telling me amongst other things that the cost of sending the letter had been debited to our account, together with a number of Christmas cards and junk mail offering ten per cent off photocopiers, fax machines and the latest craze, mobile phones. There was a letter from one client demanding something or other by Christmas Eve at the latest and three letters from Hull Prison demanding bail for the New Year.

One of the letters asked for one thousand cigarettes, another a postal order and one in particular asked for two scooter tyres and a mouth organ.

I got to court just after half past nine expecting three prisoners but there were only two at the cell area because Zippy Jones had been carted off to the local hospital to have a splinter of wood from the cell bed leg removed from the end of his penis.

My Christmas tree climber looked decidedly ill and a far different prospect than the night before. He could remember my visit but nothing before it and when I explained the facts of his case to him, he was horrified, claiming that he suffered from vertigo and couldn't stand heights. When I asked him his reasons for getting so drunk, he told me that his wife had left him that morning, hence the celebration!

Albert was much quieter than normal. He usually went about his court appearances with a rather cavalier attitude but on this occasion he was very subdued. I went into the entrance-way to Court number one to find the prosecutor, Roger Tricklebank, smoking a cigarette furiously and mumbling under his breath.

"You look pleased to be here Roger," I said brightly.

Roger looked at me, sneered and took another massive gulp of smoke from his cigarette, before pressing his glasses back to his face.

"What we doing with these buggers?" asked Roger

"Tooling is pleading guilty and will be weighed off for the tree-felling incident, Heptonstall is pleading not guilty and I'm applying for bail and Zippy Jones has gone to have his penis emptied."

"Very funny," said Roger Tricklebank, "but what is happening to Jones?"

"I've told you…he's gone to hospital to have a splinter of wood removed from his nethers."

Roger shuddered.

"Are you being serious?" he asked.

"Deadly serious," I said. "Do you think for one minute I'd joke about another bloke's hampton?"

Roger shrugged his shoulders.

"So it looks like he won't be produced today but will be back tomorrow before the ordinary court?" asked Roger thoughtfully.

"What do you think about bail for Heptonstall?"

"Is he on bail for anything?"

"No," I replied.

"Is he pending summons for anything else?"

"No," I replied.

"Are there any T.I.C.'s or just the one offence?"

"Just the one offence," I said.

"Looks a bit thin against him, doesn't it? Has he got anything wrong with his penis?"

"Absolutely," I said, "I can't understand why he wasn't bailed last night. In fact I'm going to make a song and dance about that this morning."

We agreed conditions of bail and the Clerk of the court called us in. As I was walking through the door into Court number one I saw someone arriving on the corridor. It was Caroline, Albert's girlfriend. She was the daughter of a Chief Inspector of police and one of the most attractive girls I had seen in the area. She had formed a friendship with Albert when they worked at the local animal sanctuary. It had been the making of Albert and turned him from a scruffy oik into a well-mannered, well-meaning and honest young man. Their affinity for animals had brought them closer together but the drawback, from Albert's point of view, was the fact that Caroline was the daughter of a policeman. The Heptonstall household would not approve of the relationship if they knew her background but the same could be said of Caroline's parents if they knew about Albert's past. A special meeting had been set up so that Albert could go for his tea on Christmas Day and against his better judgement Caroline had persuaded him that he should go. The rest, as they say, is history and for perhaps the first time in his life, Albert was locked up for something he hadn't done.

"Mr Smith, may I speak with you please?"

"Of course Caroline. Come with me."

I took her into the rathole interview room at the end of the corridor, opposite the courtroom. Caroline was most put out.

"Can you tell me what's going on? I've been very worried because Albert should have been at my house at teatime yesterday. I went to Mr Heptonstall's house to be told that Albert was in court today. What is he supposed to have done?"

"Well Caroline, he's supposed to have burgled a house on your road."

"I don't believe it."

"Neither do I. I think that Albert went to the wrong address, which is hardly suprising, you know what he's like, and whilst he was looking through a window to see if he could attract anybody's attention the police arrived and put two and two together and made seventy-three."

"But Albert wouldn't burgle a house on our road. What time was he arrested?"

"About half past three."

"But that's exactly the time he was due at our house. How was he dressed?"

"Well, he'd got his best suit on," I replied.

"Well, he would hardly be out burgling in his best suit and certainly not at an address on our street where he's supposed to be visiting."

"You're preaching to the converted Caroline," I said. "I don't think for one minute he's committed an offence but the problem is he didn't give a very good account of himself at the police station."

I explained what had happened.

"You see Caroline, I don't think he wanted you to be caused any embarrassment."

"If he'd have said where he was going we would have given evidence for him," she said forcefully.

"No doubt that's true," I replied, "but you see, he was frightened of what your father might think."

I felt very sorry for Caroline, particularly because I thought the relationship was doomed from the start but there wasn't a lot I could do about it.

I was called into court by the emphysemic usher and found that my not so favourite magistrate, nicknamed the Lord Chief Justice, was sitting. He was unhappy at having to work on Boxing Day morning and his attitude did not inspire me with great confidence. My Christmas tree climber was called on first and most reluctantly entered a guilty plea to his charge, and the Lord Chief decided that because there were two magistrates sitting they could dispose of the case by sentencing him there and then.

After a lengthy lecture Frank Tooling was fined £75 and told not to do it again. I turned to face the dock, not expecting thanks but just to see my client's reaction. I was not disappointed. I did not get any thanks and as he was taken away by the police officer he mumbled something about the Magistrates' parentage.

Zippy's case was mentioned next and Keith Copley, the Court Clerk, told the Magistrates that he was in hospital.

"I'm afraid, Your Worships, that we can't deal with Ian Malcolm Jones as he is in hospital having some surgery."

"What's wrong with him?" asked the Lord Chief Justice.

"Go on, tell him Keith," I thought to myself. "Let's see his reaction when he finds out that he's got a splinter shoved up him."

"Apparently the defendant has injured himself whilst in the cell and he has had to be taken to hospital for treatment," said Keith Copley discreetly.

The Lord Chief Justice beckoned Keith forward and some whispering went on between the two of them. It was clear that the Lord Chief Justice wanted to know exactly what had happened, so Keith gave him both barrels.

"Never," said the Chairman.

"Oh yes he has," said Keith Copley.

"Never," repeated the Chairman.

I resisted the urge to join in with Keith in pantomime fashion to the strains of "Oh yes he has!"

"How very odd," said the Lord Chief Justice.

"He will be now," I thought to myself.

"Your other case Mr Smith is Heptonstall I believe?" said Keith Copley.

"Yes sir, it is and I am ready to deal with that if you please."

The usher called Caroline into court and she sat at the back on one of the old oak benches.

"Who's that?" asked Roger Tricklebank spotting the blonde-haired beauty at the back of the courtroom.

"It's the defendant's girlfriend," I replied.

"Never," said Roger Tricklebank.

"Oh not you as well, another doubting Thomas."

"I beg your pardon?"

"Never mind, but that's who it is."

I decided not to go down the route of "Oh yes it is – oh no it isn't" and then Keith Copley identified Albert.

"Are you Albert Heptonstall?"

"Yes," replied Albert solemnly.

Keith asked him for his address and his date of birth and Albert dutifully replied. The charge was put to him and he was told to sit down. Roger told the court the details and suggested that the case was suitable to be dealt with by the Magistrates and they agreed. Albert was asked where he wanted to be tried and he said that he wanted to be dealt with at the Crown Court. The Lord Chief was not impressed, even though it was Albert's right.

"What do you say about bail?" asked the Lord Chief Justice.

"Well he has convictions," said Roger, "but none of recent date and he's not presently subject to bail. I would have no objection to bail providing that conditions were attached to ensure that he did not re-offend and to ensure his attendance at court."

Roger handed in Albert's considerable list of previous convictions and the Lord Chief Justice read the list thoroughly.

"He's got a very bad record Mr Smith," said the Lord Chief Justice.

"He has Sir," I replied, "but it is some time since he offended and as you have heard my friend say, he is not on bail for any other matter."

"That's not the point," said the Lord Chief Justice.

"Oh yes it is," I thought to myself, "It is entirely the point."

It was clear to me that the Lord Chief Justice was not in favour of bail and I'd got a fight on my hands to secure Albert's release. I embarked upon a lengthy bail application, pleading all the relevant facts as I knew them and the Lord Chief Justice retired to consider the application.

"Doesn't look too good for you," said Keith Copley as he mulled over his papers.

"They can't remand him, he's not on bail and his record is old."

"Yes, but you know what the Lord Chief's like when he gets a bit of a bee in his bonnet."

"Yes, and I hope the chuffing bee stings him," I said in annoyance. I must confess I was beginning to panic a little and it was almost twenty minutes before the Lord Chief Justice returned to give his judgment.

"We think that you will commit an offence whilst on bail, so bail is refused. Take him down."

I looked at the Lord Chief Justice open-mouthed and in bewilderment and felt very much like an irreverent football manager when a penalty decision had gone against him. I borrowed a phrase from the famous tennis player John McEnroe.

"You cannot be serious," I said under my breath.

"Did you say something Mr Smith?" asked the Lord Chief Justice.

For one awful moment I very nearly did and it was one of those occasions where even only a second or two's silence seemed like an age. I chose discretion as the better part of valour.

"No sir, I didn't. Nothing of any relevance anyway."

I didn't look at Albert but I turned to leave. I gave the customary bow, which went very much against the grain.

"Do you want your remand sheet Mr Smith?" asked Keith Copley sympathetically.

"Oh yes, of course I will sir yes, for the Judge in Chambers bail application," I said defiantly.

I bowed again, even more ceremoniously than before and left the court.

Caroline was waiting for me and was very upset.

"They can't remand him in custody Mr Smith, he hasn't done anything wrong."

"I know that Caroline but I'm afraid they have. Unfortunately we had a very unsympathetic Chairman who is a bit of a hardliner."

"But they should all be the same. They shouldn't have likes and dislikes."

"I know that Caroline but unfortunately it's human nature and human nature decrees that they do."

"What can we do now?"

"I'm going to apply to a Judge in Chambers at the Crown Court for bail, but the problem is that the court doesn't open until New Year."

"You mean he'll be locked up for New Year as well?"

"I'm afraid so."

Just then Jack arrived on the corridor with a red face and completely out of breath.

"They wouldn't bloody well let me in," said Jack anxiously. "I've bin 'ammering on the door for ages and no one came until this bobby said I was damaging the door. Anyway 'e let me in. What's gone off?"

Before I could speak Caroline blurted out that Albert had been locked up.

"Fuckin' 'ell," said Jack. "Oh, excuse me miss for the language," he said apologetically to Caroline, "but they can't lock 'im up for this."

"They have done Jack I'm afraid. All we can do is go to a Judge in Chambers. What really upsets me is that the prosecution didn't oppose bail but the Magistrate was against us from the start."

"Who was it?"

"It was the one that we call the Lord Chief Justice."

"Oh, that bastard. He's got it in for our family. We've never had a result from him yet."

"The only thing we can do Jack is to apply to a Judge in Chambers as I have said and I think he will grant it."

"And when will that be?"

"After New Year."

"Oh, for fuck's sake, we can't leave him in that long."

"Well short of going down and helping him to escape there's not much we can do.

"You're not thinking of helping him to escape are you?" asked Jack.

"Don't be ridiculous Jack, it was a joke."

"Ay, alreight. So what we gonna do then Steve?"

"Well Jack, I'll prepare the application today, if I have to type it out myself, and I'll deliver it to the court and we'll get a hearing on the 3rd or 4th of January."

Jack sat back in his chair and was clearly distraught but then he would be, because Albert was his number one son.

"I don't think 'e's done it Steve."

"I know he hasn't done it Jack," I said sympathetically, "but the problem we've got is in proving it."

"I thought he was innocent until proven guilty," said Jack.

I looked at him, raised my eyebrows and smiled. I did not say anything.

"Ay, alreight Steve, I get your point but 'e really 'asn't done anything."

"I know Jack, you're pushing on an open door as far as I'm concerned. What we've got to do is try to prove it."

"Well I thank you Steve anyway, you would 'ave done your best, I know that. I would 'ave felt better if 'e 'ad done it."

"I know you would have Jack and to some extent, so would I."

I had every sympathy with Jack because on this occasion I was convinced that Albert was innocent but proving it, as Jack had said, was going to be another matter.

In a most gentlemanly fashion Jack offered Caroline a lift but she declined, saying that she wanted to have some fresh air and gather

her thoughts. She probably feared for her safety because Jack's soft-top Skoda was a death trap.

Jack took me on one side.

"She's not a bad lass, is she Steve?"

"No Jack, she isn't."

"Could you give our Albert this turkey sandwich?" he said, thrusting a cling-filmed wrapper into my hand.

"Of course I will and I'll let you know as soon as I get him before the Judge."

"Thanks Steve, I only 'ope that you can get 'im out."

Jack shook hands with Caroline and took his leave.

"I'm going down to see him Caroline, is there any message I can give him?"

"Yes," said Caroline, "tell him I'm supporting him and if there's anything I can do he's got to let me know. If it helps, I'll ask my dad to give a statement to say that he was coming to our house."

I thanked her and gave her what assurance I could, telling her that I would keep her informed of all developments. I also told her what Albert had said as unfortunately I had to honour his instructions.

My visit to see Albert took only a matter of minutes, allowing us time to share the turkey sandwich. He was very disappointed with the result but philosophical and in typical Albert fashion, he thanked me for my efforts and told me that I'd done my best. Indeed I had but sometimes some clients don't always see it that way.

"What did Caroline say?" asked Albert.

"She wants you to know she's supporting you," I said.

"That's good but I knew she would. She's a smart kid but she's picked the wrong 'un this time."

"I don't want to hear you being such a defeatist Albert," I told him. "I think we've got to look forward and not back and I think we've a very good chance of Judge in Chambers bail."

Albert smiled and nodded and held out his hand. I shook his hand vigorously and told him I'd do my best.

"You always do," said Albert, "tha's the greatest."

I thanked him and told him that his father would be coming to see him over the New Year period.

As I was walking up the spiral staircase to the court, Albert shouted after me.

"'appy New Year Steve."

He wasn't being facetious; he really meant it but it would have been easier for me if he hadn't. The jailer told me that the prison bus was on its way and that within the hour Albert would be transported to Her Majesty's Prison, Armley, Leeds, a place Jack described as "a right shit 'ole" and I'm afraid he was right.

I walked into the dingy, old and crumbling courthouse soon due for closure and recalled how much time I'd spent there over the past few years. I had seen so many of the great barristers of the day who wished they were judges and so many of the judges who had forgotten they were once barristers and depending on which side you were on, some were fair and some were not. I had good results, mediocre results and some decisions I just could not possibly have agreed with. That was how it was and I suppose how it always will be.

I was called back into court by Keith Copley who had some more news.

"The defendant Ian Malcolm Jones is to be kept in hospital and then if the doctor sanctions it, he will be returned to the police station for the next available court. Have you anything to add Mr Smith?"

"No sir, thank you," I replied.

I sat down and studiously marked up my file with an explanation as to what had happened but I was disturbed by Keith who passed me a note. It read, 'Your flies are undone'.

I thought it was Keith's little Christmas joke for he was always playing practical jokes so I wrote a suitable reply entering into the spirit of the occasion. I put, 'Trust you to spot that you fucking pervert!'

I handed the note to him with a grin, only to look in horror as without looking at it he passed the note straight to the Lord Chief Justice from whence it had apparently come in the first place. I beat a hasty retreat as he opened it and pretended I hadn't heard Keith Copley shouting me to return to the courtroom. After all it was Boxing Day and I don't accept bollockings at Christmas.

Chapter 2

I GET INVOLVED IN AMATEUR BOXING AND HE IS SPARTACUS

Every so often I was given the opportunity to work outside the usual court arena and in January of that year I had to represent a young amateur boxer who found himself having to appear before a disciplinary board of his Boxing Association who were holding their meeting at the premises of a working-men's club in York.

Mohammed Razaq was sixteen years old and an amateur boxer of considerable skill. The pundits had predicted a bright future in the noble art for this young man who was a member of a well-known Sheffield gym which had a stable of up and coming boxers. Mohammed was a youth with a bright disposition and like most boxers in training was not in the least way aggressive. I have always believed that boxers get rid of their aggression in the ring so they don't appear to be much of a problem outside even when provoked, but if you've spent most of the day beating the living daylights out of someone or something, there won't be much energy left for anything else.

There is a world of difference between amateur and professional boxing. The sleaze factor which is said to attach to the professional sector is generally absent from amateur ranks, doubtless because money doesn't come into the equation. The ruling body is different too and is made up of a number of people who have varying interests in the sport at amateur level. I found the ideology to be a little archaic but they were the ruling body and what they said went and it looked very much as if young Mohammed Razaq was the next on their list.

Mohammed's problem came about as a result of incidents just after one of his contests in the October of that year. He had fought a youth from Teesside in a championship contest at Sheffield. The bout had gone against Mohammed with a points decision in his opponent's favour. All hell broke loose after that.

There was an incident in the ring between the two boxers and then afterwards in the changing rooms a fight took place involving a number of other boxers together with parents and associates of both sides. A complaint was made by the match referee about the incident in the ring and also about the incident in the changing-room because he was there when it happened. Another complaint was made by the Teesside camp. The referee claimed that when the decision was given he drew both boxers together to shake hands and something was said with the result that Mohammed had struck the other boxer with the back of his hand and walked away. "At the very least," said the referee in his report, "this represented ungentlemanly conduct."

When the referee got to the changing room he witnessed an argument between representatives of both camps. He remembered that one adult then moved towards a member of the opposing camp and there was a scuffle which led to other people becoming involved and then a large-scale fight had occurred with some of the aggression being turned upon him. He left the changing room to seek assistance from other officials but by the time they arrived the incident had finished. The referee submitted a full report to the Disciplinary Committee, setting out what he had seen and then the Teesside group had also made a complaint, saying that their boxer had been hit in the ring after the adjudication which led to the incident in the changing room, where they were subjected to abuse, aggression and violence. The Sheffield contingent made no complaint.

The secretary at the Sheffield gym received a letter from the Board calling the boxer to appear before the Disciplinary Tribunal at York and he wanted me to represent him. I had never dealt with a boxing disciplinary case before but I imagined that the procedure would be fairly similar to police disciplinary hearings of which I had experience, so I felt confident enough to accept the commission.

Gerry, my contact from the gym, was an ex-professional boxer whose love of the sport gave him sufficient interest to start his own gymnasium. On certain days when the professionals were not in occupation he allowed the amateurs to use the facilities. Mohammed was one of his star protégés who had trained at the gym for about two years and Gerry had formed a liking for him. The passion which Gerry had for the sport had been instilled into young Mohammed and he in turn had been entranced by the skills of his hero, a professional boxer called Herrol "Bomber" Graham.

Herrol was a world championship contender and had won the British and European Championships with his most unusual style of boxing. He was elusive and had been tagged by the Press as the boxer that no one could hit and Mohammed started to emulate him to considerable effect. It was something alien to amateur boxing and of course the "establishment" were unhappy to accept anything but an orthodox style. All the ingredients were there, courage, an ability to make sacrifices, the desire to achieve and above all, a deprived childhood.

Not surprisingly therefore all Mohammed's energies had gone into boxing, making him into a brilliant young prospect. It was easy to see that a disciplinary record at that stage in his career could have long-term serious effects and so Gerry thought the best he could do would be to get him legal representation.

Unfortunately Gerry didn't see what happened in the ring and only got into the changing room when the incident had finished. However he was able to say that the referee had been subjected to some abuse but not from the Sheffield camp. I told him that the case against Mohammed was a strong one and in many ways it looked as though we were faced with a damage limitation exercise but before any decisions were made I thought it best to see Mohammed himself and see exactly what he had to say. He failed to turn up on the first meeting and on the second, when I went to the gym, he wasn't there either. I told Gerry that there was little point in me getting involved if the boxer wasn't even prepared to try to defend himself but Gerry persevered and an appointment was made for the following Saturday morning.

"This is the little bugger that you want to see," said Gerry aggressively. "He's not been to training for three weeks and it seems to me that he's given up the ghost. He's running away."

"No I'm not," snapped Mohammed.

"Then why miss all these appointments? Mr Smith's a busy man, he's better things to be doing than chasing round after you."

"I didn't ask him to be involved... no disrespect Mr Smith," he said, realising he had spoken out of turn.

It was obvious to me that Mohammed thought that his fate had been sealed and this caused his frustration.

"I think it would be a good idea Gerry if I had a word with Mohammed on his own."

Gerry looked a little disappointed at having brought the lad by the scruff of the neck and I suspected that he believed that his input would be important.

"Obviously your input is important," I said, anticipating what he was to say, "and I would like to take details of that in a moment, but perhaps if I could just have a word with Mohammed so that we can break the ice as it were," I said, winking at a despondent Gerry.

He realised that I was only trying to help and he nodded his head in agreement, winking at me in return to let me know he had understood.

"Yes, of course, Steve," he said, "that's a good idea, I wasn't thinking. Yes, I'll leave it to you."

Gerry left the room and went into the waiting area where he started to look at a series of out-of-date magazines, including a copy of *Prison Officers' Monthly*, which we kept especially for our criminal clients.

I looked at Mohammed and gave him a reassuring smile.

"You know Mohammed, it's not over until the fat lady sings."

"There wasn't any fat women there," said Mohammed with a quizzical face.

"Yes...it's just a figure of speech," I said passing the comment off. "You'd better give me your version of what took place Mohammed. Start from the bout itself."

"It was a fairly even contest," said Mohammed thoughtfully. "I thought I'd won it and I've got to admit I was disappointed when they said it had gone against me and I think the other boxer thought I was showing dissent but then when he moved his arms as if to touch gloves, he just said something to the effect that I wasn't good enough and he called me a black bastard. I just pushed his hand away. I thought he'd done it on purpose, to make it look as though he wanted to shake hands to fool the referee. It was that that annoyed me, not the fact that I'd lost the contest."

"Stop there. You say that he did move as if to touch gloves?"

"Oh yes, that was part of the gimmick."

"Well why would he do that and yet at the same time be ignorant to you?"

"Well, he was being crafty. He didn't want to get into bother with the referee or the crowd and he wanted to make himself look like Mr Nice Guy but he couldn't resist that nasty remark."

"What did you do then?"

"I just turned and walked away but I admit that I turned my head and shouted something back to him. I might even have sworn at him but I'm not sure and of course the referee heard that. He'd been at me all through the fight that referee. They don't like you to dance about and show off and I suppose I did."

"What do you mean by 'dance about and show off?'"

"Well I do what the pros do, what Bomber does; it's called showboating and I'd done some of that in the fight but it's not on for the amateurs."

"Then why do it?"

"Well a lot of my friends were at the fight and to be honest I think I was just showing off. I think that cost me the bout."

"Well it may well have done because they don't like things like that in amateur ranks."

"Yea, I realise that," he said with a sigh.

"Tell me what happened in the changing rooms," I continued.

"I got into our part of the changing room and there wasn't a referee there then. Some of my friends were there, a couple of the pro boxers who'd come to see me. They were telling me that I was robbed and I was just saying that it happens. Then that lad came in an sniggered at me. I didn't say anything but I turned my back on him. He didn't like that and he said so."

"What did he say?"

"He said something about me being a poor loser and a black bastard and that that would teach me to show off."

"What happened then?"

"I told him not to swear at me again otherwise he'd be for it. I regretted it as soon as I'd said it but I couldn't let him get away with that. He walked right up to me and challenged me for a fight there and then, so I turned my back on him again. According to what one of the boxers told me, he clenched his fist and lifted his hand up as though he was going to hit me at the back of the head, so one of the boxers intervened and pushed him away, telling him not to be so stupid. The next thing, I think it was his dad came across and punched my friend and he just defended himself but then..."

Mohammed's voice tailed off.

"And then what?"

"Everybody seemed to get involved."

"And what about you?"

"I didn't. I'd got pushed backwards by one of my friends, effectively to keep me out of it I think and I'd fallen back on the bench. I couldn't get up because of all the activity in front of me."

Mohammed was the most unlikely boxer I had ever seen. He was tall and very thin and one of the most inoffensive lads I have ever met. He had a bright beaming smile with a row of beautiful white teeth which sparkled when he smiled. He was extremely courteous and polite and as I'd always believed, like most boxers out of the ring, he wasn't aggressive because he had got rid of it in training.

He then gave me an envelope containing a number of sheets of paper and a letter from the Association setting out the date, time and place where the disciplinary proceedings were to be heard. I could not find any reference in any of the documents as to "representation" and so I thought the simplest thing to do would be to write and see if there would be any objection to my appearing on his behalf.

I talked generally to Mohammed about boxing and characters and heroes for a few minutes in an attempt to establish some rapport and he spoke warmly about "Bomber" Graham and Mohammed Ali. He spoke with considerable authority and he'd obviously spent a great deal of his time reading about the history of boxing and its characters. We spoke about his future and his aspirations but there was a negative tone about what he was saying and he admitted that he thought that the disciplinary proceedings would go against him. It was a convenient lead-in to discuss the events that night.

"What happened after the decision was given to the other lad?" I asked.

Mohammed took a deep breath and shrugged his shoulders.

"It started there really, that's what caused it."

"What caused what?" I asked.

"Well it was what happened, that's what caused all the aggro."

"I know it caused all the aggro, but what I want to know is exactly what took place in that ring after the result was given."

"Well I'd been doing a bit of showboating and the other corner didn't like it, in fact the boxer sort of sneered at me when the referee brought us into the middle of the ring. I didn't take any notice and just looked to the front."

"Did you think you had won?"

"I thought I'd done enough to win on points. I think I hit him more times than he hit me, but I'd had two warnings, one for doing the Ali shuffle and the other for spinning my arm around in a circle, like the pros do."

I smiled before I spoke again.

"Well it's not professional boxing, Mohammed. You know how strict they are with amateurs."

"Yes, I know, I realise that and I should have known better. It was a silly thing to do but when I get into the ring it's as if something else takes over. I'm a different person. I'm better in there than I am out here and it's great because people respect me for what I do, regardless of what colour I am."

"Go on then. They announced the result and what's your reaction?"

"I was disappointed of course because I think that the judges had marked me down because of what had happened. I turned to shake hands in the usual way and it was funny because it was as if I wasn't there."

"You mean 'automatic pilot'."

"Well, whatever you call it but I just put my gloves forward as I did after every contest. He put his gloves forward and I thought it was just going to be the normal thing and that's when it happened."

"What happened?"

"Well he spoke didn't he?"

"Yes, well, what did he say?"

"Oh, something about me being a black bastard and a show-off.

"Where was the referee?"

"He'd already turned away from him and was going over to the corner, so he was like at the side of me and with all the noise going on, I don't think he'll have heard anything but he hadn't got quite past me when it happened."

"When what happened?"

"Well because of what the lad said I thought its ridiculous putting your hands forward to shake when you've made a comment like that and I know I'm not mistaken; I know what he said because I saw him mouthing the words as well. I just brushed his hands away...he wasn't going to speak to me like that."

"Yes, I can understand that Mohammed. He's absolutely no right to refer to you in that way but the referee says in his report that you struck the other lad when you were supposed to be shaking hands."

"Well I suppose I did but then again, I didn't."

"Well it can't be both. Which is it?"

"Well it wasn't a blow as such. I just brushed his hands away, although I did it quite quickly and it might have looked as though I was punching his hand but it was more backhanded, if you know what I mean."

"Well obviously the referee saw it," I said.

"I reckon so. I know what I did and when the referee told me about it he pointed his finger in my face. I didn't get chance to tell him what had been said, he didn't seem to want to know, and there was lots of booing like from the other boxer's friends."

"So the referee might not have heard what he said?"

"No, I don't think he did. Anyway, I just walked away from the referee."

"Did your cornermen say anything?"

"Na, they didn't hear it did they? There were lots of shouting going on but I was the only one close enough to hear and I saw him mouthing the words anyway. There was a right sarcastic look on his face."

"Right, well tell me about the dressing-room."

"I did even less there. There's not much I can add to what I've said but I went into the dressing-room and Tommy, my trainer, was asking me what the referee was going on about. I was starting to explain to him what was going on and there was some shouting from behind us. One of my friends then moved away from me but I'd got my back to them. When I turned round he was scuffling with another lad who I'd never seen before."

"Who was the lad from your camp?"

"It was a lad called Richard. He does a bit of boxing himself but he's a lot older than me and he was sort of looking after the younger ones. I've seen him since and he's told me that somebody said something about giving me a crack and he just stood in the way to stop it but then it's a bit confusing because somebody else then came across to help their man out and one of Richard's friends moved forward to help him out and before we knew it there's quite a few of them scuffling. Tommy jumped on me and kept me well and truly out of it because he thought it was me that they were after."

"So did you do anything in the incident in the dressing-room at all?"

"No, all I did was to shout, 'pack it in,' and I said something in Urdu to one of the other lads."

"What was that?"

"Same. Pack it in, in Urdu."

"Why didn't you say it in English?"

"Because I thought it might register more with him. Anyway the referee says he came in but I didn't see him and I certainly didn't speak to him."

"Well he says he saw you and he says that you were shouting and bawling."

"Yes, I was shouting. I was telling our team to pack it in."

"But he says you were acting aggressively."

"Well I don't know about that but I was certainly shouting and letting them know that they shouldn't be fighting. I don't know whether he took that to be aggression or not."

We continued to discuss the matter for some time and I used the old lawyer's trick of asking him the same questions again but in a different way and out of context, to see if I would get the same answer. Mohammed gave me the same story. I was satisfied that he was telling me the truth but would the tribunal?"

"The best thing I can do Mohammed is to see the members of your group."

"Well some of them are boxers and they are not going to want to get involved."

"Well I'm sure there will be some people who were there who weren't actually involved?"

"Well I'll ask and see who will come forward if it will help."

"Of course it will help."

"Yea, but they're friends of mine so they'll say that they're biased."

"Well they can say it but without them you simply have no case. It's hard enough as it is and it may be that they won't believe you or your witnesses but you've got to try."

"I wonder if it's worth it. I wonder if I ought to just pack it in."

I paused for a moment as I gathered my thoughts.

"Do you like boxing?" I asked pointedly.

"Yes, it's my life, I love it."

"Then it's worth fighting for, so get on with it and don't be such a defeatist. Do you go into bouts and throw in the towel if you don't win the first round?"

"No, of course I don't."

"Well, grow up then."

We concluded our business and Mohammed and Gerry left reasonably happy.

The following week I'd finished my court list earlier than usual and so I telephoned the gym to say I would be early for my appointment so I would have a look around and see the witnesses afterwards.

As I was leaving the office I noticed a man in the reception area who had given his name as Granville Hepworth. He had thick bottle-bottomed glasses that made his eyes look far larger than they actually were. He had no teeth and the most enormous beer-belly I had ever seen, which was housed beneath a T-shirt with a picture of Kirk Douglas dressed up as Spartacus and sporting the emblem "I am Spartacus" on the front. It didn't fool me and I don't think it would have fooled the Romans either! He had bright red trousers and green trainers, one with a black lace and one with a white one. He was reading the *Pigbreeders' Monthly*, which was not one of the magazines that we usually had on offer, so using a process of elimination I worked out that he had brought the magazine himself!

"Clever that," I thought to myself. "Have you been attended to?" I asked politely.

"Tha what?"

"Have you been attended to?"

"No, I'm waiting to see Smithy."

"That's me, what can I do for you?"

"Oh reight, ah, good enough. I couldn't make thee out. 'as tha got a minute?"

"Well I was just going out...."

"Thanks very much," said the man as he walked straight into the door of the interview room at the side of reception.

As he walked into my interview room I shouted, "I was just getting off for an appointment actually."

"Oh, good, thanks very much, come in and sit down. Let me tell thee what's 'appened."

Tracey, the receptionist, started to giggle and I must admit I found the situation rather amusing but I regained my composure and followed him into the room. He walked straight into the doorjamb and then tripped over a plant in the corner near the desk.

"Sorry about that, dint see it," he said apologetically.

He was about to sit down when I saw that he was going to miss the chair by a mile.

"Watch out, you're going to miss the chair by a mile."

"Oh right, thank you very much," he said as he missed the chair by a mile.

He got up and then positioned himself properly in the middle of the chair and put his arms on the desk in front. He looked at me earnestly as he knocked the telephone off the table.

"Oh, bloody 'ell," he said apologetically.

"Oh, bloody hell" I replied picking up the telephone. "That's new that phone!"

"Tha sees, it's like this Gary."

"The name's Steve," I said becoming agitated.

"Ay, Steve, sorry. It's like this. I breed animals thas sees."

"Oh yes."

"Ay, 'ave done for years. It's me 'obby and it 'elps me dole money out."

Using my finely-tuned lawyer's brain I started to piece together the facts. My erstwhile client was reading the *Pigbreeders' Monthly*. We do not keep that magazine in our reception so I concluded that he had brought it. It was a simple deduction, he was a pig-breeder.

"You breed pigs then," I said knowingly, with a self-satisfied smile on my face.

"No, whatever made you think that? Ferrets are my game."

My finely-tuned lawyers brain had got it wrong again.

"You breed ferrets?"

"Ay, ferrets. You know about ferrets don't yer? For ratting and rabbiting."

"Oh yes, I know about ferrets."

"Do yer want to buy one?"

"No thanks, no, I don't have the facilities but carry on and tell me the problem."

"Well I'll tell you what it is. I used to breed 'em on my allotment but the Council took it off me so they could build some old folks' bungalows on the land so I took me sheds down and took 'em 'ome and now I've got 'em in the garden. Trouble is, neighbours are complaining."

"Complaining? What about?"

"I'm not sure, but they said something about the stink."

"The stink?"

"Ay, the stink. I don't think they stink but then I'm used to 'em. Anyway, that's what they've said."

"Very good," I said, "and how can I help?"

"Well they've give me this."

He reached into his pocket and pulled out a motley-looking set of papers, which appeared to have been used to blot gravy. I held them with the tips of my fingers and delicately opened them up to reveal portions of partly smoked tobacco, some fluff and a live earwig. I jumped when I saw the small item wriggle across the desk as Granville attempted to crush it with his fist. Of course he missed and after about fifteen attempts the earwig got away.

"Got it," said Granville. "Anyway, what we gunna do 'bout these summonses?"

The prosecutions had been brought by the local Council, doubtless at the instigation of his neighbours and they claimed that there was a nuisance at his premises consisting of noise, untidyness and a smell.

"What do you say about these then Granville?" I asked.

I shouldn't have said it because he was going to tell me, whether I liked it or not.

"I think they ought to be shot with shit," he said firmly.

"Why do you think they should be shot with shit?" I asked.

"Because they can't leave a man to 'is 'obby without messing 'im up."

"Why is that?" I asked.

"Well tha sees, it's like this. I don't bother them and I don't mix with them. I keep mesen to mesen. I don't bother them and I don't expect them to bother me."

"Well I don't think it's about being bothered," I said, "It's about the noise, the untidyness and the smell. Let's deal with them individually. First of all, is there a noise?"

"Well there is a bit, especially when it's grub time; they get reight excited ferrets do."

"I wouldn't have thought they were big enough to make a noise?" I asked contemplatively.

"Well they're not really, it's just because of 'ow many there are."

"How many are there?"

"Fifty."

"Fifty?" I asked incredulously.

"Ah, fifty," said Granville.

"That's an awful lot of ferrets."

"Aye, it's an awful lot of ferret muck, but it's good for t' gardens. They don't complain when I'm givin' 'em that by the sackful."

"I suppose fifty ferrets all making a row at the same time is an awful lot of row?"

"Ah, I suppose it is," he said on reflection. "They are noisy at mealtimes, that's why I used to like to 'ave 'em at the allotment."

"What about the untidyness?" I asked.

"Well, I don't think it's untidy."

"But there's a statement here that says that there's cardboard boxes everywhere, a variety of dustbins and lids, sacks, rubble and all sorts of stuff."

"They're exaggerating."

"Well wouldn't it be an idea to shift it because if it's moved that gets rid of one of their complaints?"

Granville thought for a moment and then as if he had uncovered the secret of life, he spoke out with great glee.

"'ey that's a good idea. If I clean it they can't complain about that."

"Bingo" I said, "you've got it in one. Now let's have a look at the third one, the smell. What do you say about that?"

"I never notice it."

To be frank, I was not surprised but I thought the best thing was to be diplomatic.

"You see, lots of people aren't bothered about farmyard smells but some people are and if you are close to nature, as you obviously are, you're not going to notice it so much."

Granville thought for a minute.

"I see what you mean," he said. "You're sayin' that it don't really stink but to someone who dunt like stink, it stinks. To someone who dunt mind whether it stinks or not, it dunt stink as such as to a man who can't stand the stink when it stinks, sort of thing."

I didn't quite know how to answer that point. Suffice it to say that I thought it best to agree with him, even though I kept thinking it was a plot to wind me up.

"Yes... I suppose I see what you mean. What we ought to do therefore is to find some way of cleaning those sheds out on a daily basis and getting rid of the waste, if I can put it that way, so that would "spike their guns" so to speak about that part of the complaint."

Granville thought for a moment.

"Eh tha's not daft thee," he said knowingly.

"I think the best thing you could do really is to get another allotment because then you can put all your sheds up there, they can make as much noise as they want at mealtimes, stink as much as they want and you'll be as happy as a sand boy."

"That's a good idea an' all. 'as tha any idea where I can get an allotment from?"

"Not off hand, but I'll tell you what I'll do. I'll ring the Council for you."

He seemed even more impressed than with my earlier advice and on the basis that I like to see people happy, I phoned the Council. I spoke to about eight different departments before my call hit the mark and eventually I was put through to a very helpful lady who told me that she would put Granville on the waiting list but they required a letter of intent so that he could be included. I was confused as to why Granville had not done it himself, but then he wasn't an administrator, he was a ferret breeder and what he didn't know about ferrets wasn't worth knowing. Unfortunately he didn't know much about anything else so I promptly wrote out a letter and gave him the pen to sign it. He signed the back of my hand, part of the desk and the inkwell before he managed to hit the letter.

"Well done," I said, "this will get you in the queue and apparently if there's a cancellation there's a good chance that you might get an allotment pretty quickly."

"Reight cocker."

"In the meantime, if you make an effort with the rest of the things we might be able to stall the summons until you can get the ferrets out."

"Rock on! Tha'll do for me," said Granville. "I'll get stuck into it today."

"Good idea."

I held out my hand to shake his but he missed.

"Sorry about that, I'll 'ave to clean these glasses."

"Yes, I can see that. Is that why you got refused for the police force," I asked, jokingly.

"No, I never tried to join the police force," he said.

"Ah...yes, I see...," I said, realising he'd missed the joke. I was lucky he didn't take it as an insult.

"Keep in touch then Granville."

"Aye, I will and if tha wants a ferret at trade price, let me know. In fact, next time I come in I'll bring one to show thee."

"Oh marvellous, it's what I've always wanted."

"There y'are, told you you'd be interested. All reight cocker!"

"Another joke gone wrong," I thought.

He left the room and walked to the front door. He turned to wave and then walked straight into the doorframe again. He cursed and then finding the doorway by a process of elimination, he left.

"Who was that?" asked Tracey, the receptionist.

"Do you know, that man can do anything with ferrets!"

"Perish the thought," said Tracey.

I nodded in agreement and realised that she had missed the point as well.

"He is definitely a one-off and there won't be many of them walking around Rotherham...thank God. Just think of all the accidents there would be."

Just then another man walked in and for a moment I thought it was Spartacus returning to see me with an afterthought, until I noticed that he was wearing entirely different clothes. He still had the same bottle-bottom glasses and no teeth.

"He couldn't have changed in ten seconds," I thought.

He spoke, in exactly the same tone and texture of voice.

"'ave you seen our kid?"

"Your kid?" I asked.

"Ay, our Granville. He came in to see thee about his ferrets."

"And you must be...?"

"I'm 'is twin brother, Gerald."

"Get away," said Tracey and I simultaneously.

"He's just gone, you couldn't possibly have missed him. He's literally just...."

I realised he had got the same eyesight problems so he probably did miss him.

"He's just gone."

"Which way?"

"Walking towards you I think, in the direction of Canklow."

"Well, bloody 'ell, I've just come that way and I never saw 'im."

"Yes, well there you are then."

I went to the doorway and saw his brother walking in the distance.

"There he is," I said and pointed in his direction.

"I can't see 'im."

"No, I suppose you wouldn't."

I shouted after him but I realised then that he was deaf as well. I didn't quite know how to get out of this situation.

"If you run down there now you'll catch him up, honestly."

"Ay, alreight," and off he went, colliding with the doorjamb as he went.

"Of all the gin joints in all the world, they had to come into...."

Chapter 3

JIM'S GYM AND ALBERT'S FREEDOM

I told Tracey I was going before someone else got me and so off I went. Despite five sets of roadworks I got to the gym early for my appointment. It was a former school annex which had been converted into a makeshift gymnasium. There was a tarmac car-parking area, which led to two large oak doors, one of which was open. There was a big sign above the door saying "Jim's Gym".

I went inside and there in a large open area, were two boxing rings surrounded by punch-bags of all sizes and descriptions. All the windows were marked with condensation and the pungent smell of rubbing oils invaded the atmosphere.

There were about twelve boxers in the hall, two of whom were in one of the rings attempting to beat hell out of each other and the others were systematically hitting punch-bags, shadow-boxing or having large medicine balls dropped irreverently on arched stomachs, in what was described as a toning-up exercise.

Gerry was acting as referee in the gym and when he saw me he called me over.

"Now then Steve, get changed and have two or three rounds in 'ere."

He laughed as he said it and so did I. It was a long time since I'd been in a boxing ring; over thirty years to be exact, when I was a schoolboy and all the contests were rigged by the prefects so that they could act out their fantasies by beating the younger ones to a pulp.

Mohammed was nowhere to be seen.

"Give me two minutes to the end of this round Steve and then we'll have a chat."

I nodded in agreement and sat on a small oak bench near the ring. I surveyed the area and watched as schoolboys of varying ages and sizes punched mid-air punch-bags and each other. The bell went for the end of the round and Gerry congratulated both boxers, wiped their faces with flannels and sent them off to do some skipping. He walked out of the ring and came and sat next to me.

"It's a great service to the community," said Gerry. "A lot of these lads would be on street corners if they weren't in here. When they've done training they're too tired to go out looking for trouble on the streets. It's that discipline that we try to teach 'em which is the thing."

Gerry's life was boxing. He loved everything about it; the camaraderie, the combat, the rubbing-oils, the lot. He was truly a fervent disciple of the noble art and for a man in his mid-forties, he was still extremely fit and was not the sort of bloke you would want to upset in an argument; but then none of the boxing fraternity were.

"I've got some of the lads who were present that day coming in in about half an hour and they'll tell you all about it," said Gerry.

"Good enough," I said, "I'll take statements from them and if they're any good we'll take them to York with us."

"Definitely," said Gerry, "whatever you think's best; we're in your hands and we'll play it your way. If you're going to have a boxing match for someone I'd expect you to listen to me, so we're going to listen to you, OK?"

"OK."

He then thumped me in the kidneys in a friendly fashion. It made more than my eyes water.

"I wish you wouldn't do that Gerry," I said.

"Come on, don't be a wimp," said Gerry.

I couldn't understand how you could be a wimp if you were not prepared to have your kidneys thumped. It was as if Gerry had a masochistic tendency. He thought it was all one huge joke but I didn't.

"Come on, put some kit on. Let's 'ave you in the ring and see what you can do."

"Sod off," I replied, "I've just had a bacon sandwich."

Gerry laughed and picked up a plate of fruit.

"Your problem is that you don't 'ave a proper diet. You want to pack in the drink, pack in these lunchtime sessions and eat plenty of fruit and vegetables and then you'll be like me."

I looked at Gerry. He'd got one cauliflower ear, the aperture to one eye was narrower than the other and his nose had more twists and turns than the A1. It's true that he had no waistline and he had an excellent physique but his face looked as if it had been welded on by an amateur welder.

"Not for me Gerry, I just like to watch," I said hesitantly.

"You're a wimp."

"Yes, I am," I said repeatedly, thus avoiding another thump in the kidneys.

Our conversation was disturbed by Mohammed's arrival. He waved and smiled and went into the changing room, appearing soon afterwards wearing his shorts and a Mohammed Ali T-shirt.

"Excuse me a second," said Gerry. "In the ring then Mo, you and Gary can do a bit of sparring."

Gerry turned to me.

"Now watch this. Gary's a year older and just a little bit heavier and he's a good prospect, but watch Mo. I let these two spar because they're evenly matched."

They put on protective headgear and under Gerry's supervision they began to spar. I was astonished at just how good Mohammed was. He was marvelously balanced and so quick on his feet. His hands were almost a blur as he put a series of combination punches together raining into Gary's face. Just then Gary, the smaller and stockier of the two, caught Mohammed in the stomach with a heavy body blow. He winced with pain but persevered and danced his way out of trouble before planting two or three combinations firmly on the end of Gary's nose. Gerry rang the bell and the two combatants touched each other's gloves and went back to the corners.

"Right," said Gerry, "on to the punch-bags now please."

Gary held the bag by standing behind and placing his arms around it, almost like a bear-hug, whilst Mohammed hit it for all he was worth.

Just then a group of people came into the room. I guessed that they were the witnesses who I had come to see.

"Let me take you to the office," said Gerry.

We were taken to an ante-room, which had a table and a few plastic chairs and the group were invited to sit down.

There were five of them, all male, and varying in age from teenagers to middle-aged. Apparently they had all watched the fight and gone into the changing rooms afterwards. I feared that the tribunal might think that my witnesses were involved in the incident and as such their value would be much diminished. One of the witnesses was on crutches at the time, so he couldn't really have been involved in any fisticuffs. He gave a clear and lucid account of what had taken place but unfortunately for me he hadn't seen the incident in the ring. Another witness was a middle-aged man who had been helping his son to change when the dressing-room incident took place. He was useful and gave me a good statement backing Mohammed to the hilt but if I didn't have any evidence as to the ring, I was going to lose.

I left the gym and returned to my office. We had three weeks left before the hearing and at that stage I was on a loser.

About a week later I received a call from the Council to tell me that an allotment had become available in a suburb of Rotherham, not far from where Granville lived. He wasn't on the telephone so I wrote him a letter presenting him with the good news and as a result he came to see me shortly afterwards, bringing with him an assortment of photographs in the form of a "before and after" exercise on the state of his garden. The photographs he had taken before the repair work were awful. It looked worse than Steptoe's yard but the photographs taken afterwards showed a remarkable improvement. All the rubble and boxes and sheds had been removed and he had made an attempt to build a patio under the backdoor window. All the flags which had been laid were of a different colour but at least it was tidy. The ferrets were still there of course and there were a variety of photographs of them, some fifty in all, showing each one with its name and date of birth, almost like those taken by the prison with the jail numbers underneath. They'd all been named after television celebrities and Granville knew each one by name.

"It's a gift," he said with great pride.

"It certainly is," I replied, "it most certainly is."

Granville was delighted with the news of his new allotment. All I had done was to write a simple letter and by sheer fluke one became available just before he had to appear at court. He seemed to think it was some remarkable ability on my part and despite my attempts to persuade him to the contrary, he was having none of it.

"You're a genius," he said.

"Not really," I replied.

"Oh yes you are, you're the only one that could 'ave done it."

I couldn't help but smile. You can get a good result either by fluke or chance and the clients insist that it is your achievement. By the same token if you get a bad result you get blamed. On this occasion, the fact that fifty ferrets had avoided the march to Madame Guillotine made me feel good and perhaps for once I had made a difference.

I made a quick call to the Council and told them that the garden had been cleared and the ferrets had gone, thus removing the noise and the smell. I pointed out that it would be a wasteful exercise to continue the prosecution and suggested an inspection by the Legal Department before the actual hearing itself. They agreed and two days before the case was to be heard they came, they saw and they felt as though they had conquered. On the day of the hearing the summons was duly withdrawn. It was a little too close for comfort but it worked.

A day later I found a large gift-wrapped parcel waiting for me on reception. We do tend to get presents from satisfied clients which is always good, depending of course on what you get but it is always nice to get a surprise. The staff gathered round as I opened the delicately gift-wrapped item. I envisaged all sorts of things, a case of wine, a display of orchids, a piece of cut glass or a prize turkey ready for the oven but then again if it was a turkey it was still alive because whatever was in the cage was moving. I then noticed a little card which read simply, "'ave this. Thanks from Granville'.

An awful thought crossed my mind and when I opened the wrapper my worse fears were realised for there in the cage was a large fawn ferret baring its teeth and answering to the name of Doctor Who.

The following morning I set off for Sheffield and Albert's Judge in Chambers bail application. These hearings are held in private in the Judge's room in the absence of the defendant and consequently the atmosphere is a little more relaxed than in open court. My case was listed for 10.15 a.m. and experience had taught me to be there early.

I walked into the main waiting area outside Court number one where my bail application was to be heard. The corridor was littered with personnel of all sorts, shapes and sizes. To the left of me there were muggers, to the right there were mobsters and in the middle there was me. To the far end of the corridor two barristers huddled together in heated exchange, both vying for the top hand. The Clerk of the Court, resplendent in his brand new wig, paced quickly towards Court one as his heels clicked ceremoniously with a haughty display of self-righteousness for which he had become famous. He unlocked the doors and they swung open as he shouted, "Judge in Chambers bail applications this way."

Three of us walked towards the doors. I recognised the other two and gave them nod.

"What have you got?" one asked me.

"Judge in Chambers bail application," I said sarcastically.

Despite this one of the others was hell-bent on explaining his case at length, whether we were interested or not. For the first few years in the job you are prepared to listen but when you've done fifteen years plus, all that counts is your own case. I interrupted him with my excuses as pleasantly as I could and sat down to review my notes.

The Court Clerk told me that a High Court Judge would hear the applications. They are senior Judges who spend a considerable amount of their lives in the Royal Courts in London but occasionally they visit the provinces dealing with serious cases. Unfortunately they don't always fancy a fortnight in darkest South Yorkshire and it shows.

"You'll have to watch your p's and q's with this one Mr Smith," said the Court Clerk haughtily, "he's not given to frivolity and has no sense of humour."

I nodded begrudgingly as he started to look down his list, reading out the three names in order of priority of listing.

"Heptonstall, Tattershall and Gummershall," he said smiling. "All Shall's today then gentleman," he said, expecting an outburst of riotous laughter at his keen and sharp wit.

I forced a smile and nodded at him, acknowledging his brilliant one-liner and lo and behold, it worked because he put me on first.

The Clerk disappeared and returned two or three minutes later and called out my name.

"Mr Smith for Heptonstall."

I followed him to the Judge's Chambers with my opponent and we were told to wait outside until we were called.

"What's he like?" I asked.

"I haven't got a clue," said the prosecutor, "this is his first time in Sheffield. Somebody said that he's fair but others have said they didn't like him. Apparently he'll give you a fair hearing."

"Oh, that's nice, a fair hearing, very good, that's wonderful, what I've always wanted; a fair hearing."

The prosecutor missed the sarcasm.

Albert was still in Armley jail because defendants don't appear at Judge in Chambers bail applications and Jack hadn't turned up either but he wouldn't have been allowed in if he had. I imagined what it would have been like having Jack in the High Court Judge's room. He would be sitting with his feet up on the desk, smoking a Park Drive, coughing everywhere and tutting when the prosecution opposed bail. Thankfully it was not to be.

We were called into the room to see the Judge, minus his wig, sitting in his red robes edged with ermine. I don't know if it was the glow from the red robes but he had a remarkably pink face, although one old-stager once told me that High Court Judges have that complexion because of all the port they drink when they're working on circuit. They are remarkably clever with an eye for detail and there's no doubting their tremendous intellect but then there are very few duffers allowed into that magic circle. High Court Judges are always referred to as "My Lord", and not "Your Majesty", as one wag once put it. They earn a good salary and they are also given a knighthood, which must be very nice. I would like one.

We were invited to sit at a small table near his desk but he did not look up as he busily scrutinised his papers. His silver-coloured hair was well groomed and he was clean shaven, with bright blue eyes which moved from left to right under a pair of horn-rimmed spectacles as he devoured the information before him. He had very sharp features and a pointed nose, turning over the papers with bony fingers with well-manicured nails. My opponent and I sat quietly at the desk, watching his every move and waiting for our opportunity to speak.

"Let me see his record," said the Judge coldly.

"Certainly My Lord," said the prosecutor deferentially and handed over Albert's list of convictions.

Unfortunately there were a lot of them and the Judge made rather a meal of reading them out.

"Burglary and theft of thirty boxes of shoes?"

He looked at me over the top of his horn-rimmed spectacles, anticipating a comment.

"Yes, My Lord, they were taken from a shoe shop but they were all actually left feet as he'd taken display boxes."

The Judge sighed, stared at me and then looked back at the record.

"Theft of five thousand wire coat hangers?"

"Yes, My Lord, they were in a box with a picture of a Zanussi washer on it. He took it from outside a dry cleaner's shop thinking it was a washer but when it was opened they had just simply used the box to put five thousand wire coat hangers inside."

He sighed again and looked back at the sheet.

"Theft of four...ducks?"

He looked at me again with a perplexed stare.

"Yes, My Lord, that was something of a prank." I declined from telling him that he got "bird" for that offence.

"My goodness me, what on earth is this? Theft of a chemical toilet?"

He looked at me even more intently than before.

"Yes, My Lord, that was a portable toilet which he took for his allotment."

"Another joke?" asked the Judge.

"Not really My Lord."

"No, of course not," he replied.

I then saw the Judge suppress a smile before he made another comment.

"According to this," he said brightly, "there was someone in the toilet when they drove it away."

I grimaced.

"Yes, My Lord, I'm afraid there was."

"Must have been a considerable surprise for him then?"

"It was a considerable surprise My Lord, yes."

"Was the toilet actually in use when it was towed away?"

"So to speak My Lord."

"What do you mean, so to speak?"

"Well, yes, you're right My Lord, it was."

"Your client appears to have little regard for the law."

"Well yes, it seems that way My Lord, but his offending is fairly minor and you'll notice that there are no dwelling-house burglaries on that list and substantially over the past year or so he's been quite quiet."

"What do you mean, quite quiet?"

"Well, there have been no offences."

"Um," said the Judge thoughtfully. "He doesn't appear to offend whilst on bail."

"Certainly not My Lord," I replied confidently.

"But he does the rest of the time," said the Judge sarcastically.

"Yes, My Lord." I'd long since learned not to argue with High Court Judges.

"Might I respectfully suggest My Lord...?"

"No you may not, I've heard enough."

My heart sank. I had not been able to mention any of my prepared submissions and the Judge was cutting me off short.

"But My Lord, if I may...?"

"No, you may not," snapped the Judge, who then began to write some notes on the paper in front of him.

I was straining at the leash because it looked very much as though I'd lost my bail application and I hadn't been allowed to make my strongest points.

"Were the Koi Carp recovered?" asked the Judge.

"I beg your pardon My Lord?"

"One of the convictions; it appears that he stole a number of Koi Carp from an ornamental pond. Were the Carp recovered?"

"They were recovered in full My Lord."

"You mean he cut them up into pieces?" he asked, smiling sarcastically.

"No, My Lord, I meant they were all recovered and returned to the pond from whence they came." I said forcing a smile.

The Judge nodded thoughtfully.

"Well Mr Smythe?"

"Begging your pardon My Lord, it's Smith."

He looked at me and then looked back at his papers and thought for a minute.

"Well Mr Smythe, I'm going to grant your client bail but there'll be conditions on it."

I breathed a deep breath out of relief.

"He'll have to reside with his parents and he'll have a curfew. I'm not having him wandering around at night, stealing livestock, so there'll be a curfew from 8pm to 8am and he can report to the police every Sunday between 6 and 8pm. That's all, thank you, you may go now."

I thanked the Honourable Judge enthusiastically and left his room. I paused at the door, turned, bowed and said,

"Good morning My Lord and thank you."

The Judge did not answer, continuing to read through papers on his desk.

"Ignorant git!" I thought to myself.

When I got outside I went to a telephone box and contacted Jack to give him the good news.

"Hello Jack, this is Steve Smith, the solicitor."

"Hey up Steve, 'ow's tha gone on?"

"I'm pleased to tell you that Albert's got bail but it's subject to conditions."

"Bloody great," said Jack, "I'll get off to Leeds and fetch 'im."

"You don't need to do that Jack, he'll be given a travel warrant and put on a train back to Rotherham."

"Alreight me old cock, that'll do for me," said Jack.

We discussed the application and I told him how good and clever I was to outwit the High Court Judge and he loved it.

I made my way back to the car park and set off for Rotherham and the Magistrates' Court. I was late and due for a telling-off but at least Albert was free and I was getting used to bollockings for trying to be in two places at once.

Chapter 4

STING LIKE A BUTTERFLY,
LIKE A BRICK

It was the week of the amateur boxing tribunal and Mohammed's date with destiny. I had built up a case which I hoped would prove that he could not have been blamed for the incident in the changing room but I only had his evidence for the incident in the ring. I was mulling the evidence over in my mind on the night of an amateur boxing show in Sheffield. I was attending as Gerry's guest and I'd bought some other tickets so that my friends Wilf, Bader, Tom 'The Hemingfield Fussilier', Goody and Jarvis could share the entertainment. It was a bow-tie do and we enjoyed a pleasant meal before the start of a schedule of eight amateur boxing bouts. They started with the juniors and worked their way through to the seniors and then the heavyweight contest.

There seemed to be something gladiatorial about these contests as the boxers were urged on by an ever-eager bloodthirsty crowd, most of whom were inebriated. It was, of course, illegal to gamble in that setting and as all gentlemen of sport and honour would, we all put money on each bout. I was about even by the time the sixth contest took place but heeding a call of nature I left my place and went off in search of a loo. On my way back I noticed a young boy of about fourteen or fifteen years in a wheelchair. He was carrying one of the latest video cameras and was filming the fights. His legs were wrapped in a blanket. I tried not to stare but I enquired about him back at our table when Gerry came to see me.

"I'm not sure what they call him. He comes to all the boxing matches. He wanted to be a boxer when he was younger but unfortunately he got polio but now his father brings him to the fights and he always has that camera."

I kept an eye on the lad during the evening and noticed that he filmed all the fights and results. He'd got a ringside seat in a slightly elevated position, which helped him with his filming. Just before the last fight I saw his father go to the bar. It was just a hunch but I decided to follow and engage him in conversation whilst we were waiting.

"It's been a good night hasn't it?" I said brightly.

"Yes, they're always good do's these. We come to them all."

"Do you really?"

"Yes, I come with my son. He used to be a schoolboy boxer."

"Did he?" I asked pleasantly.

"Yes but he got polio and now he's in a wheelchair. That's him sitting over there by the ring," and he pointed him out.

"I'm very sorry to hear about your boy," I said. "He looks a good-looking lad."

"Yes he is, he's very courageous. He just desperately wants to be part of something but when he watches the other boys…."

His voice tailed off.

"I understand; or at least I think I do."

"He films the fights and then he plays them the film afterwards and he analyses where they're going wrong. He's become quite an expert on boxing."

"Is that his camera?" I asked.

"Yes," said the man, "why do you ask?"

"Well I've been thinking about getting one myself but I don't know the first thing about them."

"Oh, you want to ask Archie, he can take one to bits and rebuild it. I'll introduce you to him if you want and he'll show you his camera."

"That's very nice of you," I replied.

"No, not at all. Archie will be thrilled to bits, he does all his own editing. He likes to show what he can do. There's not much else for him these days."

I deposited my drinks at the table and then went to meet the young man. He was a good-looking boy with a pleasant smile but his eyes were full of sadness.

"I'm sorry, I don't know your name," said the man.

"My name's Steve Smith."

"Well then Steve Smith, this is my son Archie. Archie this is Steve."

We shook hands and I warmed to the young fellow immediately.

"Your dad's been telling me that you're a bit of a camera buff."

"Well, I've got this video camera now but I had an old movie camera before that. I've got used to this now and I can put titles on the screen."

"What do you mean by that?" I asked, showing interest.

Archie was delighted to tell me all about his camera and he welcomed the attention that I gave him. He went into great detail about what the camera was capable of and whilst he spoke I had a hunch.

"Do you come to the boxing often?" I asked.

"I've been to every one this year except one," said Archie.

"And when you come do you always film?"

"Oh yes, that's why I come, to film all the boxers and then me and my dad watch them back at home. I can pick out the good points and the bad ones as well."

"You say that you've been to all the boxing matches?"

"Yes, all except one when I wasn't very well."

"You mean that you film all the fights?"

"Yes, each and every one and then I get the result and sometimes I'll get them going up to get their trophies."

"Do you ever show these films to the boxers?"

"No, because I don't know any of them."

"It would be a pretty good idea for them to watch their fights and they could see what mistakes they are making," I said.

"Yes, I suppose they could. I'd like that but I daren't ask."

I couldn't resist the question.

"Did you film the fight about two months ago?"

"Would that be the October one?"

"Yes," I said expectantly.

"Ah," said the boy, "that was the one that...."

"Just my luck," I thought, "he's going to tell me that that was the one he didn't see."

"That's the one where there was the trouble."

"Yes, that's right. Were you there?"

"Oh yes, I was there," said Archie. "I filmed the fights."

"You haven't still got the film have you by any chance?"

"Yes, I should have it somewhere, unless I've taped over it, but I would have to check."

I thought I ought to explain why I was showing such an interest. I told Archie and his father that I was representing Mohammed.

"Oh, that's the showboater," said Archie, "he's very good, he's probably the best one in his age group."

"Oh you like him then do you Archie?"

"Well I don't know him, it's just that I've seen him fight before and I think he's a great prospect."

I decided to lay my cards on the table and so I told him about the case.

"Can you help us?"

Archie's eyes picked up and a flash of excitement shot across his face.

"I'd love to help but what can I do?"

"Well for a start you can find the video, you can have a look at it and see if you recorded the fight. You could let me know. I might even have to call you as a witness to prove that you took the video."

"I'll do that," said Archie excitedly.

I gave him my telephone number and he promised to contact me the following day.

"Well done Archie," I said, "I'll look forward to seeing you again."

We shook hands and then I went back to my table. I could not believe my luck.

The following day I was sitting in my office waiting for Jack and Albert to call to take Dr Who to the allotment. We had closed up the office at five-thirty and so I sat downstairs near the front door so that I could hear when they arrived and whilst I was using my dictating machine I became aware of a presence behind me. It was the cleaner, Vera. A wonderful, hardworking character, the 'salt of the earth' and an expert at making hangover remedies.

"Hello Steve," she said in her slow drawl.

"Hello Vera," I said, "are you alright?"

"Not really," she replied.

"Why's that?" I asked, dreading the answer.

"I've got a problem."

"Oh dear," I said, "is there anything I can do?"

"Yes, will you help me blow my tubes out?" she asked.

"Blow your tubes out?" I replied, wondering what on earth she was talking about.

She then produced a vacuum cleaner and told me that the machine's tubes were blocked and she needed my help to assist her to unblock them. Breathing a sigh of relief I took the object and laid it on the table in front of me and using my non-existent mechanical wizardry I managed to free Vera's tubes, much to her delight. I gave her the vacuum cleaner back and assumed she had gone about her business and so I continued to dictate a very important note on a murder case that I was dealing with when I became aware of someone's presence. It was Vera again.

"Will you have a cup of tea Steve?" she asked in that slow drawl to which I'd become accustomed.

"No thanks Vera, I'm desperate to finish this dictation.

"Two sugars Steve?"

"No, it's alright Vera, I'm going to finish this dictation, it's important."

"Milk?"

I took a deep breath and sighed.

"Oh yes, fine," I said, giving up the ghost.

"I'll go and fetch it then," she said.

"Yes, alright Vera," and I turned back into my chair, looking at the papers on my desk and continued dictating the note.

"...do you think I ought to serve the pathologist's report on the prosecution because the stab wound which had been inflicted had not drawn blood. It occurs to me that the victim must have been dead at the time the blow was delivered."

Just then I heard a voice in a slow drawl speak out.

"Well it's up to you Steve, I can't help you with that one. If you think you should serve it then that's the best thing you could do."

I stopped and put my dictaphone down. I turned around and saw that Vera thought I had been speaking to her and she was doing her best to answer my query. I sat open-mouthed as she gave me her opinion. I could just imagine when she got home she would be telling her family how Steve Smith had difficulty with a murder case and so she'd had to sort it out for him. I realised it took all sorts to make a world, so I smiled and thanked her for her opinion, telling her that it was very helpful.

"That's alright Steve, here's your tea." She put down the cup and placed her arm on my shoulder. "Just do your best," she said earnestly.

"I will," I replied, "I will."

Just then I heard a knocking at the door and when I opened it, in walked the redoubtable Jack Heptonstall and his number one son, Albert.

"Now then Steve, what's to do?" said Jack.

"Alright Jack? Alright Albert? How are the two musketeers today?"

"Not bad," said Albert "but me dad 'as got this real bad cough. I've told 'im to pack the Park Drives in but 'e won't. I've told 'im to go to the doctor but 'e won't go there either."

"Leave it alone Albert, it's just a cough that's all, it's nowt to worry about."

"Yea but sometimes Steve he can't see fer coughin' and then 'e's out of breath and in a right state."

"Well it's probably a bit of inflammation in his chest. Might be worth checking it out Jack."

"I'll get round to it as soon as I can. Anyway, more importantly, what's tha' want?"

"Well I'll tell you why I've asked you here lads, it's to sort Doctor Who out."

"Sort bloody what?"

"Sort Doctor Who out."

"Which doctor?"

I laughed.

"Witch doctor. Someone else fell for that last week," I said continuing to laugh. Jack and Albert completely missed the point.

"And who the f...'ell is Doctor Who when 'e's at 'ome?" asked Jack.

"He's none other than this ferret. I held up the cage and Doctor Who was still gnashing his teeth.

"Sod me, that's a beaut," said Jack.

"Oh, he's beautiful," said Albert.

Jack put his hand towards the cage and the ferret went for him.

"See what I mean Jack?"

"Ay, I see what you mean. Let Albert have a crack at 'im."

Sure enough, Albert walked forwards towards the cage and almost as if in slow-motion, he opened the door. Jack and I stood back waiting for the ferret to pounce as Albert reached into the cage. We held our breaths as the ferret arched his back in readiness for a concerted assault but then, as if by magic, the animal sniffed at Albert's hand and allowed himself to be lifted out of the cage. Albert whispered to him and stroked the back of his head. The ferret curled its tail; it was responding. Albert had conquered a wild animal with razors for teeth and jaws powerful enough to bite through a finger like a knife through butter.

"How does he do that?" I whispered to Jack.

"Good i'nt 'e," said Jack proudly. "'e's always 'ad that way with 'im. Summit about 'im...'e does better with animals than 'umans...'e 'as an understanding tha sees."

"I quite understand," I said smiling, "he's truly a most remarkable young feller."

"There y'are Albert," said Jack.

"How's Madge," I asked.

Jack paused for a minute as if troubled.

"She's not reight good Steve," said Jack. "I don't know what it is but somethin's causing problems. We think it's a bit of blood pressure; she's got vertigo we think, but we're not sure. I keep telling 'er to go to the doctors but it's like talking to a brick wall, she's always got too much to do."

"Well you can't mess about when it's your health," I protested.

"You try talking to 'er, next time you see 'er, you tell 'er, she might listen to you but she won't listen to us."

"OK Jack, next time I see her I'll have a word with her."

"Reighto. By the way, tha don't want to buy a rabbit 'utch does tha?"

"No, I haven't got a rabbit."

"Ah, well that's where I come in," said Albert, "I've got fifteen."

"Yes, and you can keep them as well. No thank you, I don't want a hutch, a rabbit, a ferret, a goose, a rotweiller or a giraffe. I'm out of the market for animals but thank you very much."

"Ah well we'll be off then," said Jack.

He paused for a moment before he turned, laughing.

"Ay it's good that."

"What is?"

"Witch doctor. Brilliant that," said Jack and then they left, laughing together. I shook my head in disbelief.

The next day I received a phone call just after the switchboard opened, at one minute past nine. It was Archie, the lad in the wheelchair. He was very excited indeed and so was I when he explained that he'd found the video of Mohammed's fight. He told me that it was extremely clear and he would bring it round as soon as his father returned from work. I thanked him and we arranged to meet just after five o'clock when my appointments had finished.

All day I thought about the video, wondering whether or not it might give us a lead and sure enough at five o'clock Archie and his father came into the office. Archie greeted me with a very bright smile.

"I've got it, it's here," he said excitedly.

"Well done Archie, you've made my day."

I had taken the video player downstairs, Archie hurriedly unwrapped the cassette and after some jiggery-pokery with some wires and his camera, the television set was ready and Archie triumphantly pressed the switch for the film to start. He had arranged for the video to start at exactly the beginning of the fight. It was a very clear picture and had been well taken and I told him so. Archie smiled again and his father put his arm around his shoulder, glowing with pride.

There was a fair amount of niggle between the boxers during the fight and that was evident at the end of each round but the important part was the end of the fight when the referee called the boxers together. Just as this was happening someone had walked in front of the camera and I got a remarkable picture of the back of a bald man's head. I moved as if to try to push him out of the frame but then, fortunately, he leaned to one side and the camera had a clear view. Within seconds the announcement of the winner was made and the other lad's arm was raised abruptly.

The next piece of film was worth a fortune for it showed Mohammed's opponent push out his fist and catch Mohammed at the top of his chest, pushing him backwards. The other boxer clearly then mouthed the words, "black b..." and with that Mohammed brushed his hand aside, just like he'd said to me in his statement.

It was not easy to see at first but then I knew what I was looking for and on the third or fourth rerun it became apparent that Mohammed was right and the other boxer had provoked him. Of course over all the noise he wouldn't have been heard and indeed on yet a further rerun, I saw the referee's attention being distracted to one side, returning only to see the aftermath of Mohammed having brushed the boxer's arm aside. There could be no doubt that the referee had got the wrong impression.

I put my arm around Archie and told him what a brilliant young man he was. He was thrilled.

I rang Gerry at the gym and gave him the news, telling him that the case had been cracked by a very bright young man who might just have saved Mohammed's career and then I took Archie and his father to the Italian restaurant close to the office and regaled them with stories from the courtroom and then at the end of the night I watched as Phil pushed his son out of the restaurant. He got to the door, swiveled his chair round and waved, giving me the thumbs up sign. It spoke volumes that this nice young man who was without one hint of bitterness, would spend the rest of his life in a wheelchair. On my way to the car park I saw two youths fighting ferociously outside a public house but, of course, they were fit and well and not dependent on a wheelchair.

In the short term Archie was going to York as my star witness. I was calling Mohammed himself to give evidence, together with Archie to prove the video that I was going to play and I would also call two witnesses as to the incident in the locker room if necessary. If the Board believed them and accepted the video, we were in the clear. If they had already made up their minds and were antagonistic towards us, we would lose and Mohammed's career would be over.

The hearing was set for 6pm, which I thought was unusual but the Board consisted of twenty-odd members, some of whom worked during the day, hence the late listing. I set off about three-thirty in the afternoon because I had to travel through Leeds onto the main York road. I anticipated that there would be problems with traffic and I was right. The other difficulty was the weather because the forecast predicted snow. It took me over an hour and a half to get to York and half an hour to find the venue but when I did arrive I met up with the others who were waiting for me in the car park. Gerry had brought all the witnesses in a transit van and I had brought one of the new-fangled television and video recorders combined.

We carried our various items into the Club and were directed to the top of a set of stairs and as there was no lift it was necessary to carry Archie in his chair. The corridor led to the Boardroom where the hearing would take place and we were greeted by a gentleman who I thought was the concert secretary of the working-mens' club. I was wrong and in fact the man was the secretary of the local Boxing Board. His greeting was not the most pleasant and welcoming.

"You can't bring all them people in 'ere. It's private."

"Well I'm the solicitor representing Mohammed Razaq, this is the boxer himself and these are my witnesses."

"I don't care who they are, they're not comin' in."

"Forgive me, I don't wish to be awkward but they are coming in because they are my witnesses and I am calling them to give evidence."

"This is a private hearing and alright you can come in if you're representing 'im but the others can't."

I didn't want to argue because I didn't know if he was part of the ruling body and if I offended him I would start off at a disadvantage with having one member voting against me before we had even got going, so I bit my tongue and asked that I be allowed to make some preliminary submissions before the Board itself.

"You'll 'ave to ask them, not me," he said dismissively and with that he vanished.

"Well it's nice to be made to feel welcome Mohammed," I said to him sarcastically. He smiled and shrugged his shoulders.

Archie had brought a spare copy of the video just in case, together with the original film and the camera that took it, so there could be no possible problem with establishing the veracity of the film.

After about ten minutes my name was called out and I walked down the corridor to a double set of wooden doors. I was shown into a large boardroom with a massive table, which had about thirty people sitting around it. Two seats had been placed inquisitorially at the bottom end of the table; one I presumed for Mohammed and the other for me. I was directed to sit at the bottom of the table where the two seats had been placed and told to sit down when the Chairman addressed me in a rather gruff, uncompromising voice.

"We don't usually 'ave solicitors at these meetin's," he said firmly.

I didn't know whether he was stating a fact or asking me to comment on it but before I could say anything he spoke again.

"However, this lad's sixteen so I suppose if he must 'ave someone speak for 'im, he must but we're not 'aving anybody else in."

"Ah, now that's a point I would like to clarify, if I may Mr Chairman," I said respectfully. "You see, I have a number of witnesses to call and I have some evidence in the form of a video film."

There were gasps around the room and they all looked at the top of the table where the Chairman was sitting with other of his distinguished brethren, who then whispered together for some little time. The whispering stopped as the Chairman moved his seat forward and everyone's eyes focused on me.

"Yer say witnesses?"

"Yes Mr Chairman, I say witnesses."

With that the Chairman pushed his chair back again and the huddled whispering continued, only to be stopped when a man in an ill-fitting dinner jacket walked in and asked for the bingo machine. Eventually the Chairman pushed his chair back to the front of the table, allowing the bingo machine to pass him and he questioned me further.

"Who are these so-called witnesses?" he asked as his eyes followed the bingo machine through the door.

"These are people who witnessed the incident in the locker room and someone who witnessed the incident in the ring and also took the film of it."

"Took a film? We're not 'aving any film in 'ere," he said.

"But you've got to see the film," I said, "It is compelling evidence; it's of the incident itself and if the prosecution (I couldn't think of any other name for the people who were opening the case), intend to rely on their witnesses as to what happened in the ring, I think it only fair that I be allowed to counter it by showing you the video because of course, as it is said, the camera cannot lie."

"No, but it can certainly confuse things and we don't want any confusion in this 'earing," said the Chairman defiantly.

"Mr Chairman, far be it from me to tell you how to run your own Board but I would have thought that if Mohammed has any information relevant to this case and complies with the rules of evidence, even though this isn't a court as such, that evidence should be seen and heard, otherwise it is not a fair hearing," I said as politely as I could.

"We're not 'appy about the video," he continued.

I took a deep breath.

"Well in that case, you're not allowing me to put my case, so consequently I intend to say nothing and call no witnesses. If you then find him guilty of the complaint, I shall appeal by way of case stated to the Queen's Bench Division of the High Court."

There was a lot more whispered discussion and more of the Board became involved in it. I was asked to leave the room whilst a discussion took place and I did so. There were many heated words emanating from the room and we tried hard to listen, to see what was being said but the actual words were not discernable except for 'dinner jacket', 'bingo caller' and 'smarty twat' which must have been a reference to the bingo caller.

After about half an hour I was called in again and the Chairman told me that they were going to listen to the witnesses and would be prepared to watch the video, providing that they could be assured it related to the same incident. I thanked them profusely.

A member of the Board outlined the allegations against Mohammed, saying that he had shown ungentlemanly conduct in the ring and had then been involved in a very nasty incident in the changing room. A report was read out from the referee who had not attended to give evidence, so consequently I couldn't cross-examine him and there was also a letter submitted by the other boxer and members of his camp. I protested that the Board should not place too much reliance on mere letters and that the veracity of that evidence had been called into question by their very absence and unavailability for cross-examination. The majority of the Board stared at me as though my trousers were undone and I was not wearing underpants and I saw one of the members lean across to another and mouth the words, "smart-ass". I knew from thereon in, that we were up against it.

The Chairman then announced, "It's up to you," which I took to mean that they were ready to consider my evidence and with that I called Mohammed to explain what had happened. He gave a good account of himself and despite being asked a number of questions by the Board, I thought he came over very well.

I objected to one questioner who asked Mohammed what he thought the other boxer would have felt like in the locker room but in as mild a way as possible, pointing out that Mohammed wasn't in a position to speak of what he thought was in someone else's mind. The Board member threw his pencil down in disgust.

"That's two of them that's against me," I thought. "Only another eighteen to go. I wonder if I should undo my trousers again?"

I then called the two witnesses to the incident in the locker room who also gave a good account of themselves and then finally I called Archie. He was nervous but resolute. He seemed to have found some inner strength, which I suppose had been provoked by his desire to help and in a way gain some acceptance from other members of the club.

Archie was absolutely brilliant and despite attempts by certain of the Board members to suggest that it could be a film from a different day than the one in question, he rose to the occasion and I'm quite sure satisfied all the doubting Thomas's.

I then asked Archie to produce the film and he did so with a flourish. I addressed the Chairman once again.

"Before I ask to play the evidence," I said, "this is a video taken of the incident in the ring and if I may, I will direct your attention to certain points. You will need to view it more than once because there's so much happening in the picture it's difficult to take it all in. I suggest that we concentrate on individuals to see the extent of their role in what happened and thereafter take a more general view."

"We don't 'ave a TV," he said sternly.

"No, but I do," I countered.

The Chairman reluctantly agreed to watch the film and the video was placed on the desk, to much mumbling and shuffling from the assembled throng.

"That's three down, seventeen to go," I thought to myself.

"It's not usual to have witnesses remain when they've given their evidence," said the Chairman.

"I appreciate that," I said, "but I think Archie ought to stay just for any clarification points and also he can show me how the video machine works."

Certain of the members smiled in appreciation, so perhaps I wasn't doing so badly after all.

We played the video through about eight times, during which I pointed to the important individuals so far as our case was concerned and let the members see exactly what each party did. The incident in the ring was the easiest to deal with and I pointed to the other boxer's behaviour. More of the Board nodded in approval. I felt the old swingometer moving in my direction.

"I particularly want you to watch exactly what the other boxer does, both before, during and after the announcement."

We showed the video on a number of occasions until finally the Board was satisfied that they'd seen enough. Ironically, no one had any questions for Archie and the fact that he wasn't going to be cross-examined appeared to disappoint him. I called my other witnesses who gave their evidence well.

It was then my turn to make my submissions and I suggested to the Board what they had to find proven, to say that Mohammed was guilty.

The Chairman kept tutting to himself in disapproval at just about everything that I had to say but I noticed that more and more of the members had ceased to be hostile towards me, although they hadn't really much option because the video spoke for itself. I praised young Archie for having taken the film in the first place and then for saving it and producing it at the hearing. I rather hoped to engender some agreement from the Chairman to the effect of "yes, well done lad", or "if you 'adn't done what you done we wouldn't 'ave known whether he was guilty of anything or not," but it was not to be. My last act was to submit three written references. I had got them mixed up and submitted two copies of one of the references. The Chairman couldn't wait.

"I've got two copies of this reference," he said sarcastically.

"Oh, thank you for pointing it out but I did know; I thought the reference was so good that you'd like two copies."

That one comment broke the ice and the Chairman laughed and with him the rest of the committee.

The Chairman then spoke.

"You'll 'ave to go outside now."

As we were leaving, the dinner jacketed man entered the doorway and enquired,

"Any balls in 'ere?"

"Yes," I whispered, "they're sitting around the table."

He missed the point.

We discussed the hearing outside whilst we were waiting and it was at least half an hour before we were called back in.

"I speak on behalf of the majority of the committee," said the Chairman, "and I 'ave to say that we deplore bad behaviour in

63

amateur boxing. It's rare it ever occurs and when it does, we find it very upsetting. The problems that seem to stick to football are now spilling over into our sport as well. The fact that an incident occurred afterwards in the locker room is, in our opinion, reprehensible and we're going to stamp it out before it gets popular."

"Which way was he going?" I wondered to myself but then he put me out of my misery.

"On this occasion we've looked at the video and as Mr Smith says, a video camera cannot lie, although it can picture people in compromising situations when they weren't compromised at all but by and large we tend to accept your case and we reluctantly find you not guilty of the charge."

Mohammed jumped to his feet as did Gerry and all our supporters stood up and shouted in unison.

"YES!"

The action brought a rebuke from the Chairman, who said he hardly felt that that was behaviour suited to the occasion. I apologised for everybody and whisked them outside as quickly as I could. Everyone was speaking at once and not making much sense, suffice it to say that they were all delighted. Mohammed had the widest smile on his face that I'd ever seen and Gerry shook my hand with such force that it crushed my fingers.

We walked to a small anteroom and en route the secretary passed me on the corridor. I saw no mileage in gloating, so I simply looked the other way; after all, I never knew when I might have to go back!

Everyone congratulated everyone else but the main recipient of the slaps on the back was Archie. I took Gerry to one side.

"Isn't there something that you can do for that young lad?" I asked, seizing the moment and thus the opportunity.

"What do you mean?" asked Gerry. "I don't think there's anything I could train him to do. The poor lad's not able to walk is he?"

"No I realise that," I said, "but surely there is something that could be done. Can't you let him be a honorary member?"

"Well yes of course, he's more than welcome if he wants to come."

"Good. I think you could make use of his abilities with that video camera."

"In what way?" asked Gerry sympathetically.

"Well, what I would do is to let him film the training sessions and let the boxers see it. He's very knowledgeable and he's got some good opinions about boxing, so let him talk them through it and he can show them where he thinks they are going wrong. Not only that, it would be good for the boxers to see what they're doing and I'm sure it would help them improve."

"That's a bloody good idea," said Gerry, "I never thought about that...yes, he could be very useful...and of course he could film all the fights in the championships and if we pay for the film he can run copies off for the boxers to keep."

"That's a good idea, it will give him something worthwhile to do and something to look forward to. I think it would be nice to get him involved in the camaraderie."

"Great idea," said Gerry, "I'll ask him about it next week."

"I'll tell you what Gerry, why don't you ask him about it now? Don't put off what you can do today until tomorrow, or whatever the saying is."

"Yes, alright Steve," said Gerry, "I will. I'll take him and his father on one side."

"Good idea. Thank you for that Gerry."

Gerry went up to Archie and when he'd finished speaking to all his other new found friends, he took him and his father on one side.

Five minutes later they returned to our room and Archie's face was beaming and so was his father's.

"You'll never guess what's happened," said Archie excitedly.

"No Archie, what is it?"

"Well Gerry has asked me to get involved in the club. He wants me to be on the committee and take all the films. I can film the sparring and the fights and show the boxers in special film sessions after the training. He says he wants me there three nights a week on the sparring sessions and at all the fights and championships."

"Well, well, well," I said, "what a good idea. Do you fancy that?"

"Of course I do, I think it's a great idea. My father's getting me some new film and I'm going down next week. I'll edit all the films as well so that they're not boring. I've been learning how to do edits and I can put titles in as well."

"Well I think that's a great idea and if you're prepared to do the work, then so be it."

"I'm prepared to do the work," said Archie, "and I'll be a member, just like the other lads. Obviously I won't be able to do the boxing but I'll be able to do everything else."

"And a bit more besides," I said, "especially with the filming. What a fantastic idea."

"Yes, he's clever that Gerry and what a smashing bloke too," said his father.

I smiled and suggested to everyone that we ought to make ready to leave because I'd looked out of the window and seen that the snow was coming down quite heavily and even worse, it was beginning to stick.

We all gathered together outside and said our farewells. Mohammed went away happy, Gerry was very happy and Archie and his father were delighted.

The last I heard of Mohammed was that he was to turn professional. Gerry had built up a fantastic stable of highly successful boxers, aided and abetted by his assistant, a young man called Archie who, whilst in a wheelchair, was an absolute genius with a video camera. He had undertaken all sorts of courses in relation to boxing training and was well on the way to becoming an Approved Trainer.

Some time later his father sent me a copy of Archie's diploma and I understand that he now helps and manages a number of boxers. From time to time I see him at championships in the fighter's corner. He has an assistant who films the fights. He's a nice young man who, regrettably, is confined to a wheelchair.

Chapter 5

BATSOID AND DINGLEBERRY

One of the interesting things about my job is that you meet all kinds of people, from representatives of the Devil Incarnate to some of the nicest folk you could ever wish to meet. There is a very old saying which says "but for fools and rogues, lawyers would not exist" and I suppose that is true but we are introduced to more than just clients who need our services. We come into contact with a whole range of people from various walks of life, which in itself affords a marvelous education. It can also create paranoia.

There is a tendency to form opinions of people's characters, working on the basic premise that you cannot trust anyone, but the profession makes you very cynical and because you see the very worst of human nature, there is a tendency to tar everyone with the same brush. I remember saying to one of my heroes, the great Wilfred Steer QC about one case "he doesn't look like a murderer to me". Wilf replied as only Wilf could, "Neither did Crippen."

So I've had a hard education in the school of knocks but every so often the better side of human nature shows itself, which to some extent restores your faith. Having said that, my hatred of injustice and simply growing old and infirm has never left me and for years I've lived in fear of having to deal with those twin evils. This was never more so than in the case of Batsoid and Dingleberry.

Who are they? Well, these are not their real names but those titles stuck one day because our hard of hearing stand-in receptionist had misunderstood what two other equally hard of hearing people had told her.

I was sitting in my office one afternoon when the receptionist told me that Mr Batsoid and Mrs Dingleberry were waiting to see me. I must confess the names meant nothing to me, except they were particularly unusual and so I went into reception to check the visitors' book. Sure enough, Mr Batsoid and Mrs Dingleberry featured at the top of the page so I looked into the waiting room and there saw a very elderly man and an elderly lady smiling and nodding at me. I returned the smile and the nod and out of their earshot questioned the receptionist.

"Are you sure it's Batsoid and Dingleberry?"

"Is it what?" she asked being unable to decipher my whisper.

"Could I have a quick word with you if I may, in this room?" I asked, taking her on one side so as not to embarrass my clients.

"Is that right, Batsoid and Dingleberry?"

"Well that's what they said," she said. "Really two very nice people but they both seem to be slightly deaf, or rather she is but he's…well…how can I put it…I don't think he's a full shilling."

"A full what?"

"You know what I mean, not the sharpest knife in the drawer; not a full picnic, or there's a brick missing out of the wall."

"What on earth are you talking about?" I asked her.

"Well you know, crackers."

"Crackers!" I exclaimed.

"Yes, in a nice way but I think he's lost the plot."

"Oh, I see. Have they got any papers that have their name on because if I refer to him as Mr Batsoid and I've got the wrong name, he might not be very happy about it," I said, trying as delicately as I could to explain the position.

"Oh, I see…yes…I'll ask them," she said.

I waited at the side of reception and at the top of her voice she shouted,

"Mrs Dingleberry, have you got any ID?"

"Any idea about what?" she asked pleasantly.

"No, any I.D.?"

"I said, any idea about what?"

"No, identification," she said pointedly.

"What do you want me to identify?" asked Mrs Dingleberry.

I couldn't stand this any longer because we were getting nowhere and the lady was more confused that I was. I returned to reception, smiled and shook hands with them both.

"Good afternoon, I'm Steve Smith."

Mr Batsoid looked at me, smiled and then continued to read his newspaper, which I thought was rather odd. I directed my remarks to Mrs Dingleberry and said,

"Hello, I'm Steve Smith, good afternoon to you"

"Get away," she said, "you look much older than your photograph."

"Photograph?"

"You what, love?"

"Photograph!"

"Have you? That's very nice of you, thank you very much."

"No, I think we're at cross purposes."

"There's no need to get cross."

"No," I said laughing. "I think we're both confused now."

"Oh, he is, he's been like it for years but he's got steadily worse as he's got to eighty."

"Yes, yes…I understand. Would you like to come with me?"

"Where are we going?"

"Shall we go into my room?"

"Oh, that's very nice of you. Will Mr Smith come and see us there?"

I looked at the receptionist and she looked at me and smiled.

"Please come in," I said, smiling and guiding them into my room. I cleared my throat and made an announcement.

"I am Steve Smith."

The lady looked at me as if studying what I had just said.

"Did you say you were Steve Smith?"

"Eureka!" I said to myself. "Yes, that's me. I'm very pleased to meet you."

"Oh, lovely," she said. "George, this is Mr Smith."

"Who's he?" he replied, unhappy at being distracted from his newspaper.

"He's the solicitor."

"Well he'd best go and see one then."

"No, he's the solicitor we've come to see."

"What have we come to see him for?"

"You remember George, about the wills, we're going to have the wills."

"The wills? I've got the wills?"

"Not yet you've not, but you're going to get it in a minute."

"Oh yes," I thought to myself, "you're going to get it alright."

"Leave it to me Jack, you read your paper."

"Alright my love," he said smiling. He winked at me and then lifted his paper up to conceal his face.

They were actually quite charming people. He was an old gentleman who was somewhat confused and his wife had a hearing problem. So far, so good. I hasten to add that I do not make light of their difficulties, neither do I take the mickey but the situation was very amusing and I like to think that I was laughing with them, not at them.

Mr Batsoid handed me a number of papers that bore the name "Holroyd". I suppose it was similar to "Batsoid" in that it rhymed, but that was all. George Arthur Holroyd, who Mrs Dingleberry referred to as Jack, was eighty-two years old. His wife, whose name was on some of the papers, was Diane Cherry Holroyd, which nearly rhymed with Dingleberry.

Our receptionist had had an infection in both ears and having used some drops, the ear canal had been plugged with cotton wool but unlike many who would have gone sick, she had turned up so as not to leave us in the lurch. In doing so, because she couldn't hear anything, she thrust us into the lurch. There is no greater compliment to an employer than someone who turns up for work when they could have avoided it. Henceforth Mr & Mrs Holroyd became known as Batsoid and Dingleberry. After a while it became clear that they had come to make a Will. Wilf was on holiday and consequently I got the job.

The couple had been married for sixty years but had had no children so there were no little Dingleberrys running around to inherit their estate. Dingleberry handed me a list of at least fifteen different charities.

"Would you like this sandwich?" asked Batsoid, smiling and offering me a paper bag.

Dingleberry laughed as though he was making a joke, thus concealing that poor old Batsoid had become gloriously but harmlessly confused.

"We don't have any family," said Dingleberry and so we'd like these charities to benefit from what we've got left when we've gone. George has got a half-brother who lives somewhere in South Africa if he's still alive, but they never got on and we've never been to see them, so we think these charities ought to benefit," she said with a self-assured smile.

"That's a wonderful thing to do Mrs Holroyd," I said.

"You don't smoke Woodbines do you?" asked Batsoid.

"No, I'm sorry, I don't Mr Holroyd. I'm sorry about that."

"Neither do I," he said, "filthy habit. I stopped smoking in the army....bad for the chest."

I nodded and smiled.

"Hates smoking, does George," said Mrs Holroyd. "Saw a lot of it in the army. Filthy habit."

"It's usual to have an Executor to ensure that the will is performed correctly," I said.

"Can anybody be an executor?" asked Mrs Holroyd, turning up her hearing aid.

"Of course. It's usually a member of the family or the solicitor can do it if you wish."

"Oh that would be excellent, don't you think so George?"

"The sergeant used to smoke Woodbines in our tank. It used to be terrible, the smell of smoke and grease," he continued.

I nodded and smiled again.

"He was in the Tank Corp you know," said Dingleberry. "He fought in North Africa, didn't you George?"

"No, not me, I was in the Tank Corp in North Africa. "Have you ever been on a camel?" he asked seriously.

"No, I don't think I have Mr Holroyd."

"It's bloody uncomfortable, especially if the driver smokes Woodbines. The smell of the smoke used to mix with the smell of the camel...they have syphilis you know."

"Who had, the driver?" I asked, trying to placate him.

"No, the camel. Camels carry syphilis. They're bloody aggressive and they're always spitting."

"Who's that, the camels?"

"No, the drivers. Terrible people."

"Is it a long job to prepare wills?" asked Mrs Holroyd, changing the subject.

"Not really. We should have them ready within the week."

"Oh that's good. We want to get everything tidied up. We've been putting it off for a long time, haven't we George?"

"No thanks, never use them," he replied sternly.

"Yes, you're quite right," said Mrs Holroyd, pleasantly disregarding Batsoid's comment.

"We've had a marvelous life together, haven't we Jack?"

"No," replied Batsoid casually.

"We travelled the world when we were young you know. We even went back to North Africa to see where George served in the war." She smiled as she reminisced further.

"One afternoon he took me on a tour and showed me all the buildings he'd blown up. He was a dab-hand with that tank you know."

I nodded and smiled thoughtfully.

"Have you any special or specific requests?" I asked, "You know the sort of thing, if you've any item of jewellery that you want to go to any particular person?"…"or a tank or a camel....?" I thought to myself.

"No thank you," said Dingleberry. "Everything to the charities, they can sell everything and do whatever they want, but I have got a very nice vase, now I come to think of it. It's Dresden or something and about two feet high. It's quite a collector's piece. I'd like you to see that that goes to our doctor, Doctor Hargreaves; he's always admired it. Oh, and then of course there's George's medals."

"Medals?" I asked.

"Yes, George's medals. He picked a few up in the Second World War. They're wrapped up in a nice presentation box. We'd like to send them back to the army. He doesn't have a son to pass them on to so we thought that they might like them."

She didn't have details of the regiment in her possession but she said she would telephone me later that day with the information. We concluded our meeting and it was resolved that I would try to have everything prepared by the weekend. We made an appointment for them to call back but when the weekend arrived, Mrs Holroyd telephoned me to say that her husband had flu and wouldn't be able to travel, so I agreed that I would call on them later.

That night it was one of our monthly soirées at Ranulphs Restaurant in Sheffield, run by my old friend Bob Ego and his wife Lynne. All the gang were there; Goody, Pagey, Jarvis, Bader and Wilf, who had returned from his holiday minus a suntan and most of his money, which had been spent on Diacalm following an argument with some dodgy cuisine. As ever it was an evening to remember, which ended with a guitar solo from Honest Ernest Booth, our travelling troubadour. We were thrown out about two in the morning and when I set off for work six hours later, I felt like death. Instead of a Saturday morning in bed I had to visit Batsoid and Dingleberry.

The short journey to the outskirts of town took me to the Holroyds' residence. It was a large detached house with a large garage in a pleasant suburb. I rang the bell and was directed to the back door. I walked along the path at the side of the house, to witness the most magnificent garden, which featured pools, a series of fountains and a large commercial-size greenhouse. At the furthest end of the garden was a vegetable plot and beyond that a small but magnificently kept orchard. I was looking at the garden when the back door opened and Dingleberry greeted me.

"Hello Mr Smith, please do come inside."

"I must compliment you on your garden Mrs Holroyd. It's absolutely magnificent."

Mrs Holroyd turned to face me.

"What do you think to my garden then? Isn't it magnificent?"

I paused before I spoke as clearly she hadn't got her hearing-aid switched on. I approached the problem as diplomatically as I could.

"Have you got your hearing-aid switched on Mrs Holroyd?" I asked.

She looked at me intently and realised I had finished speaking.

"Oh goodness me, I haven't got my hearing-aid switched on. I turn it off when nobody's in because I like the silence."

Just then Batsoid walked past the door.

"Are you from the Salvation Army?"

"No, I'm not...."

"You remember Mr Smith, don't you?" asked Dingleberry.

"Never heard of him," and he continued off through a side door.

To conceal her embarrassment Dingleberry pretended that her husband's unusual behaviour was his way of enjoying a joke.

"Oh, what a character he is. He'll do anything for a joke," she said.

I just smiled and nodded in agreement.

"Please come into the drawing room and sit down and I'll fetch you some tea."

"Oh, there's no need to bother Mrs Holroyd, I'm perfectly alright."

"Two sugars?"

"No, really, I'm fine."

"Milk?"

"Certainly," I said.

I was shown into a beautifully decorated and furnished room, and there in the corner was a magnificent baby grand piano, which dominated the corner of the room. It housed a number of framed photographs, which featured the Holroyds from years gone by and one of them had Mr Holroyd in full uniform. I noticed that he had the rank of major. He looked resplendent in full dress uniform, wearing all his medals. Just then in he walked, carrying the back half of a car exhaust.

"Have you got any matches?"

"No, I'm afraid not Mr Holroyd. I don't have a lighter either because I don't smoke. I'm sorry about that."

"Did you say you don't smoke?"

"Yes, that's right."

"Good," he said. "Woodbines; terrible things. Had them in the army you know."

I'd no doubt that in his confused state he had a perfectly good reason for wandering around with a car exhaust in his hand, in the drawing room but I couldn't work it out.

I was fascinated by the photographs and noticed a selection with the couple pictured in some of the most famous places in the world including the Sphinx in Egypt and what looked to be the Great Wall in China.

Dingleberry joined me with tea supplied in a bone china tea service.

"I couldn't help noticing your photographs, Mrs Holroyd. I hope you don't mind."

"Don't mind what dear?"

"Me looking at your photographs."

"Oh, of course not, they're from a long time ago now."

She moved towards me and looked and there was a hint of sadness about her eyes.

"They were wonderful days. Jack was very handsome then. He was quite a catch you know at the time."

I smiled and nodded.

"I've noticed the photograph with the medals. Are they the ones you wanted to leave to the Regiment?"

"Yes," she said, "I'll show you them dear, I've got them here."

She went to an ornate inlaid wooden box, about a foot in length by about four inches wide. It was opened to display a set of medals in pristine condition. The first was the campaign medal 1939 – 1945 but along the row there was one which caught my eye.

"Isn't that the Military Cross?" I asked, expressing some surprise.

"Yes, it is dear, how clever of you. He was actually awarded that medal twice and mentioned in dispatches."

"When did he get that then?" I asked.

"Oh, it was towards the end of the war in the desert."

"Really." I said, full of admiration. "That's a very high honour."

"Yes," said Dingleberry, handing me a cup of tea, "he must have been terribly brave don't you think?"

"I don't think Mrs Holroyd, I'm sure, and the other medals…he's got the DSO as well."

"That's right dear," she said smiling. "Have you been in the army?"

"No, but my father was. He had medals too."

"Yes, that's right dear."

"I would really like to know about that Military Cross."

"There's very little point in asking him dear," she said pleasantly, which was the first acknowledgement that she had given me that her husband had any form of problem.

"Sit down dear, let me explain. You see, George is not what he was. He's alright of course but his memory's not as good as it used to be. We try to humour him; it keeps up his spirits you see."

Here I was, listening to this lovely old lady telling me about her war-hero husband and I had had the audacity to smile at his expense when they first came to see me. I felt rather ashamed until Batsoid walked into the room, this time carrying a steering wheel. He interrupted us.

"Have you seen the rest of this dear?" he asked, holding out the steering wheel.

"Not just yet Jack, I'm speaking to Mr Smith, the solicitor. We'll have a look for the rest of it when he's gone."

"Very good."

Courtesy had forced me to stand up when Mr Holroyd walked in, urged on by some small measure of shame and embarrassment. If ever anyone had gone up in my estimation so quickly, it was him. He turned, looked at me, nodded and told me to "carry on". I was almost tempted to say "certainly sir," but I didn't want Dingleberry to think I was taking the mickey. I just smiled and nodded deferentially. I looked again at the photographs and saw a splendid fellow in his thirties or forties, straight-backed and proud with medals for valour and here he was in his dotage, a prisoner to his own condition.

"Well I've prepared all the documents Mrs Holroyd and here is yours to sign but we ought to have two witnesses. Is there anyone who we can call upon?"

"No, I don't think there is dear. Oh wait a minute, there's my next door neighbour and her husband, I'm sure they will help."

The problem was that I wasn't sure that Mr Holroyd was of sound mind, which of course was necessary if the will was to be valid. I didn't quite know how to broach the subject because the last thing I wanted to do was to cause any offence but I had a job to do and so the problem had to be tackled.

"In dealing with these wills Mrs Holroyd, they have of course to be legal otherwise it could be challenged."

"Yes, I see, I understand that."

"So you may have to bear with me because I'm simply trying to protect your interests."

"Yes, of course, thank you."

"I've no problems with your will at all but I'm just worried about Mr ...."

Before I could say anymore Mrs Holroyd smiled.

"I know what you're trying to say Mr Smith," she said, "but if this helps you, George knows what we're doing and he understands it. I'll prove it to you. GEORGE…"

Mr Holroyd entered the room.

"George, you know that Mr Smith is a solicitor and we are going to make wills don't you?"

"Yes," said Batsoid firmly.

"And who do you want to leave your money to?"

"Well you of course, there's nobody else," he snapped.

Mrs Holroyd looked at me and smiled.

"That's good enough for me Mrs Holroyd."

"Look, it's nearly time for luncheon," said Mr Holroyd, looking at his watch. "Got to call the troops to order."

"I've outstayed my welcome Mrs Holroyd," I said as I prized myself out of a luxurious armchair.

"No, you're welcome to stay for lunch if you want, we're having meat and potato pie."

I faltered in my step because the mention of that wonderful delicacy had my mouth watering.

"There's plenty, and you'd like my pie. I've won prizes at the Women's Institute for my meat and potato pie. I use the best steak and new potatoes."

The last thing I wanted to do was to cause offence and miss the chance of meat and potato pie, so I gave in.

"Don't be alarmed," said Mrs Holroyd, "we have a ritual...we don't actually have a dinner gong, we have something else but please sit down and have a glass of sherry."

I was given a glass of sherry and Dingleberry went through a door into what I presumed was the kitchen. The smell of freshly baked meat and potato pie met my nostrils. I should imagine the effect was like that of a junkie who had just secured a well-awaited fix. I then heard Dingleberry shout to her husband.

"I've set the table George, everything is ready."

Just then Mr Holroyd entered the room and blew about a dozen notes on a bugle. My sherry went down the front of my shirt and I jumped up with such speed that I felt a twinge in my back, as though I'd pulled a muscle. Mrs Holroyd entered.

"That's the dinner gong," she said smiling.

I nodded in agreement as though it was a perfectly natural thing to do as I put my finger in my left ear and wriggled it about to try to re-establish my hearing. Mr Holroyd marched into the dining room and I followed him. There was a silver service set for luncheon with the most magnificent bone china plates and Mrs Holroyd saw me admiring them.

"They're Japanese," she said, "we have the full set, minus one or two plates which we've lost along the years but it's very unusual isn't it?"

"It must be worth a fortune," I replied.

"Yes, we've collected a lot of artifacts over the years. In fact, even George's bugle is a collector's item. They say that it was used at Rorkes Drift."

"Really," I said. The fact that it was still around Batsoid's neck worried me that at any minute he might be likely to play it again. In the event I enjoyed a sumptuous meal and when I was finished I sat back in my chair.

"That is the best meat and potato pie I've ever eaten," I said.

"Good," said Dingleberry. "He enjoyed the pie Jack."

"Good," said Batsoid, "you need plenty to eat, you never know when you've got to go out on patrol."

Dingleberry went into the kitchen to fetch some coffee and being intrigued by Batsoid's war record I just couldn't resist asking him about the Military Cross.

"I couldn't help noticing the Military Cross medal Mr Holroyd," I said, trying to engage him in conversation. For one moment Batsoid looked as though he had understood everything I had said. Surprisingly the rather blank look on his face disappeared and was replaced by a wry smile.

"It was a long time ago. It was in North Africa," he said thoughtfully. "It was the Tank Corp you know...we had to fight our way out of a tight corner. We had two Tiger tanks, one at each side of us," he said excitedly as he set out a reconstruction on the tablecloth in front of him. An orange took the part of one tank and a pear the other. The salt pot acted as the British tank.

"Our tanks were no match for the Jerry's," he said, "but they forgot who they were dealing with. We knocked one of theirs out before they blasted the tracks off ours. The tank caught fire and we dashed out and as we did so they started on us with the machine guns. There was only one way and that was that we'd got to knock the tank out. We got a bazooka...you know what a bazooka is don't you corporal?"

"Yes I do Major," I said entering into the spirit of the discussion.

"Very good," said Mr Holroyd, adopting a military tone. "I got the bazooka and we'd only got one shell...I took aim...and fired. I hit the Tiger head on and it caught fire. I took the only rifle and what bullets we had and I don't know what made me do it...fear I suppose…but we charged the tank and knocked the Jerries off one by one."

"Were you injured?"

"Yes, I got one in the shoulder and one in the thigh but they weren't serious injuries and funnily enough I didn't notice them until I sat down but it bloody hurt I can tell you. But then the armoured car came with four of them. I had only four bullets left…."

"What did you do then?"

"Well, they were soldiers just like me, with families and what have you…but it was us or them."

"So what did you do?" I whispered.

"Shot the buggers…yes, shot them…," and on that Dingleberry arrived with the coffee.

I was offered a brandy and Batsoid proposed a toast to the Regiment and we all joined in.

I left shortly after lunch had finished because I had an afternoon court and when I got back to the office I took the wills and gave them to one of the secretaries to put into the vaults. I have very fond memories of that afternoon with Batsoid and Dingleberry. We were to meet again but the circumstances were not to be as pleasant.

Chapter 6

STUTTERER'S LAMENT AND
ALBERT'S TRIAL

After one of the evening soirées I was having one of my headaches. Vera had brought me her usual concoction of tincture of bat, goose grease and elderflower oil, which she forced me to drink out of a massive spoon. If the intention was to make you vomit and detoxify, it worked.

Nevertheless I turned up for work early and ready for action at the local magistrates court. If there was a day when I would have been entitled to a sick-note, I think that was it. What I found most exasperating was that I turned up with flu, coughs, colds, gout, cartilage trouble, ulcer problems and the like, whereas some defendants didn't, even though they were on bail.

It occurred to me that the majority of the criminals in Rotherham suffered bad health because from time to time most of them submitted sick notes in one form or another but quite how they got them always baffled me. Gastroenteritis was high on the list of popularity because it was very difficult to disprove. It would take a doctor of rare quality to perform the sort of inspection that would satisfy even the most doubting Thomas. I've had them all in my time, with such diagnoses as 'tired and listless', 'sore testicles', and even 'feeling unwell', and those maladies remind me of Angela Ricketts. Her son, Todd, was due to appear in the adult court at Rotherham but his mother appeared in his place to tell the court of his illness. The Chairman of the Magistrates was an old friend of mine called Oscar Hartley. He had been the Mayor of Rotherham and a councillor for many years and was probably one of the most popular magistrates that we ever had, and even though he is no longer with us, his memory lives on in the Rotherham court.

I told him that Todd was unwell with a savage ailment and watched Oscar's eyes crinkle as he tried to suppress a smile.

"I have the defendant's mother here sir to confirm the malady as I have no sick note to put before you." I turned to the public gallery from where Angela shouted straight on cue,

"'e's got bleeding piles!" she shouted.

Even though it was Oscar and he liked a laugh, I avoided the strong compulsion to say,

"And he's got a chuffing cough as well."

Oscar hid his face behind his court list, pretending to read it, until he had composed himself.

"I'm told sir that his condition is such that he would have difficulty in walking into court, let alone enduring a bumpy ride on a bus through Rotherham," I continued.

Oscar's eyes narrowed and it looked as if he was going to tick me off for being cheeky.

"It's not an ailment you should make light of Mr Smith," said Oscar sternly.

"Of course not sir and I apologise if I gave that impression. I should imagine it is very nasty."

"You can take it from me," said Oscar, "it certainly is."

I decided to leave it at that and avoid discussing Oscar's medical problems. The rules and regulations imposed by these boffins from London tend to stereotype court users and all the dearth of training preached to magistrates, tends to bog everybody down with statistics, targets and points systems and the real job tends to take second place.

The defendants don't change however, and as we hurtled on into the 1990's a new spectre appeared to dominate the courts. Drugs had become fashionable and had achieved cult status, bringing with them the speculators who plied their filthy trade on every street corner, creating and facilitating a drug-related culture. There were still the traditional offenders who were just after the quick buck and one of them was Derek Otley, known to his friends by his nickname "Mirra", a shortened form of the word mirror. Nobody understood how he got that name but that's how he was known. He was also known as a prolific burglar with no hint of concern for those who suffered at his hands.

The first time I met him was in the height of summer when we were enjoying a rare heat wave. He'd left some papers on my reception from the CPS. They had photocopied the file and for some reason it had been served upon him. The offence was a "sneak-in" burglary, which means that he entered a house unlawfully and without consent, stealing something in the process. He had stolen a purse from the kitchen table but as he was leaving he was confronted with a rather large and fearless lady who didn't take kindly to being burgled. She challenged him but he claimed that he had gone into the wrong house by mistake. She gave a fairly detailed description of him but remembered in particular that he spoke with a pronounced stutter.

Tracey, our receptionist, told me of his arrival and I walked to reception. He smiled, nodded and followed me into the room, sitting down on the chair opposite my desk.

"It's Derek Otley isn't it?"

"Yep," came the reply.

"I think you've been charged with burglary, is that right?"

"Yep," came the reply again.

"I'll fill your Legal Aid documents in first if I may?"

"Yep," came the reply yet again.

I asked him for his National Insurance card, which he handed over and I took the majority of the particulars I needed from the charge sheet which had been rolled up inside the statements.

"Are you unemployed Derek?"

"Yep," came the reply.

"Are you in receipt of DSS benefit?"

"Yep," came the reply.

I busily ticked all the appropriate boxes in the Legal Aid application and asked him to sign it.

"Would you just sign between these two crosses on the sheet and be careful, that's my best pen...when you've done I'd like it back please...that's how I got it," I said, trying to lighten the subject.

"Yep," came the reply yet again, disregarding my humour.

I began to summarise the evidence and explained the case to him.

"They say, Derek, that you sneaked into a house in East Herringthorpe and took a purse from the kitchen table. As you were leaving, the owner of the house came into the kitchen and confronted you. She says that she can give a good description of you."

I looked at the description written in the statement and then looked at him.

"It looks fairly accurate to me but she goes on to say that the man she spoke to had a pronounced stutter, what do you say about that?"

"W..w..w..w..well,.. th..th..th..th..that leaves me ou..ou..ou..ou..out th..th..th..th..then doesn't it?"

I lifted my eyes up from the sheet in front of me and looked at him with a curious stare.

"I'm f..f..f..f..fighting this one th..th..th..th..this time," he continued.

I wondered how I could break the news to him that he had got major problems with the evidence. I didn't want to insult or embarrass him concerning his affliction but it was my duty to point out the difficulties in the evidence.

"The lady says that the man had a pronounced stutter."

"S..s..s..s..so?"

"Well, if I can say it without causing offence, I've just detected...." I looked at his face and he was clearly embarrassed, which made it even worse for me and so I continued,

"Well you see, you appear to have what I would describe as...a sort of ...a kind of gentle but likeable...very likeable in fact...sort of...stutter really."

He didn't reply and looked at me in horror.

"Not that it's a bad one you understand but it might just be sort of apparent to the court and when you have to give evidence in your defence, they might actually just pick up that there is a slight difficulty...about your speech...if you see what I mean."

"Oh, f..f..f..f..fuck it. It's only wh..wh..wh..wh..when I am st..st..st..st..stressed."

"Yes I see and I can sympathise but you are likely to be under stress when you're being cross-examined and as she's got the description pretty accurately...," but then I pulled myself up sharply because when I finished reading the statement I noticed that she had completed her description by saying that the man had "sort of an ugly face". I was just about to read that point out when I realised that she had got it absolutely right; he was a bit of an ugly bugger but how could I broach that point?

"Far be it from me to put a dampener on it Derek," I continued, "but I rather think if this lady comes up to proof, or should I say sticks to her evidence, you have, not to put too fine a point on it..., shit it."

Derek looked at me rather despondently, as if he really hadn't understood a word I'd said but there was little point in beating about the bush and looking stupid trying to cross-examine this lady on the question of whether Derek had a stutter or not.

"Are you with me Derek?" I asked sympathetically.

"I..i..i..i..in a w..w..w..w..way," he said, calming down slightly.

"It's the stutter point that worries me most, to be perfectly frank with you," I said, gaining in confidence. "I wouldn't want you to go into that courtroom and come a cropper."

He looked at me with a blank expression.

"And mark my words you will...the minute you open your mouth."

"Well, I'll n..n..n..n..not give evi..evi..evi..evi..evidence then."

"Well, you could do that, or rather not do it if that was your choice but the magistrates will be suspicious and they'll think you're refusing to give evidence on purpose, thus covering up the stutter. Of course you're not obliged to and they can't criticise you for it but they're going to smell a rat."

Derek thought for a moment with his head bowed.

"There is another point," I said.

He looked at me rather expectantly.

"Well, you…er…," trying to think of something else to say, "if they find you guilty after pleading not guilty, the sentence will be much worse."

"Will it go to Cr..Cr..Cr..Cr..Crown?"

"Hopefully not and if we put in a guilty plea we might be able to keep the sentence down a bit but I'm afraid it's got "bird" written all over it," I said.

He had grasped the point. The last thing he wanted was a lot of "bird" (common parlance for a prison sentence).

"So what do you think then Derek?"

The odd thing about some defendants is that even though they have done it and even though the evidence is overwhelming, it is almost as if it is against their religion to say the word, "guilty".

Derek thought for a bit longer before agreeing to plead guilty but he was clearly unhappy about it.

"Wh..wh..wh..wh..what will I h..h..h..h..have to s..s..s..s..say?" he asked.

"All you say is "guilty" when they put the charge to you and then leave the rest to me," I said confidently.

"F..f..f..f..fuck me."

"Yes, I see what you mean," I said thoughtfully, but I couldn't help thinking that somebody would if he didn't plead guilty.

I changed the subject by asking him a little about his background and eventually I got the story out of him that he had been to prison twice, been on probation three times, had failed to do his community hours, had been to a detention centre when younger and had spent considerable periods in the care of the local authority. In short, he was a recidivist.

"You are becoming a bit of a recidivist," I said without thinking.

"What the f..f..f..f..f… does that mean?"

"It means someone who …well…someone who's used to spending their time in prison and who can't get out of the habit."

He went on to tell me in his own way that the courts always sent him down and never gave him a chance. He thought the courts sent him to prison for the hell of it.

"You don't actually help yourself," I said firmly.

"Oh, y..y..y..y..yes I do…it's h..h..h..h..helping myself that got me into th.th..th..th..this m..m..m..m..mess in the f..f..f..f..first place."

His comment broke the ice and we both laughed. I had got through to him after all.

We were at court the following week and I asked the Court Clerk just to confirm his date of birth and address and not put him through the embarrassment of having to say it, particularly as we'd only been allotted fifteen minutes for the case from start to finish

Of course he pleaded not guilty at first, forcing me to give him a gentle reminder and then with a deep breath and the greatest possible reluctance, he used the magic word, "g…g…g…guilty" and he was allowed to sit down.

The case was before my not so favourite magistrate, the Lord Chief Justice and after the Prosecutor had outlined the case he referred to the stutter as being the clincher from the point of view in establishing guilt. It was ironic because the prosecutor, Herbert Casson also suffered from a slight stutter which became apparent when he was giving the court details of the offence.

"…and the worse thing of all, Your Worships, was that he left the hallway and he shat…shat…he shat…"

I looked up from my notetaking wondering what the hell the defendant had shat on, until I was put out of my misery.

"He shat… he shattered a window in the conservatory."

"Thank the Lord for that," I said to myself. I resisted the temptation to laugh.

I stood up to mitigate and by some remarkable coincidence I stuttered on only my second word. It was a most unusual thing for me to do but I think it was just a coincidence. I was convinced that the Lord Chief Justice thought I was taking the mickey and he gave me a very nasty look. The prosecutor told me that he thought the way I started my mitigation was very funny and I ought to be on the stage but I didn't appreciate his point and asked him if he would like a copy of the Magistrates Handbook shoving up his arse. He didn't take too kindly to that and funnily enough has not spoken to me since.

Derek's case was adjourned for the Probation Service to see him and see what they could come up with in their "bag of miracle cures", for after all, Derek didn't want "bird" again.

"Bird" was on Albert's mind as well, for the last thing that he wanted was prison.

During the weeks building up to the trial he'd lost contact with Caroline and had kept the date of the court hearing a secret. Unfortunately her father, the Chief Inspector, had found out about Albert's past and had forbidden Caroline to have any contact with him. Since the parting, Caroline had got a place at University to study veterinary medicine but Albert had taken to travelling about on motorbikes, which had led to all sorts of problems with the police and the magistrates who had banned him from driving and subsequently he was unable to drive to see her. Like many young men, however, he found the attraction of riding motorcycles so great that he was caught driving a tracker bike from a field to his home whilst disqualified. Fortunately because it was only a short distance the magistrates decided not to send him away but they warned him that if he did it again he would go to prison.

We had a listing for Albert's trial in front of a recorder whom I had never heard of. Recorders are barristers or solicitors who sit as part-time judges. I'd been warned that he was trying to find his feet and make a name for himself and was suffering from "Judgitus". "Judgitus" is a peculiar condition of the brain, which affects some judges but fortunately not all. It's a form of paranoia which induces feelings of grandeur and superiority, to the extent that they become, what is known in legal circles as "shit bags".

This Recorder had caught the disease at a very early stage in his career and he was hell-bent on pulling rank on others of his colleagues in much more lowly positions. We had drawn the short straw and he was to conduct the jury trial.

The case started on the Wednesday morning and the jury had been sworn in after a late start. Albert had missed his bus and was late, which caused the recorder to lose his temper and tell Albert that if he were late again, he would lock him up for the duration of the trial.

The prosecutor, Mr Harley-Dobbs, outlined his case to the jury with great gusto, suggesting that Albert was as guilty as sin and had no defence to the charge whatsoever. One by one the witnesses were called as Albert sat, a lonely figure, in the huge dock in Court number one at the Sheffield Crown Court. I was sitting behind defence counsel, and was as confident as one could be in a jury trial, until the prosecution case began to unfold. Unfortunately the evidence made Albert look guilty. By the end of the prosecution case we'd all but put the rope around Albert's neck and convicted him.

It was then the turn of the defence. We had one witness, or at least that's what we thought at that time and Albert went into the witness box most reluctantly. He had a fairly quick and agile mind but he was more streetwise than clever and I worried what sort of impression he was going to give. Albert had always pleaded guilty every time he'd gone to court, basically because he was guilty but on this occasion he protested his innocence and what made it worse was that I believed him. I was worried that he might be found guilty and because his record was extensive the sentence would have been increased but he would have gone to prison for something he hadn't done. I felt the weight of responsibility very greatly and as I looked round the courtroom I could see Jack and his family in the gallery giving Albert the thumbs-up sign as he marched to the witness box.

Counsel took him through his evidence carefully and Albert did extremely well but the biggest test would be the cross-examination. Mr Harley-Dobbs went about his work with ruthless efficiency and did his very best to tie Albert up in knots but he stuck to his guns and did reasonably well until he was asked about defence witnesses. His voice bellowed out and reverberated around the high ceilings of the courtroom.

"If you were visiting your girlfriend's house, as you appear to reluctantly accept, is your girlfriend going to give evidence to confirm that this is correct?"

"She can't," said Albert nervously.

"Why pray is that?" asked the Prosecutor, tugging at his gown impatiently.

"Because she's at university."

"She doesn't exist does she?" said the prosecutor firmly.

"She does exist but I don't want her to be upset or embarrassed by people like you," said Albert.

This was the first time that he'd shown any signs of getting annoyed or upset. The prosecutor pounced on the point.

"Of course there is another explanation isn't there?" he asked.

"I don't know what you mean," said Albert.

"I think you do," said the prosecutor thoughtfully. "The other explanation is that this girl does not exist and neither do her family. Perhaps you'd like to tell us why they haven't been called."

I was willing Albert to tell the truth and say that her father was a policeman and he didn't want him to get involved but Albert wouldn't answer and I noticed the jury were beginning to shuffle in their seats with discomfort. The trial was moving in favour of the prosecution.

"For God's sake Albert, tell him," I kept saying to myself.

Just at that moment the usher brought me a note. It said that someone wanted to see me outside but I was in no mood to leave the trial at that point and so I disregarded the piece of paper and listened intently as Mr Harley-Dobbs continued his cross-examination.

Albert was getting upset and flustered and didn't know how to handle the situation but then he made the cardinal mistake in giving evidence by losing his temper and answering back. The prosecutor smiled, as he realised he had touched a nerve and it was only going to be a matter of time before the humiliation was complete.

The usher came to me again with another note saying that it was most important for me to go outside. I tutted angrily and stormed outside. When I opened the large door I was confronted by a very good-looking blonde girl. It was Caroline.

She told me that she'd made enquiries about the trial but Albert had deliberately given her the wrong date. By chance she'd found out about the hearing that day, had travelled from Leicester and insisted upon helping.

"I want to give evidence Mr Smith," she said. "It's the very least I can do, I simply can't stand by and watch Albert be found guilty."

I smiled and nodded in agreement and made my way back into the court; not for the first time I was going to act contrary to my instructions. By the time I returned to court, Albert and Mr Harley-Dobbs were arguing "hammer and tongs" and the Recorder was getting a little tired of it.

"Heptonstall, would you kindly calm yourself down and answer the questions without being so rude."

Before Albert could comment I informed our barrister what had happened. At the end of the cross-examination he rose to his feet and told the Judge that his witness had arrived and the defence wanted to call her. The prosecutor coughed and spluttered and complained bitterly, saying that the defence had not given prior notice of the witness.

"Did you say you had another witness?" asked the Recorder.

"Indeed we do, Sir. I apologise for her late arrival but I'd like to call Caroline…."

The jury were already in mid-discussion and it looked as though they were making a decision there and then but one by one they stopped their conversation and looked towards the witness box as the beautiful Caroline took the oath. She said it so sweetly and gained a number of admiring glances from the younger male members of the jury. She gave an extremely good account of herself, telling the court in no uncertain terms that Albert had indeed been invited to her home on Boxing Day. She said that he had been expected at 3.30pm but hadn't turned up. She was cross-examined but when witnesses are telling the truth, it is impossible to catch them out. She looked, sounded and indeed was, extremely honest and the main plank of the prosecution's case, that Albert couldn't prove where he was going, had gone.

When Caroline's evidence had finished, the Recorder decided to adjourn the case until the following day for speeches and summing-up and with the Judge's words ringing in his ears, Albert left the court. Caroline was waiting for him outside and they left together.

The following morning the jury returned to their places, both counsel were ready to start but Albert was nowhere to be seen. Just as the Clerk of the Court called upon everyone to stand for the Judge, the doors to the court burst open and Albert ran in, perspiring freely.

"Where the bloody hell have you been?" I whispered to him.

"Me dad's Skoda wouldn't start.

"So how have you got here?"

"Well...I er...I drove my motorbike.

"Bloody hell, Albert."

"Oh it's worse than that."

"What do you mean?"

"Well...the coppers pulled me up coming into Sheffield."

"Oh, Albert...."

"I'm sorry Steve...."

"Sorry, what's sorry?"

"But they didn't know I was banned."

"But what if they check?"

"They won't."

Famous last words...

The defence counsel summed up to the jury and after a long and tedious summing-up by the Recorder they were called upon to consider their verdict.

It was one of the longest three hours wait that I have ever experienced. I spoke first with Caroline and then bought her a cup of tea from the WRVS kiosk in the main foyer. She told me that she was enjoying university but for some reason peculiar to her she missed Albert.

"I know he's a rogue...but he's got so many good points. All he needs is a direction. When he's with me he never presents a problem."

"I know that Caroline. The problem is that you're not always there, and then what?"

"I know but I have to think of my career. I have asked Albert to come to Leicester but he finds it difficult to relate to the other students. When I'm on holiday I come home and see him but he's distant. He says he's glad to see me but I'm not sure. I wonder if he has lost interest. Do you know Mr Smith?"

"I don't I'm afraid but I will find out," I said apologetically.

"Thank you Mr Smith, I am grateful for all you have done. I'll wait until after the trial. If he's found guilty I'll stand by him. If he's acquitted I'll wait at my friend's house for him to come to me. If he doesn't come I'll know; you see he's not very good with words."

There was nothing I could say.

I left Caroline and went to the holding cells to see Albert. He was sitting in his cell staring at the floor as I walked in. He looked up and smiled.

"What's it look like Steve?" he asked.

"I don't know Albert, I simply don't know. I think we've done enough but you can never tell with juries."

For the next two hours or so we played cards. When the prison officer came to the cell I had lost the equivalent of eighty pounds.

"The jury's back," he said breathlessly.

"This is it then Albert, best of luck," and we shook hands. In doing so the ace of spades dropped out of his cuff. He laughed nervously and I shook my head.

I walked upstairs and into the main courtroom and we all took our places as the jury filed in one by one. The prosecutor looked extremely confident and sneered at his opponent on the defence bench. I sneered back and the prosecutor looked away.

"Will the foreman of the jury please stand," said the Court Clerk ceremoniously. "Mr Foreman, have you reached a verdict upon which you are all agreed?"

"We have," said the foreman.

"How do you find the defendant Albert Heptonstall, guilty or not guilty?"

There was a short pause as if the foreman had forgotten the verdict. You could have cut the air with a knife, such was the tension, and then he said the magic words,

"Not guilty."

I took a deep gulp of breath.

"And is that the verdict of you all?" asked the Clerk.

"Yes it is," said the foreman.

Defence Counsel rose to his feet and asked the Judge if Albert could be discharged.

"Yes, I suppose so," said the Recorder reluctantly and Albert was freed from the dock to cheers of "Good old Albert" from the public gallery.

Albert walked past me and winked and I just smiled. When I went outside I saw him with his family. Caroline had gone.

"And now Albert, that's the end of trouble for you."

Albert smiled and nodded appreciatively.

"Now there's the little question of Caroline. She'll be waiting at this address."

I handed him a piece of paper with the directions.

"She'll wait until eight o'clock. If you go she'll know you are still bothered; if you don't' she'll know it's over. It's as simple as that."

"Wasn't she great Steve?"

"She certainly was."

"I think she's the greatest. I've kept out of the way because I didn't want to cock-up 'er studies. She's gonna be a vet and I was gonna 'elp 'er set up 'er own outfit."

"Why have you avoided her Albert?" I asked.

"Well, I let 'er down, getting locked up and if she's gonna be a vet she's not gonna want to be 'eld back by a burke like me. It wouldn't look reight good would it, 'er boyfriend in the nick? Nobody would trust 'er and that's not fair. And there's another point...."

"What's that?"

"Well it's not reight easy to say..."

"Try me."

"Well, I'm not in 'er league like...I'm...."

"What?"

"Well, the sort of people she mixes with won't take to me. I'll 'old 'er back. It's not fair. I can't 'old 'er back Steve, I can't but I'll go because I can't 'elp meself."

I might not have accepted what he was saying but I understood. For the second time that day there was nothing I could say.

I left Albert and his family at the court and set off for the office. At about twenty past eight the police rang me to say that Albert had been arrested just after 7 o'clock at his home for an offence of driving whilst disqualified. He had been taken to Attercliffe police station in Sheffield where he was being detained for court the following morning. Apparently Caroline caught the eight fifteen train for Sheffield and the connection to Leicester. She was unaware of Albert's arrest.

Chapter 7

DRUGGED UP AND WASHED OUT

Heroin addiction has been around for ages but as the 1980s disappeared into the history books and the 90s began, drugs were more readily available to the masses. A steady supply into the country from eager hands to even more eager distributors meant that more and more of the wretched stuff was being introduced to a largely unsuspecting section of our youth who felt that they had every reason or excuse to try it. Once snared, they were fair game for evil suppliers who profited greatly from their trade in misery.

The police did their best but were losing the one-sided battle which made fortunes for the unscrupulous who left the middle man to take the risks and the mugs to serve the prison sentences when they were caught. Information came to the police from a variety of sources, particularly the addicts themselves who would sell their souls for the next fix.

I had more and more cause to study the drug culture as its subjects invaded the court lists. I represented so many of them from the big time suppliers to the "also rans" and the ordinary users, ever-growing in number, who formed gangs for there was safety in numbers as they plied their trade in protection. Then of course there were the casualties; not the users themselves for they had a choice but the parents and siblings. They were usually the ones who were most sinned against and the least likely to complain.

One such family was the Hopkins. Arthur, the father, a steelworker in the mid-forties; Eunice, his wife, of similar age and their two children Tanya and David completed the household. They lived in a three-bedroomed semi in a pleasant suburb of Rotherham. Arthur and Eunice were good people, honest and hardworking and had done their very best for their two children. David was sixteen, a good scholar with a bright future and then there was Tanya. She was spoilt as a child with doting grandparents in whose eyes she could do no wrong, or so they thought.

Tanya had a good childhood, doing well at school with parents who were proud of her, particularly Arthur who doted on her. Arthur's world was particularly insular. He had his work, his garden and his family; he wanted nothing else. He had worked all the overtime available to ensure that his children had all they needed;

the very best of everything – nothing was too much trouble as he watched his children grow into adulthood, but he found it difficult to accept that it had actually arrived.

The Hopkins's house was neat and tidy and the rooms were bedecked with family photos, including one enlargement in an expensive frame; Tanya on her eighteenth birthday. It had pride of place over the fireplace in the front room, which Arthur and Eunice had furnished and decorated with the proceeds of a matured insurance policy to the tune of eight thousand pounds.

Arthur was a tall well-built man, whose body had been honed with years of manual work. His hair was thick and wavy, just turning grey. He had a quiet manner, was shy and did not mix well but was well respected by his workmates and neighbours as a thoroughly decent man.

Eunice was six inches shorter with an expanding physique which, she said, had been caused by the "change" but she had lovely auburn hair which had retained its natural colour despite everything else "going to the dogs" as she so often put it. She had a winning smile but was shy like her husband. In short, they were an ideal, well-matched couple. Everything in the Hopkins's household was fine and rosy; that was until Tanya met Jodie.

Most mothers have nightmares about their children and Eunice was no exception. Her personal nightmare came in the form of Jodie Cliffe. He had been experimenting with drugs as he indulged his passion in all-night parties and taking amphetamines, initially to stay awake and latterly because he had to. He progressed into opiates and heroin took charge becoming his master and he its ever-willing servant. As with most addicts he felt the need to persuade someone else to share in the misery.

Despite his unruly nature, he attracted local good girls like a magnet. Perhaps it was something new, a break from the traditional lifestyle that Tanya had been used to but Jodie's "devil may care" attitude appealed to her. He was not studious or boring like most of the local lads who were at university or were holding down jobs and perhaps that is why Jodie seemed different. He had a flashy car, designer clothes and a penchant for making girls laugh, funding his expensive lifestyle by selling drugs. He was street-wise, quick-witted and well able to look after himself in fights.

Drug pushers are extremely territorial and dislike intruders straying onto their domain. Jodie's entrepreneurial skills had led him into many crises but he coped by utilising the talents of local yobs who fought his battles for a handful of silver.

Eunice and Arthur were very polite and welcomed him into their home, unaware of his character. Initially they were won over by his good Latin looks and smooth tongue, which superficially at least endeared him to the family, but Arthur felt there was something about this young man that did not add up. Jodie was perceptive and sensed Arthur's concerns but he knew how to please and for a time Arthur and Eunice were placated by his easy-going manner.

Just after Christmas I was appearing at the magistrates court with Albert who was entering a not guilty plea to a motoring charge, when Jodie came to court. He was carrying the customary pink charge sheets handed to him at Rotherham police station. There were four charges, three for possession of heroin, cocaine and amphetamines and one for possession with intent to supply. I looked at the charge sheets and looked at Jodie.

"That's a lot of drugs."

"You're right," said Jodie.

"The possession charges are not much to worry about, but the intent to supply, that's a major problem," I said.

Jodie's case was adjourned because the prosecution had a lot of paperwork to give us so we could establish exactly what we intended to do with our case. Jodie breathed a sigh of relief because it had put off the evil day.

When I went outside I saw a very pretty young lady waiting at the end of the corridor. She appeared to be waiting for Jodie. I explained to him that I would want to see him again as soon as the documents had been received and he went on his way. I noticed that he took the girl's arm and led her away.

A few days later I received a large bundle of documents including statements and exhibits, all appertaining to Jodie's case. I wrote to him and sent him an appointment so that we could study the documents together. Within two or three days he was in my office and the same young girl I'd seen at the courtroom was sitting with him in the waiting room. I invited him into my room and just caught the words,

"You stay here."

Jodie entered my room on his own and I asked him if he wanted his guest to join us. He was most hesitant about it and said that she would be quite happy where she was. I concluded that his reluctance meant that he did not want the girl to be party to our conversation and thus become aware of the evidence against him.

I gave him a brief summary of the evidence, telling him that the police had kept observations on his flat for a period of over a week.

They had gained access to an empty house across the way, from where their observations were carried out, taking a series of photographs using a telephoto lens which were all timed and dated. There was no argument about that because his property was the only one in the block with the main door leading to the street and if you were using that door you were visiting that flat. There were photographs of at least eighty people visiting the house over an eight-day period, an average of ten per day. Some of the photographs showed the visitors with bank notes in their hands and some with small packets on their departure. Jody was seen in the doorway on at least half of the photographs. Interestingly his Morgan sports car was parked outside.

The statements consisted of twenty youths and girls all of whom had admitted buying drugs from the flat. Almost half of those witnesses named Jodie as the supplier. The other part of the case consisted of statements from police officers who had visited the flat with a search warrant and found drugs with a street value of over five thousand pounds, together with drug paraphernalia and cash to the tune of two thousand pounds in used notes. The police had also found a number of DSS payment books. The suggestion there was that the payment books were in lieu of repayment for drugs bought on credit.

Jodie had been interviewed at the police station in the presence of a solicitor from another firm and he had said that the drugs were for his own use and that the cash was a loan from people he didn't wish to name, which was owed to a drug dealer. He told the police that the visitors comprised of friends and people who had come to visit Jodie's dealer.

His former solicitor had advised him that the evidence was overwhelming and he should plead guilty to the charges but it would have meant a substantial prison sentence and Jodie did not want that. He was trying to delay the proceedings as best he could, although for what purpose I wasn't sure, although I suspected that he just wanted to avoid the inevitable.

After I gave him an explanation of the state of the evidence he asked me my opinion.

"What do yer think?"

I thought for a moment before answering because this was a problem that needed to be looked at very carefully to avoid the stalemate that was achieved with his former solicitor.

"I think the evidence against you is very strong and my real fear is that if you fight the case and are convicted you will get a longer sentence."

Jodie did not like the advice he was being given and the look on his face made it obvious.

"But I'm not guilty," he said.

It was never our duty, contrary to popular opinion, to force people to plead guilty, although there was a growing band who thought that that was the case. We were failing in our duty if we didn't advise people as to the strength of the case against them and we also had to warn them about the reduction in sentence they would get if they pleaded guilty first time. Eventually it became a legal duty imposed upon us to advise as to the reduction. When cases were listed for a trial (a not guilty plea) the court asked us if that advice had been given and they wouldn't proceed unless it had.

I could understand Jodie being disappointed because there are very few who actually want to be sent away but I felt at that meeting that to have pushed the point even further would have only sought to alienate him from me completely. When I read out the statements of the witnesses who had named him, his eyes narrowed and I could see the hatred in his face, which totally belied the "hail fellow, well met" character that he tried to portray. I could see him systematically noting the names of the witnesses in his memory bank and when the conversation was complete he asked me to remind him of the names to see whether or not he could remember any of them, or so he said. I was unable to recall them.

A week later Jodie was back in court and Tanya, his girlfriend, was with him. She looked anaemic and there were blotches and spots on her face, which made her look decidedly ill. She wore the telltale signs of drug addiction, with her slurred speech and her movements slow and deliberate. As Jodie and I were talking she was closing her eyes and seemingly nodding off. Her hair was unkempt and she looked as if a good bath would not have gone amiss. I'd seen many people in that state before and as the years wore on I was to see many many more. I couldn't resist a dig at Jodie.

"Is she not well?"

"No, I think she's got a virus," he said hesitantly.

It was remarkable how addicts so vehemently deny that they were addicts. I got no sense out of her at all because, to use a colloquialism, she was "out of it".

Jodie told me that it was vital that his case be adjourned.

"And what reason shall I give for the adjournment?" I asked.

"Anything," he said forcefully. "I just can't be dealt with just yet, I've got to have some more time to get my things in order."

I was aware that we'd not actually received all the papers and it would have been possible to ask for an adjournment so that we could see everything before any final decisions were made and so I made the application at court and the magistrates adjourned the case for three weeks. Jodie had got his adjournment and three weeks to get his house in order. When I went outside he was waiting for me.

"Do you think we'll be able to get another adjournment next time?"

"I'm afraid not Jodie," I said, "there's no prospect of that. The case will have to proceed. They'll decide to send you to Crown Court and then the case will have to be adjourned for six to eight weeks anyway for the committal papers to be served, so that's your adjournment."

"How long will it be before I'm at Crown after that for my trial?"

"Well if you're pleading not guilty possibly another six weeks after that, but before you decide on that course I want you to have a conference with the barrister I am going to select for you and let him advise you as to how you stand. I think this is definitely a case for a second opinion because you don't seem to be impressed with what I've told you."

"It's not that but you must understand, I've got to look after myself on this one."

I was tempted to say that he would be extremely good at doing that but there was little point. Tanya by this time had come round.

"What about you then Tanya? You don't look too well to me."

"I'm alright, I've just got a virus," she said, repeating her mentor's words.

"How's your mum and dad?"

"Well I haven't seen them for a bit because they're decorating and everything, so I've just kept out of the way while they get straight."

It was clear to me that she was lying.

Jodie seemed agitated when I mentioned Tanya's parents. He looked at his watch quite dismissively and said that it was time they were on their way. It was as if Tanya wished to say something but before she had the chance, Jodie took her arm and gently pulled her away.

"Come on, we've got things to do."

They set off but as they were walking down the corridor Tanya turned and looked at me rather sheepishly. There was nothing I could do. Her situation looked hopeless.

Three weeks passed remarkably quickly and despite our previous discussions Jodie was more agitated than before as he demanded yet another adjournment.

"Well, we've got witnesses to see," he said.

"What witnesses?" I asked.

"Witnesses, to say that I'm not dealin'."

"And who might they be?" I asked.

"Well, there's the neighbours for a start, they'll be able to help on that."

"But the neighbours are people who've been seen visiting your house."

"Well, of course they do, they come to borrow milk."

"Don't they ever buy any?" I asked.

"What do you mean?"

"Well they must visit your house at least twice a day."

"Well, we're friends aren't we?"

"As you please. Well, they've not given a statement to the prosecution that's for sure. I'll certainly see them but we can do that during the time that we're waiting for the case to appear in the Crown Court list."

Jodie was unhappy but then that sort of person always is when things don't go absolutely their own way. Tanya wasn't with him and I asked after her, only to be told that she had gone to see her parents. I accepted what he said and we went into court. The prosecutor outlined the case and not surprisingly the magistrates said that Jodie would have to go to the Crown Court to be dealt with as the case was too serious for them.

That afternoon I received a telephone call from Mrs Hopkins.

"This is Mrs Hopkins, Tanya's mum."

"Good afternoon," I said.

"I'm sorry to bother you but I wonder if you might be able to give me some information if possible."

"Certainly, if I can Mrs Hopkins. It depends what it is."

"Well, we haven't seen Tanya for over five weeks now and we know that you're representing her boyfriend. We wondered if you could tell us what's happening?"

"Well I can't tell you about the case I'm afraid because that's private to Jodie but I can tell you that I saw your daughter the other week, she was with him at court."

"Was she alright?"

"Well I didn't really get much time to speak to her but to be perfectly frank, she didn't look at her best, no."

"That's because of the drugs, we know that," she said despondently.

"But I understood that she was with you yesterday?"

"No, that's not true at all. We were at home all day yesterday but we haven't see her."

"But you've been decorating haven't you?"

"No, what makes you say that?"

"Oh, it was just something that was said. I must be mistaken."

"I've got to ask Mr Smith, and forgive me but she is our daughter; is she in trouble too?"

It was obvious that the lady was distraught. They were a good hard-working family and their daughter had gone astray in the worst conceivable way. She had brought much shame and concern to her parents and it did not seem fair.

"How is it that a girl like her could get involved with someone like Jodie,Mr Smith?" she asked. "Is it our fault...have we let her down...have we not been good enough parents?"

"Not at all Mrs Hopkins, let me assure you. I get lots of kids in here from all sorts of homes, good and bad, and it's wrong to try to blame the parents."

"Arthur thinks it's his fault. He told her she'd to get out of the house you know, because of the drug thing. She was stealing money out of our cupboard and then on one occasion she actually took the video and sold it. The worst thing was she took my engagement ring and sold that too. She denied it of course but we saw it in the local pawnshop and they told us that she'd taken it there. That was bad enough but the fact that she continually denied it was the final straw and Arthur effectively kicked her out. We've lived in torment ever since."

She began to whimper over the phone and I was aware of my inadequacy at being unable to intervene or to assist.

"Would you just do one thing for me, Mr Smith?"

"Yes certainly, of course I will, what is it?"

"When you see her, tell her that her father and me still care and tell her that whatever we can do to help her, we will. We'll get some money together and we'll pay for her to go to a clinic or something. She's asked us for the money already but we know it will go on drugs but if she'll only...."

Her voice tapered off and I could tell that her concern had got the better of her, so I interrupted.

"Mrs Hopkins, I'll do my very best. At the very least I will speak to her."

"I know you can't discuss her boyfriend's case but we think that if he's out of the picture she'll be alright. Is he going to get sent to prison?"

I was torn between my duty to my client and a moral duty to these people who had been so badly treated.

"I think I can say this Mrs Hopkins. It's common knowledge that Jodie is charged with possession and supply of drugs. The charges have been read out in court and it is an open forum, so that information is public knowledge. If someone were to ask me as a general proposition, what sentence would someone get for such offences, I would have to say that more likely than not they would get sent to prison. So far as Jodie's case is concerned, I can neither discuss it or speculate beyond what I've told you. I'm sorry to sound so glib but there are rules and I'm stuck with them."

"I understand," said Mrs Hopkins, "I'm sorry that I should be so presumptuous as to ask you but I'm sure you can see our position."

"Of course," I replied, "and believe me I have every sympathy."

"Oh thank you, Mr Smith. Don't forget if you see her to tell her that we asked about her."

"Rest assured I will," I said.

She put down the phone and I imagined what sort of agonies that poor woman was going through. Whilst it wasn't my place, sooner or later I was going to see what I could do about it.

Eventually Jodie was committed to the Crown Court and was listed for the Monday morning but he didn't turn up and a warrant was issued for his arrest. I presumed that he was still getting his house in order. Nevertheless, a week later he was arrested outside the DSS and taken into custody.

Tanya had tried to interfere and got herself arrested for obstructing a police officer and when she was searched they found drugs in her pocket. She was charged with possession of heroin and the following morning she was placed before the magistrates' court. Jodie was taken straight to Sheffield and after much deliberation agreed to plead guilty to a charge on an agreed basis, that is to say he admitted supply but on a much smaller scale. He was sentenced to three years' imprisonment and Tanya had her case adjourned for a Probation Report and to be seen by a drug counsellor. She was placed in a bail hostel during the adjournment and shortly afterwards returned to court, having failed to turn up for her probation appointment. Mrs Hopkins had contacted me in the meantime and offered her support but driven by feelings of guilt and disloyalty, Tanya had declined the offer of a room back at home.

I saw Tanya at New Hall Prison near Huddersfield. What a place and an experience that was!

On the day of Tanya's sentencing her parents turned up and were sitting in the waiting room outside. I felt so terribly sorry for them as they sat there waiting and worrying.

Tanya had been sitting in the dock and was unaware of her parents' presence. She'd had three weeks without any drugs and had started a course of substitutes. The drug agencies were pleased with her and were prepared to continue the course. The Probation Officer made a very strong recommendation for a Probation Order and residence in a drug rehabilitation clinic for a period of six months. She had every prospect of beating the problem but it was going to be very hard and so the case was adjourned for an assessment to take place.

I saw Tanya in the office late one afternoon and for almost two hours we discussed her case, her life and her family. She told me that she was upset and disappointed in herself for the way she had treated her family and all the indications were of genuine contrition but so often drug addicts will protest their desire for rehabilitation and in the next breath they will let everyone down. I have seen children from good families steal from their parents, even to the point of using violence. They would sit on street corners and beg, harass and even sell their bodies for the next fix. A massive proportion of all our crime was drug related and over the next ten to fifteen years we were to see it escalate into epidemic proportions.

I put all these points to Tanya who listened courteously, nodding at the appropriate times and expressing her desire to go onto any course or receive any medical treatment that could be offered to her.

At that time courses for drug addiction were few and far between but Mr and Mrs Hopkins decided to use what money they had left from Mr Hopkins' insurance policy to give their daughter the start she so badly needed. The cost of the course would amount to thousands of pounds but the despair that her parents felt could only be erased by this last ditch attempt to save her. I could not fault their compassion but there were those who said that they were wasting their money on a lost cause. The Probation Service discussed Tanya's case with her parents and were aware of the efforts that they were prepared to go to, to jump the queue and pay privately for her treatment. They recommended a Probation Order with a condition that she live at the private hospital where she would be treated. The course would take six months during which time she would be an in-patient and for three months she would not be allowed any home leave. In many ways it was as bad as a prison sentence but at least they would look at the root cause of the problem and try to deal with it.

It was no surprise to me that the court gave her the benefit of the doubt and, impressed by her parents' efforts, they made the order and Tanya was freed. Before they took her away I went to great pains to explain what would happen if she failed to observe the conditions of the Probation Order.

"It's going to be very, very difficult for you Tanya," I said firmly.

"I don't care," she said, "I'm going to get well and I'm going to get back to work. I also want to continue my education."

"I hope you do Tanya, I really do because if anything, your parents deserve it."

She nodded in agreement and within minutes she'd said her farewells to her parents and off she went to face the hardest six months of her life.

The advance payment left Mr and Mrs Hopkins virtually destitute and the long cruise that they'd promised themselves throughout their married life had gone. They made no complaint, in fact in many ways this positive action had removed any blame that they so wrongly thought was theirs.

Tanya kept in touch by telephone every day and after a very shaky start, she began to respond to treatment and month by month she grew fitter, stronger and healthier. Towards the end of the six months' period Mr Hopkins contacted me and told me how well his daughter was doing. He spoke with great pride and confidence, saying that whilst the treatment had taken all their savings, it was worth every penny. They had just enough left to take their special trip.

Their "holiday of a lifetime" was spent in the Lake District. He told me that they'd had more pleasure, peace and rest there than they would ever have had on any cruise because Tanya had beaten her addiction. I was delighted and I told him so. I expressed every hope that when she came back into the community, Tanya would be able to remain drug free. Jodie, her mentor, was still inside and there were moves to sell their house and move away before his release. It looked as if there was going to be a happy ending. On one occasion I bumped into Tanya and her mother who were shopping in town when I was on my way to court. She looked wonderful; her eyes were clear and bright, she had put on weight, she was clean and well turned out. She told me that she'd enrolled at the local college to continue her studies. She appeared to be happy and with that dreadful phase of her life behind her, she looked forward to a brighter future.

As I walked up the steps to the court I couldn't help thinking that for once I had actually helped to make a difference. It was a good feeling.

I didn't see Mr and Mrs Hopkins again as my services were no longer required, but there will always be someone to take Tanya's place on the never-ending story of drug-related crime. Only the names change, the faces and the attitudes are always the same.

About a year later I was in the Sheffield Magistrates' Court one morning, waiting for my case to be called on. It had long been my habit to look at the court list to see if I recognised any of the names on it. As the years rolled by, more and more names went into my memory bank and my powers of recall being reasonably good, I could remember most of them. Midway down the list for my court that day was an entry bearing the name of Tanya Hopkins. Her address was given as Sheffield and the charge was possession of heroin and amphetamine. I never found out if it was the same girl.

Chapter 8

FAREWELL TO MADGE

Albert had appeared at Sheffield Magistrates Court in respect of the driving whilst disqualified charge and despite my efforts he was sent down for four months. I saw him in the cells afterwards.

"I don't think there's an appeal in it Albert. You'll have to serve about two months of it."

"Don't worry Steve, I'll be alright. I'll do it standing on me 'ead."

Somehow I didn't believe him.

"I take it you didn't go to meet Caroline."

"I didn't get chance, they arrested me at 'ome," he said despondently.

"Albert, I must ask you, would you have gone before eight o'clock?"

Albert didn't answer.

"Were you going or not?"

He shrugged his shoulders and said nothing. We were disturbed by a prison officer.

"We're on our way now Mr Smith. I'm sorry but I'll have to ask you to go."

I got up, shook hands with Albert and left. Once again there were circumstances which I couldn't understand. That old so-and-so called Fate had played the wrong cards yet again. Albert was sent to Armley jail at Leeds and this time it was for something he had done but that didn't make it any the easier. I thought four months was too long but then I would, I was on his side.

I saw him once during one of my visits. He was in reasonable spirits but had lost weight. I realised I ought to spend eight weeks there and if the diet didn't kill me, the boredom surely would.

Albert was about one month into his sentence when I got the sort of phone call that turns the stomach and dries up the throat. This time the caller was Jack and he was the bearer of grim tidings. Madge, his devoted wife of almost thirty years, was dead.

"It was last night," said Jack tearfully. "She'd been complaining of 'eadaches for weeks. I tried to get her to go to the quack's but she wouldn't 'ave it Steve, she wouldn't 'ave it."

"I know Jack, I know."

"If I'd 'ave insisted she might be alive now," interrupted Jack.

"You can't say that Jack."

"I can, I 'ave...."

"What on earth happened?" I asked.

"She 'ad a stroke Steve...a stroke...she just went to sleep and never came round...she tried Steve...we all did...oh God...what about Albert? What shall I say? What shall I do?"

"Do you want me to tell him?" I asked as sympathetically as I could.

"No Steve...thanks...really, thanks...but it's got to come from me."

"Thank God," I thought to myself, "that was one job I couldn't face".

Jack gave me as much information as he had. Dear old Madge had had a stroke and had died quietly and painlessly at home amongst her family, all except Albert and now Jack had to tell him. I could not think of a grimmer task.

I sat back in my chair as the realisation came to me that Madge had actually died. It was the suddenness of it and after all she wasn't old. And what about Albert? How do you tell a child that their mother's dead, and yet it is one of life's events that we all have to face.

Jack and I spoke for half an hour. He told me of the good times and the laughs...such laughs. He just confirmed how devoted to each other they were but then the reality had to be faced. The funeral was to take place the following Monday and my task was to try to persuade the authorities to let Albert out. It wouldn't be easy but I was determined that Albert would be there. It took ten telephone calls and three letters, and they required proof. I submitted a copy of the death certificate, the funeral booking and a letter from the undertaker and it worked. Albert got his permission.

I wasn't able to see Albert before the funeral, there simply wasn't time, but the Monday came soon enough. I walked down the tree-lined pathway to the crematorium where the leaves had all but completed their life. Those that remained were brown and curled but underneath the new shoots were waiting to burst into life when nature decreed herself ready. The west wind caused me to shiver and fasten my topcoat. I realised that winter was on its way and in a matter of only weeks the path would be white with snow.

The nearer to the chapel I got the louder the music. It was a sort of Irish lament played on a solitary violin that gave an eerie feel to that bleak grey afternoon in late November. I waited as one by one

Jack's relatives and friends gathered, heads bowed in grim acceptance of their mortality. A Ford Escort arrived and parked near to the slip road leading to where I was standing and two large gentlemen got out, one from the front and the other, who had been sitting with someone considerably smaller, from the back. They looked like prison officers and I was right. The smaller man was Albert. I breathed a sigh of relief.

The officers were in plain clothes but I could not help but see the handcuffs despite the attempt to conceal them.

"Please don't make him sit with those on," I thought to myself so I decided to try to persuade them to unshackle him during the service.

I went to meet them. Albert's face brightened a little when he saw me.

"Hello Albert," I said grimly.

"Hello Steve. Thanks for coming."

I smiled and directed my attention to the guards.

"Hello. My name is Steve Smith. I'm a solicitor and I act for the family. I wonder if I could speak to you about Albert?"

"Certainly," said the spokesman in a most polite manner.

I took him to one side leaving Albert handcuffed to his colleague.

"Look, you know it's Albert's mum's funeral don't you?"

"Yes."

"Well look, Albert's only got three weeks to do, he's not going to run off...not today...come on, unlock him...I'll sit with him if you like, but don't make him go in there in handcuffs."

"Well I don't know...if he runs off...it's my job."

"Look, unlock them at the door, let him sit with his family. There's no other way out."

"Look Mr Smith....I don't want to be the bad bugger...."

"Well don't then. Just let him grieve without the bloody handcuffs."

"OK, OK, but if he does a runner, he's dead."

"Fair deal. Let me speak to him."

I walked back to where Albert was standing.

"Albert, this gentleman is going to let you out of the handcuffs for the funeral. I've given him my word that you won't do anything foolish."

The other guard looked surprised.

"Don't worry Steve, that's the last thing I'd do today. I'm out in three weeks anyway and besides not today, especially not today."

"OK, that will do for me. Now go down there and look after your dad when he comes. I think you'll find that he needs you."

The handcuffs were unlocked and Albert walked to the entrance and then the cortege arrived. One stranger nodded in my direction and his friend did the same. I returned the greeting as the first car containing Madge's coffin pulled up at the door. The second car contained Jack and five of his children. The third car had the rest crammed into it with Morris sitting next to the driver who was looking decidedly unhappy with so many passengers. Morris pressed some of the buttons on the centre console causing the driver's seat to move up and down at regular intervals, much to the driver's annoyance. Jack was suitably attired with a black suit and tie. The rest were wearing their Sunday best. No one spoke although Jack managed a reluctant smile in my direction. I estimated a gathering of about sixty people and if the devil could have cast his net at that moment, half the petty crime in Rotherham would have ceased.

Albert was silent even when he came face to face with his father. There was nothing to say. The moment had robbed them of a greeting.

Six of the boys took the coffin with Albert at the front, freed from his handcuffs by his reluctant guards who shamefacedly concealed the offending items in their pockets as they followed the gathering to stand at the back at a discreet distance.

The first hymn was the stalwart *Abide with Me* sung entirely without gusto by a reluctant choir of family and friends, all of whom wished this day had never risen. Some sat in tears and some in disbelief as the vicar delivered his eulogy from a makeshift pulpit erected pending repair to the real one, which lay discarded on its side near to the entrance.

"A family orientated woman....," said the vicar, and he should. After all Madge had twelve children and you couldn't get more family orientated than that.

"...brought up for the whole of her life in Rotherham without aspirations to live anywhere else...."

"Not quite right," I thought. There was the time when she packed everyone off to Northumberland when Jack became a member of the working class, even if his job was as a pigeon-fancier's mate.

"...she enjoyed a good meal with friends...."

That she did, but quite how she managed the whelk stew was beyond me.

"...she worked hard for her family," continued the vicar.

"That she did," I thought again, "generally helping in the acquisition of other people's property."

"...she was an accomplished gardener with a remarkable allotment."

Yes, and geese which would have outshone any Rottweiler.

"...and a remarkable gift she shared with her husband for training and breeding racing pigeons, especially a champion of rare quality...."

Yes, but don't tell anybody he had named his best pigeon "Arse!" What a name for a pigeon; what a name for anything except an arse!

"...a woman who would do anything for her family...."

"That's true," I thought to myself. What a nice way to finish for no one could have accused her of anything else, especially when she helped Jack to flog those Cuban cigars from off the back of a lorry to just about every smoker in Rotherham.

"...she will be sadly but well and truly missed."

Of that there could be no doubt. Madge was very special. One of the most likeable villains' molls I had ever met and for all that she was a rogue, she had a sense of values. She would never have robbed a house or an old person but "commercials" were fair game.

As the vicar finished speaking Madge's favourite tune played over the tannoy, *Moon River*, the orchestral version with the choir. It seemed particularly poignant.

I listened intently to the beautiful collection of musical notes magnificently sung by a most impressive selection of voices. I was so impressed I was minded to get a copy, such was the quality of the performance. Everyone in the congregation thought the same but then the violins conspired together to wrench at the heart strings when the hitherto sombre mood changed. Handkerchiefs made appearances up and down the aisles and even Billy-One-Leg, Jack's next door neighbour and enemy, was affected. He brought out what looked to be a well-used oil rag as he dabbed his eyes to stem the flow of tears. I had a lump in my throat larger than a golf ball and found myself looking for my handkerchief. Seeing my difficulty Billy-One-Leg handed me his oily cloth. Kind thought though it was, I declined the offer graciously clearing my throat in the process just as the service had finished, and then one by one the congregation, urged on by the funeral director, turned and walked away, first Jack, followed by the children. Albert remained where he was watching as the coffin disappeared from view behind the curtains. Eventually everyone except Albert and his two guards sitting in the back had left the chapel.

The guards moved slowly to the end of their aisle, stopping only when I held out my hand to persuade them to stay where they were. The music continued as I walked down to the front of the aisle to where Albert was sitting. I stepped over an array of hymn books and one copy of the Beano before sitting myself down at his side, looking forward as though there was something to see. Albert broke the silence between us.

"I let her down Steve…being in prison and all when she was dying."

"No you didn't Albert, there was nothing you could have done."

"Yes I could. I could 'ave been at 'ome."

"And done what?"

"Just bin there."

Albert's eyes were red and his eyelids swollen as he tried hard to hold back his tears.

"She thought the world of you Albert," I said to reassure him.

"How do you know that?" he asked expectantly.

"She told me."

"When?"

"Just before she died."

Albert paused as he tried to regain his composure.

"Well if she did I didn't give her very much to be proud of."

"Your mother was so proud of you she never stopped talking about how good you were with animals…she told everybody."

Albert turned to face me.

"Did she, did she really?" asked Albert, desperately seeking the answer he wanted.

"Yes, definitely," I replied, giving him the very answer he needed.

Albert forced a painful smile as relief was etched across his face, and he looked forward once again. Fearing he would be disturbed by the guards, I wanted him to move of his own accord and not face the indignity of being placed back into handcuffs.

"It's time to go Albert, there's another funeral after this. It's someone else's turn now. I think it's for someone else's child."

I lied, but then everybody was someone's child once and all's fair in love and funerals.

Albert dried his eyes and stood up. I stood with him.

"Goodbye mum," Albert whispered.

"Yes, goodbye Madge," I said, joining in Albert's farewell.

Looking back I suppose it was a silly thing to say but at the time it seemed wholly appropriate and Albert definitely appreciated it.

As we walked back from the aisle Albert stopped and turned towards the curtains once again.

"Did she really say all that Steve?" he asked pathetically.

"Yes Albert, I wouldn't lie to you about that."

"No you're right Steve. She liked you, trusted you, like us all. Thank you."

"You don't have to thank me Albert."

"For 'er then."

I smiled and nodded.

As we left the chapel Madge's favourite song, *Moon River* was just about to finish and the lump in my throat had returned. I thanked Albert's guards for being so sympathetic and was delighted to be told that they were going to allow him to go home for one hour provided he didn't cause any problems and he left when they asked him to. They knew that Albert was a low risk and even they had not been left unmoved by the ceremony. I had learned that day that death is a great leveler. No one is spared from the inevitable and I never felt more like living for the day than at that moment.

"Are you coming back to our 'ouse?" asked Albert.

"No thanks Albert, I've got to go to court this afternoon. I'm representing Billy-One-Leg's son and some other choice subjects."

"OK," said Albert despondently. "Fancy Billy-One-Leg turning up. I didn't expect 'im."

"No neither did I. More reason to bury the hatchet."

"Bury the what?" asked Albert.

"Never mind, it's just one of my funny sayings."

"Oh, I got yer."

Just then Jack appeared and he and Albert embraced. It was a most touching moment. Then Jack embraced me.

"Thanks for coming Steve, she would have been so pleased."

I didn't reply but just nodded thoughtfully.

He turned to walk away. How his life would be changed, and changed for ever.

"Never hurt me once you know Steve, although there were times when I deserved it but Madge wasn't like the rest."

"You're right there Jack."

Albert interrupted us.

"Do you want a lift Steve?"

"No thanks Albert, I've got the car. I'll see you another day."

"OK, I'm out soon. I'll come and see you but it won't be for anything criminal I've done. You can say I've retired, I owe her that."

Just at that moment my attention was drawn to a beautiful blonde-haired girl who had been sitting at the back during the service. It was Caroline. She moved forward and she and Albert embraced. I could not resist a smile. Albert then turned to face me and held out his hand. There were tears in his eyes. We shook hands and there were tears in my eyes too, so much so that I turned immediately and walked away along the tree-lined walkway. A leaf had blown against my chest so I took hold of it and continued to walk towards the car park. A solitary bird was singing on a nearby branch. I stopped and looked up as it continued its melancholy tune and then I heard the sound of a vehicle behind me. The engine noise was familiar. It sounded just like Jack's transit van and when I turned to see it, I was right, it was Jack's van. I stopped on the grass verge to allow it to pass and I recognised the two men in the passenger and front middle seat. They were the prison officers who had escorted Albert to the funeral. Jack and all the children were in the back but I didn't recognise the driver straightaway until I heard the sound of the horn and then as it drew close I realised who it was. I was open-mouthed in amazement. He was serving six months for driving whilst disqualified and there as large as life with two prison guards for company was Albert, driving the bloody van. He waved as he passed by and as ridiculous as this sounds, I waved back.

Chapter 9

BIG GEORGE GETS HIS... AND ARISE
SIR DUMBLEOID

It was a Monday. I don't like Mondays. It is always a stressful day and it began with a three-handed case, which means that there were three defendants, all charged with the same or similar offences. It was a public disorder matter where the prosecution alleged that my client, known by his nickname "Big George" and his erstwhile companions had been drinking in a public house in Dinnington, a small hamlet not far from Rotherham. There had been an altercation in the pub which spilled over onto the forecourt outside. My client was alleged to have punched two men in an attempt to knock their heads off, followed by a similar attempt on their private parts.

The police arrived on the scene in the Black Maria and tried to arrest Big George but they realised that it was not going to be easy because Big George didn't want to be arrested. He explained to the police in fairly graphic terms what he would do if they tried to lay their hands on him but Big George had consumed twenty-three pints of lager and was not at his best and so he was no match for four burly policemen who hadn't been drinking at all. As Big George was being placed in the Black Maria some of his friends took exception to the rough way in which he was handled, consequently they began to interfere. Comments such as 'I say you fellows, I think you are being rather rough with Big George' would have been better used by Harry and Alvin Willoughby who chose instead to inflame the situation further.

"Get off 'im you black pig-fucker," came from Alvin, whereas his brother was a little more graphic.

"If tha dunt get off George I'll shove (and then pointing to a form outside the pub) that bench up thee arse."

The police claimed that they advised Alvin and Harry to desist from using such appalling language but not surprisingly PC Bayldon didn't want a wooden bench shoving up his arse so an arrest followed, which prompted another of the group to complain about it. He apparently repeatedly gesticulated with the middle finger of his right hand thrust upwards, shouting, "Swivel on this." He was arrested as well.

They were all charged with threatening behaviour and of course by the time they appeared at court they were sober and moderately contrite. The prosecutor was Herbert Casson, the lawyer with a slight stutter. He was addressing the magistrates about a shoplifting case which had been called on first.

"The store detective went to the back of the store and stood watching the defendant sitting on the toilet...the toilet...sitting on the toilet...toiletries section on a stool used by the staff for stacking shelves. He was to shove a bottle of aftershave up his ar... ar... the armpit of the jumper he was wearing. He left without paying."

Herbert was very entertaining, especially if he was under stress, when his little problem got the better of him.

The Bench retired only to return and send the unfortunately shoplifter to prison for twenty-eight days.

I had the next case which involved Zack Wolstenholme. He was supposed to be appearing from Leeds prison on a charge of burglary but the prison reported he was in the hospital wing after having swallowed two batteries the night before.

"We had better adjourn the case for seven days to see what his condition is," said the Chairman of the Magistrates.

Quick as a flash I responded.

"Could you make it a fortnight sir? I understand they were Duracells!"

My joke went down like a lead balloon as the magistrates just stared at me dismissively.

The court retired again for a 'comfort break' and when they returned it was George's turn. The case was adjourned so that we could consider the prosecution evidence and when it arrived I studied it with some amusement. I don't suppose it was very funny to the police at the time but to read the summary of events did make me smile. I think it helps to be able to see the funny side of things, or at least that's my story and I'm sticking to it.

For all his size and aggression Big George was terrified of being sent to prison and I could not help thinking that he presented an entirely different kettle of fish at the court than he would have done outside the Falcon Arms in Dinnington. He had been charged with assault occasioning actual bodily harm on both unfortunate complainants. The other three defendants were represented by a foreigner, or another solicitor from out of town, to use a common parlance. I had not seen the "foreigner" before and looking at his age I guessed he was fairly new. He was what we called in Rotherham an "awfully awfully", which is a rather sarcastic bite at the so-called bourgeoisie.

The prosecutor had decided that the charges which had been laid did not truly represent what happened in the incident and that a slightly less serious charge would be more appropriate so far as the Willoughby brothers were concerned. Big George had no option but to plead guilty and his case was going to be adjourned so that the Probation Service could see him and try to come up with a non-custodial option.

The Magistrates came back into court and the "foreigner" was mulling over what the prosecutor had said. Just as the defendants were being identified by the Court Clerk, the "foreigner" appeared to be in some difficulty in making a decision. He had been concentrating so hard upon the dilemma that I do not think he realised that the magistrates had returned to court and so in more than a stage whisper he shouted across to the prosecutor, "I'm not sure Alvin Willoughby should plead guilty to breach of the peace because all he did was shove his finger up."

"Up what?" I asked in a stage whisper of equal measure.

The chairman of the magistrates and his male colleague tried hard to stifle a laugh but the female representative was not impressed and looked down her nose.

The "foreigner" then, in support of what he had to say, started gesticulating with his middle finger in exactly the way that I suppose his client had done on the night in question when he had invited the police to "swivel on it". The sight of him giving that rather rude gesture in the face of the court brought even more hilarity to the proceedings.

"It can't be breach of the peace, just shoving your finger up," he said, missing the joke entirely. The Court Clerk was aware that the whole proceedings were going to turn into a shambles unless he brought the hilarity to an end, so he asked the Bench to retire while the "foreigner" and the prosecutor resolved the problem. As the Bench walked out I couldn't resist it. "We'll see if we can resolve the problem sir," I said with a straight face, "and we'll try and find out exactly what my friend's client's finger was shoved up."

All I could hear was the sound of muffled laughter from the magistrates' retiring room. Some minutes later when everything had been resolved the magistrates came back in, refusing to look at me for fear that they would start laughing again. Eventually my attempt at humour had got through.

I should explain that there is still a great deal of humour in the courts despite attempts these days to stifle it. The way to try to get away with it is to deliberately make some form of innuendo, as in this particular case, but do it with a straight face so that you always have the defence that you hadn't realised what you had said. If you did it with a grin, or even a laugh, you leave yourself open for rebuke. The problem is in keeping a straight face.

Big George had his case adjourned and the others were "weighed-off" with fairly large fines. Interestingly, the defendants completely missed the humour.

"That was funny about the finger wasn't it?" I said to George.

"What was that Steve?" he asked.

"Oh, never mind," I said, "it was just my attempt at humour that appears to have missed the mark."

"Missed the what?"

"Never mind. Anyway your case has been adjourned Big George. When the Probation Service send for you, you must turn up to see them and they will discuss the case with you. Then they'll make a recommendation."

"Recommending what?"

"Well, it could be anything. It could be a Probation Order, a Community Service Order, a suspended sentence, forty lashes on the Town Hall steps, an enforced enema or just having your left bollock amputated."

George missed the point again and screwed up his face in confusion. For one awful minute I thought he'd actually believed what I'd said.

"I was only joking about the bollock."

"What...Oh, aye...I see what you mean," said George missing the point completely.

"It's in your interest George to see them, because often they will make a good recommendation that can mean the difference between bird and freedom."

"Bird?"

"Yes, bird; nick."

"Nick?"

I was getting exasperated.

"Yes, bird, nick, slammer, jug, the pen...oh alright, if I must, JAIL!"

"You mean...going to prison?"

"Yes," I said excitedly, as though I had unraveled a major dilemma.

"There won't be any prison in this will there?" asked George pathetically.

"Well the magistrates said that they could not rule out custody, which means that they can't rule out prison."

"Bloody 'ell, I only brayed them."

"I think you did a bit more than brayed them George, in fact they're lucky that they didn't suffer a serious injury."

"They're lucky I didn't give them a good 'iding."

George's idea of a good hiding was not an attempt to knock their blocks off or remove their genitals, he meant really serious harm, as in death!

"Well, I've told you all I can George, you know what you've got to do. See the Probation and do your best."

"Ay, but I'm not having any prison."

"I'll tell the magistrates that," I said, "and hopefully all will be well."

"Ay," said George thoughtfully and then walked off to join his friends.

"And thank you very much for everything," I shouted after him sarcastically. "Don't bother to thank me, despite the fact that I did my best...missed my lunch...fell out with a colleague....."

George was leaving by the double doors and again totally missed the point.

"And thank you for knocking those men senseless and trying to remove their wedding-tackle...." My words tailed off into despair.

I remember the words of my former mentor, George Tierney, when he told me "Don't do this job for thanks because you won't get any". He was right. Perhaps I was becoming a little cynical, after all I had been self-employed for some time and a little of the edge had gone off it.

The problem I fear is that there is a proportion of the general public who have certain expectations of the welfare state.

I've dealt with many criminals over the years; some I have liked some I have disliked, some I could tolerate and some I could not. There were those for whom I had a great deal of sympathy and some I could not pardon for their wrongdoing was so evil. There have been the clever criminals, the witty criminals, the bright, the not so bright and then, of course, there's the Dumbleoid.

A Dumbleoid is a name given to someone who perpetrates a crime so naïve of nature that the prospects of him getting away with it are less than nil. Their offending ranges from the ridiculous to the sublime and over the years I have had the joy of being entertained by these remarkable people. There are, of course, some who find themselves · in the court arena for whom you have the greatest sympathy. I think of people whose patience has snapped at provocation so great that they have been led into violence or dishonesty which is totally and completely out of character, but the Dumbleoids are something else.

One such character was Martin Hacksey. Martin had never been to school but then to qualify that, I think he went once but he didn't like it so he never went again. His mother said it didn't matter because he wouldn't have been able to learn to read and write anyway but he had an endearing personality and everybody in the office liked him. I think the best way I can describe him was to say that he was an extremely thick Albert and whilst basically harmless, he had a penchant for committing silly offences, which inevitably ended up with him being caught. He spent most of his day watching television and most of the night roaming the streets. This pattern had begun as a child when, at the request of his mother, he was sent out, usually at about ten or eleven in the evening, to play whilst his mother entertained a succession of what she described as "uncles". They always left some money on the sideboard and they were rarely ever seen to visit again. Martin therefore boasted of being a member of a very large family, although he could never quite remember their names. He would return in the small hours of the morning whereupon he would catch up on the night programmes via his video player, which his mother had bought him for raising no objection to her shenanigans.

Martin was a likeable lad, with that sort of persona that made you feel sorry for him. He was always immaculately clean, reasonably well dressed and well groomed. He had a pleasant face, the whitest teeth I'd ever see but a vacant look which only altered when he smiled. He was generous to a fault and he was regularly taken in by his peers who used him as their entertainment but when the laughter ceased they promptly left him on his own. Nevertheless, there was no hint of aggression although he did have a tendency to be light-fingered. I found that with a view to gaining acceptance he often found himself as the "fall guy" for those much more criminally minded than he. It wasn't a case of him being bullied but more used in an unholy union which inevitably led to trouble.

He made an appointment to see me because he was appearing at court the following week on charges of theft and deception. He had built up an array of convictions over the years, usually for minor pilfering. He always got caught and he always pleaded guilty and this particular occasion was to be no different from the rest, which earned him the coveted title 'Dumbleoid of the Month'. Nevertheless it was always a pleasure to see him and, being interested in his welfare, we always had a long conversation, usually about nothing in particular. I would try to talk him out of his silly ways but would fail dramatically in the process.

He had a passion for Tracey our receptionist, who he thought was "swell". Like many of the youths in that era, he had been subjected to a surfeit of American television programmes that were "hip" and the fashion was to use some of the American terminology and slang sayings, with comments such as "it's cool man" and the use of the word "like" at every conceivable opportunity grated on my nerves. Martin had fallen foul of this as well and on his arrival he swaggered into the office and his face lit up when he saw Tracey sitting on reception.

"How's the coolest chick in town?" he asked rolling his head from side to side.

With amazing repartee Tracey countered,

"I don't know, I'll ask him when he comes in."

Martin was bewildered. All he could think of to say to Tracey's sparkling rebuff was,

"Like...cool...like."

Tracey smiled at him and showed him through to the interview room.

"Now then Martin, come on in, what's to do?" I asked, shaking his hand firmly.

"Cool brother," replied Martin in his latest Americanesque.

"Yes," I said nodding contemplatively. "I understand you've got a new summons Martin?"

"Ah," he said and handed me some dog-eared pink sheets.

"They've got me for theft and deception...like and like...well like...."

"Cool," I replied thoughtfully.

"Ah," replied Martin.

"What's it all about then Martin? I asked.

"Well it's like this," said Martin. "Somebody nicked this Giro like and gid it to me like, so I went to try to cash it tha sees like."

"Who gave you the Giro?" I asked.

"It was one of the lads like but I ain't sayin' who 'cos Jed Parker will be mad!"

"OK, that's fair enough," I said, "and the deception I presume is taking the Giro to a post office and cashing it."

"Well ah," said Martin, "well, trying to cash it."

"Trying to cash it?"

"Well ah, they wouldn't give me any money."

"How did the postmistress twig it?" I asked.

"She were a bit smart like and said she weren't givin' me any money 'cos she didn't think it were my Giro," he continued in his slow drawl.

"Was that because you didn't have any ID?"

"What's an ID when it's at 'ome?" asked Martin.

"ID means identification, something to show who you were."

"Well it were no good showing 'er who I were, were it like? She wunt give me owt then."

"No, I didn't mean that. What I'm saying is, did she "twig it" when you didn't have any ID?"

"No, it didn't get that far."

I was confused so I thought I'd try from a different angle.

"I'm struggling a bit Martin, give me another clue."

"Well, I gid 'er the cheque reight?"

"Yes, so far so good."

"Reight...like...then...like...I handed it o'er and she took it like."

"Excellent, we're getting there. And then?"

"Then she looked at me like, like looking down at me sort of thing."

"Was she tall?" I asked.

"No," said Martin looking perplexed. "It were a funny...like...look that sort of said... tha're a twat."

"Who said that?" I asked.

"Well she didn't say it but that's 'ow she looked."

It was my turn to be perplexed.

"Then what?"

"Then she told me to wait a minute and she went into t' back. I thought she'd twigged it."

"So what did you do then?"

"I shouted t' back to say I was gettin' off and she told me to wait there."

"What did you say?"

"I told 'er to fuck it."

"You told her to what?"

"I told her to fuck it. I meant like forget it, so I legged it."

"Where did you leg it to?"

"Out of the shop."

"Where did you go?"

"I went to Jed's car and told 'im that they wouldn't gi' me owt and he weren't 'appy so he kicked me out the car and fucked off, leavin' me to it. I weren't sure what to do so I sat on this wall next to the shop thinking about it, do yer know what I mean?"

I nodded.

"And that were it."

"What do you mean, that were it?" I asked, realising that pulling teeth would be easier.

"Well, I'd blown it 'adn't I? The cops came and went in the shop and in the post office."

"What did you do?"

"Nowt."

"Then what?"

"The cops came out and nicked me."

"Didn't you think to leg it when the cops came and went in the shop?"

"I never thought about that," said Martin, "I were a bit slow there weren't I?"

"Well just a little, but what did you do when you got to the police station?"

"I didn't do owt."

"No, I meant what happened when you were at the police station?"

"They put me in a cell and that were it."

"But there must have been more to it than that?"

"Well, ah, they interviewed me like."

"And what did you tell them?"

"Oh I were smart there," he said smiling.

"Why, what did you do?"

"I told them it weren't me but that old bird from the post office pointed me out, so that caused me to think."

"What did you think?"

"I thought, I've fucked it now," said Martin shrugging his shoulders.

"So what did you do?"

"I ain't got any option. I coughed it so the coppers bailed me and 'ere I am."

"Yes, here you are," I thought, "back in trouble again, in breach of a conditional discharge which the court gave you only three months before."

"Do you remember being put on that conditional discharge?" I asked him.

"Ah," said Martin shrugging his shoulders again.

"Well you know what that means this time don't you?"

"I'm in bother."

"Right first time. I think the best thing we can do is to fill in all the forms and then I'll get your old file out and see what information we can get from that."

I asked him his date of birth and his proper address and post code and then I proceeded to ask him about his personal circumstances.

"You're not working are you?" I asked.

"Nope."

As I was busy writing I noticed that Martin had gone back to his full-blown Yorkshire accent and the American seemed to have slipped away for the moment. I then proceeded to ask him about his income and I needed to know what sort of benefit he was claiming because the form required me to say so.

"I'm just asking about your personal circumstances Martin. Right, what are you on at the moment?"

"Nowt much."

"But you must be on something."

"Argh, I am."

"Well, what then?"

"I 'ave a bit of cannabis but I don't take heroin or anything."

I put my pen down and looked at him.

"No, I meant what type of benefit, not what bloody drugs you take."

"Oh," said Martin laughing, "I thought you meant…."

"Never mind Martin, just tell me what benefit you get."

"Er…disability."

"Disability?"

"Argh."

"How come you're on disability?"

"I'm disabled," he said defiantly.

"I realise that you burk, but how?"

"Depression."

"Depression?"

"Argh…it's not nice, depression."

"Who says you suffer from depression?"

"Doctor did."

"Which doctor?"

Martin started laughing.

"Now what's funny?" I asked.

"Witch doctor," said Martin.

"What?" I asked, in a state of confusion.

"Witch doctor, that's a good un, that is…witch doctor."

I completed the paperwork and Martin left, wolf-whistling Tracey as he walked to the door. She just looked at him with contempt written all over her face.

"Told thee she likes me," he said winking at us both.

That evening I went to play football at the Herringthorpe Leisure Centre on the outskirts of Rotherham. We were playing a large firm from Sheffield who had a number of players to choose from. We did not have a full squad so Bader Lidster had to persuade one of his friends to play in our team. Bader told me that he wasn't a very good footballer but he was an excellent kick boxer.

"Brilliant," I said to Bader "if we should be losing we can send him to beat everybody up."

"Fair dos," said Lidster believing I meant it.

We won the match five nil; that is to say that five of them were injured and none of ours were, although the teams scored two goals each. There was little chance of a return match because the other side did not like our "ringer", the kick boxer and what's more they did not accept our excuse that he had bad eyesight and kept missing the ball and kicking them.

After the match I stayed for a drink and then went to meet Goody, Jarvis, Wilf, Pagey, et al for one of our monthly soirées at our friend Bob Ego's restaurant, Ranulph's, in Hutcliffe, Sheffield. Bob is a brilliant chef and his food was and is famous throughout Sheffield. The other good thing about his place is that you are allowed to take your own wine. The other customers looked in amazement as bag after bag of grog was shipped into the little restaurant from our eager brethren. After we'd placed our order I went to the washroom and bumped into an elderly lady. I stood aside to let her pass and she smiled at me sweetly before speaking.

"Are you Mr Smith, the solicitor?" she asked.

"It depends whether you're friendly or not," I said with a smile.

She smiled again.

"I've heard a lot about you," she said, smiling sweetly. "I understand that you're very good."

"Flattery will get you absolutely everywhere," I replied. "Are you here for a special party or something?"

"Yes," she said, "It's my birthday today and some of my children have brought me out for a meal."

I recalled that I'd seen a group of other diners in the restaurant, about eight in number, and she must have been with them.

"Are you in the large group?" I asked.

"Yes."

"Are they all your children?"

"Yes, they are and I'm very proud of them."

"Goodness me, that's quite a considerable family," I said.

"Well they're not actually my children," she said, "they were fostered by me over the years and they've all got together and brought me out."

"What a very nice thing to do," I said. "I do hope you enjoy yourself."

"Yes," she said, "I certainly will."

I turned to leave and she spoke again.

"Oh, before you go, can I be cheeky and ask for one of your business cards. I don't want to talk business today when you are out socially but I have a young man called Graham Taylor who's fostered to me now, who's got himself into a little bit of trouble and I'm very anxious to help him. I understand that you cover the Sheffield Magistrates' Court as well."

"Yes, I work throughout Yorkshire but I don't think I have a card with me," I said reaching into my jacket pocket. I took a paper napkin from a table nearby and wrote out my name and telephone number and gave it to her.

"Thank you very much," she said, "I do hope you have a pleasant evening."

We shook hands and she had a remarkably firm handshake for a woman of that age, particularly as she had such small hands. Her fingers were child-like and you couldn't help noticing just how small they were. I wished her well and returned to my table thinking what a charming old lady she was.

I took particular notice of the table where she had been sitting and noticed a cross-section of people. They varied in age I would have said, from their forties to early twenties. They were all smartly dressed except one, the youngest, who had an ordinary T-shirt and chino trousers who looked out of place in comparison with the others.

We had a splendid evening with much revelry but before it came to a close the old lady and her group had departed. As she walked past me she waved and I stood up to bid her goodnight.

"I'll give you a ring next week if I may," she said, "to see if you can help me with this problem."

"Of course you can. What name is it so that I will remember you," I said.

"Anne Goodyear," she said, "Anne Beatrice Goodyear. My friends call me A.B."

"Good, I'll remember that. Goodnight."

She smiled sweetly, the young man in the T-shirt held the door open for her in a most gentlemanly fashion and they left. I was *compos mentis* enough to take note of her countenance, in particular the fact that she looked to be the epitome of the perfect grandmother. I remember one of the group asking me who she was and I told them that she was a foster parent and obviously a very nice lady.

The evening ended with Pagey giving us a rendition of the Dubliners' hit, *Seven Drunken Nights* made more interesting by virtue of having eight verses.

The following day I was subjected to one of Vera's miracle cures of tincture of bat and once again I wished I was teetotal. On my way to the magistrates' court I was approached by a young man whose face was vaguely familiar.

"Excuse me Mr Smith, can I give you this letter?" he asked.

I took the letter from him and looked at him quizzically. I've been asked to give you this letter by A.B."

"By A.B.?"

"Yes, Mrs Goodyear."

"Oh yes," I said and then remembered that he was the young man in the T-shirt and chinos from Ranulph's the night before.

"Do you need a reply?"

"No," said the young man, "she said she'll wait to hear from you," and with that he left.

I opened the letter on the way to court and it was about three A4 pages of quite beautiful handwriting on a very expensive parchment-type notepaper. Balancing my files in one hand I read the note with the other, which explained that she had taken to fostering children on a voluntary basis and over the years she had cared for nearly a hundred children, most of whom still kept in touch with her. Her husband had taken out a number of insurance policies so that she had been left reasonably well provided for and providing she was prudent she would survive reasonably well on the interest. She had no children of her own but had taken to fostering to fill a void in her life. She had adopted Alan, her first foster child and how proud she was of him. She said that he was training to enter the priesthood and from being a problem child he had turned into a well-balanced boy who had "seen the light" and had pursued a future "in the cloth". It was clear that she was a very proud lady and justifiably so.

She said that she had only one foster child left at home, namely the young man who had delivered my letter. She told me that his name was Graham Taylor and he had had an unhappy childhood, having come from a broken home. He had lived with her in foster care for three months. Unfortunately he got himself into trouble and had to appear at the Sheffield Magistrates Court charged with burglary. My role was to represent him at court.

Mrs Goodyear and her adopted son Alan were there to support him. Alan having taken time out of theological college just to be at home to give such support as he could and so I was most impressed.

Chapter 10

DON'T TAKE A FENCE

Graham Taylor attended early for our appointment, accompanied by Mrs Goodyear and her adopted son Alan. He gave me his papers, which showed he had been charged with a rather serious dwelling-house burglary where jewellery to a value of nine thousand pounds was taken and there was no doubt that the only place he was going was to the Crown Court.

I took the appropriate details from him and noticed he looked rather nervous. I put that down to the fact that he'd no previous convictions and had never seen a solicitor before but as he spoke he constantly glanced at Mrs Goodyear for encouragement, especially when we referred to the offence and to where the property had gone.

"Was the property recovered?" I asked.

"No, it's all gone."

"Did the police ask you where the property had gone?"

"Yes."

"Do you want to tell me what happened to it?" I asked.

"It's gone, that's all I can say," he said with his head bowed. "I gave it to somebody to look after and I've not seen them since but I don't want to say who they are for fear of reprisals."

I did not accept his explanation. It was all far too stage managed for my liking and so I persevered.

"What did you tell the police about the property?"

"The same," he said.

"The difficulty you've got Graham is that the property remains outstanding and you've done nothing to help with its recovery. That is what we call an aggravating feature, which means it will be held against you when the court comes to deal with the case. I'm not suggesting for a minute that you should shop your mates but I just want you to understand where you stand with this case."

"Yes, thank you," said Graham politely, "I know I'm in trouble and I know I'm going to get a prison sentence."

A.B's son Alan had said nothing, although he had listened intently to what had been said and had not involved himself in the conversation until then when he interrupted.

"You see Graham, Mr Smith is trying to act in your best interests. It's a two-way thing; you can't leave it all to him, that's not fair. Please help him to help you and start by telling him the truth."

"Thank you Alan," I said gratefully, his input was most welcome.

Graham sneered. I realised he was not impressed with Alan's interjection but then as a trainee priest he was on a hiding to nothing.

"Alan is right," I said trying to smooth troubled waters. "Everyone here has your best interests at heart...all they want to do is help."

"I know," said Graham, "I'm sorry...I've let everybody down...I'll do my best to make amends."

"OK Graham, let's get some information to paper and sort this lot out."

Graham nodded. We were all agreed but perhaps the tension had got to us all.

I continued to complete all my paperwork and told the young man that I would wait for the evidence to be served and then we could discuss his case again. Mrs Goodyear interrupted us.

"Graham is from a broken home and he's had rather a terrible life."

"Yes I appreciate that Mrs Goodyear, that's what we call mitigation and it means that we can tell the court about his background and try to explain why he's got involved, but really I think we ought to see the paperwork before we go any further."

"Oh, I understand, forgive me, I'm not well up on these things."

"No, that's alright. If you've any queries please don't hesitate to ask me. Are there any more questions while we're here?" I asked.

"No not really, it's just that whilst Graham has been with me he's been very good and very well behaved and I think I can do something with him."

"Yes, I'm sure that's right Mrs Goodyear."

"By the way Graham, where are your parents?" I asked.

"I don't have anything to do with them. We fell out and I left home and that's when I came to A.B.'s."

"What was the problem?"

"We just didn't get on. Mainly it was my dad. He drinks a lot and always causes problems at home and then one day he thumped me in the face and that was enough for me. I've not been back since."

A.B. smiled sympathetically and touched his hand for reassurance. He turned, looked at her and smiled and then bowed his head again.

"Do you have no contact with them at all?"

"No, not at all," interposed A.B. "We don't think he should be made to suffer because his father has a drink problem so we thought it better that, for the time being at least, he keep well away."

"It's just very unusual to find somebody with no previous convictions whatsoever getting involved in a serious burglary.

"He was very silly," said A.B. "and from what I can gather, the jewellery was just laying about in the bedroom, in boxes. If he'd have wanted to have done a professional job he would have taken all sorts of things I would have thought."

I knew that professional burglars who concentrate on jewellery are not interested in videos and televisions because they're too bulky and slow their escape. I looked at Graham once again and couldn't help thinking that something was not quite right. I'd no idea what he'd got himself involved in and he wasn't going to tell me.

We agreed that we would meet again later and they left to go to the front door. A.B. paused and allowed the youth to walk on in front of her.

"Could I just have a quiet word with you Mr Smith?" she asked.

"Certainly Mrs Goodyear, please come back in."

She spoke to me in a half-whisper.

"He's a good lad really you know but I think those beatings by his father have had quite an effect."

"Why should he get involved in something as professional as this?" I asked.

"Well I don't know about that but I'm convinced that it's just a one off and those rings and necklaces were just lying about."

"Yes, but you can see what I'm getting at?"

"Oh yes, of course, I understand exactly what you're saying but perhaps he'll open up to me as we go along and if he does, don't worry, you'll be the first to know. I'm keeping my eyes and ears open."

"Watch out for any particular callers that come to see him and note who they are because I suspect that there'll be a fence somewhere."

"A fence?" she asked, "What do you mean by that?"

"Well, a fence is a handler, a person who receives stolen goods."

"Oh I see," she said, "I understand. You mean someone who's had the property?"

"Yes, quite right," I said.

"But he said he gave it to somebody to look after who he's not seen since."

"Yes I know but I suspect that that's the handler. You don't just hand jewellery to somebody; it doesn't stack up."

"I see what you mean. I must say you've opened my eyes but then I'm not used to this sort of thing. Thank you so much Mr Smith, we'll keep in touch."

"Yes, and thanks for coming with him to offer support."

She smiled and we shook hands again and she turned to walk away. Unfortunately she went in entirely the wrong direction.

"No, the front door is that way," I said smiling. "You'll end up in our basement and you wouldn't like it there."

She laughed and then went to the front door, courteously thanked the receptionist and she was gone. This was an unusual case with more to it than met the eye. I thought of nothing else as I made my way to court until a transit van pulled up at the side of me with the legend emblazoned on the side, 'Jack's jacks'. It was Jack Heptonstall, Albert's dad.

"Is that a different van?" I asked him.

Jack peered out of the window with his Park Drive cigarette burning in his mouth and began to cough.

"These bloody Park Drives," he said, "I'm gonna pack these in one day."

He took the cigarette from his mouth and ran his hand across his nose.

"I've got a big consignment of car jacks," said Jack. "I bought a job lot...there's 'undreds of 'em. I've got one for you free of charge."

"That's very good of you Jack," I said, "but I've already got one, it came with the car."

"Oh not to worry," said Jack, "but there's one 'ere if yer want one."

"Thanks very much, I'll bear that in mind."

I then looked at the sign on the side of the van, which I realised had been painted on by hand and not by a professional either. The apostrophe was missing between the 'K' and the 'S' of the first word but I didn't expect Jack to look for niceties.

"Jack's jacks," I said, "yes, it's got a nice ring to it."

"Ay," said Jack. "By the way, before yer go let me introduce you to my mate. This is Nob."

A face appeared from behind Jack. He looked like a former professional boxer. He had a shaven head, which was unusual in those days, a boxer's nose and two cauliflower ears. There were scars above and below his eyes, giving a rather frightening countenance.

"Nob's setting himself up in business," said Jack, "'e's goin' on the markets with bankrupt stock."

"I'll bet he is," I thought to myself.

"How do you do Nob, it's nice to meet you."

"Ey, alreight?" said Nob. It was clear that he was a man of few words.

"What sort of stuff are you going to be selling then Nob?"

"owt really, door handles and brass plates for doors and hinges and all that."

"That's a good idea. Where are you off to now then Jack?" I asked.

"We're off to a bankruptcy sale, there's one in Retford that Nob wants to 'ave a look at so I'm takin' the van to 'elp 'im transport it."

"Oh that's good, well best of luck with the sale and I hope you get what you want."

"Ey," said Jack, "anyway we'll call in to see thee next week. Nob's got some motoring charges for you to look at and I've got some smashing rolls of lino that would be alreight for your office. Just 'ave a look at that square in the back, it'll go down a treat in your office."

I looked in the back of the van and there saw a sample of lino. It had a picture of Batman and Robin on it.

"Yes, that would look good," I said, "when the building society manager comes to call, with Batman and Robin everywhere, what a good idea but I'm not sure if it's actually what you expect in a solicitor's office," I said to Jack. He was most disappointed. He thought it would have looked good.

"Never mind, the thought was nice."

"Ay, OK," said Jack, "but I've got some more coming next week."

"Oh what's that?" I asked.

"Kids go mad over it, it's that Walt Disney thing, Dumbo."

"Oh that would go well next to Batman and Robin, Dumbo the elephant!" I exclaimed.

"Ay, I never thought about that," said Jack, "Ey, thanks for that, we'll use that as a sales pitch Nob," he said, turning to his friend.

"Good idea, 'e's a bright bloke that solicitor of yours," said Nob, winking.

Nob was not the sort of man with whom you would want to argue and if he thought it would look good, that was good enough for me providing that it wasn't in my office.

About a fortnight later I received the documents from the CPS about Graham Taylor's case and read them with great interest. He had very skillfully taken a pane of glass out of a ground floor window at the back of a detached house and gained entry. The owners were still in the house but had not engaged their alarm because they didn't expect anyone would try to get in while they were downstairs. I suppose they thought burglars only came out at night. Graham had acted with remarkable coolness and having seen where the occupants were, he cheekily crept upstairs and rifled the bedroom, putting things away so as not to give the impression of disturbance. He made good his exit by the same window. The occupants only realised what had happened the following day when they saw the damaged window but by then of course it was too late. The police were called, and a check was made of the house and the occupants found that the jewellery was missing. What confused me was how he knew where to look for the property. I also wanted to know how he had learned to remove glass and not to leave fingerprints. The police felt that this was a high-class professional burglary. Something somewhere did not add up.

The following day I was in the Magistrates' Court and I bumped into one of my colleagues from the Crown Prosecution Service. I knew that he was the lawyer designated to deal with Graham's case and so I asked him about it. He told me that it was a professional burglary and that the police suspected Graham of other offences but couldn't prove them. He told me that whilst no fingerprints were found at the scene there was a footprint on the ledge where the window had been taken out. Apparently the footprint was photographed and had been sent to the forensic science laboratory at Wetherby where it was to be compared with a similar footprint at another burglary. I knew that Graham's trainers had been taken by the police because it was mentioned in one of the statements which I had been given but it would take some time for the forensic science laboratory to confirm their findings. To quote a well-worn phrase used by CID officers everywhere, 'He'd been bang at it'.

I did not pick up Graham's case papers again for the next fourteen days or so but he was due to call to see me one Friday afternoon. He was the last appointment of the day, just after a visit from Norbert Jacques, better known as Jack's friend Nob. He was being prosecuted for driving a transit van with the following faults.

1. Defective tyre.
2. Defective lights.
3. Defective windscreen washers.
4. Defective windscreen wipers.
5. Dangerous parts.
6. No insurance.

7. No valid vehicle excise licence (tax disc).
8. No driving licence.
9. Driving whilst unaccompanied.
10. No L-plates.
11. No seat belt.
12. Fraudulent use of a tax disc.
13. Insecure rear seats.

I looked through the summonses and then at Nob.

He was a large man, over six feet tall, powerfully built and a face that looked as though it had been gouged out of rock. He spoke with a growl and a marked Cockney accent.

"Come in Mr Jacques," I said, smiling.

"Yus, alright," he said.

"Please take a seat. As you know I'm Steve Smith and I think you're Jack's mate aren't you?"

"Yus, that's right."

"Well I've been given a lot of Summonses Mr Jacques…"

He interjected, "Call me Nob, everybody else does."

"OK, Nob," I said reluctantly. "I assume you have come about these summonses?"

"Yus, that's right."

"Well I've looked at the charges and I've looked at the papers and to be quite frank with you, there are so many things wrong with this van, it looks as though the police are saying it's a death trap."

"It was in good nick."

"Well are you saying that the wipers worked?"

"They worked a bit," he said. "It just so 'appened that when the old bill came they weren't workin'."

"What about the dangerous condition? According to this, a whole wing was hanging off."

"Yeah, that's an exaggeration. I pushed that back in and it was perfect."

"And the tyres were bald."

"I agree they were not that healthy but they weren't bald, they were more…balding than bald."

I then found a thirteenth summons.

"Oh, unlucky for some, this thirteenth one says you'd got faulty brakes."

"Never."

"Yes, that's what it says. Apparently the handbrake was not effective."

"Oh, is that all, I thought they meant the ordinary brakes, there were nothin' wrong with them, I've just done 'em and put new shoes on. They were perfict, but the handbrake didn't work, but when do you use a handbrake these days, let's be fair."

"Then there's the tax disc," I interjected.

"What's the problem with that?" asked Nob.

"There wasn't one, I replied. Well there was one but it was bent. It had got the wrong date and registration number on it."

"Never," said the astonished Nob.

"Yes, and what's more the registration number on the tax disc had been altered to fit the registration number on your van," I continued.

"Never."

"How do you account for that?"

"Never...I mean who would 'ave done that? Somebody must 'ave bin tinkerin' about with the van."

"But do you think that somebody would break into your van and alter your tax disc and then leave it in your van? Who would benefit from that?" I asked.

"There are some funny people about."

"Yes, but who would do such a thing?" I continued.

"Well it weren't me," protested Nob.

"Well who else has access to the van?"

"Only Jack and Albert," he said.

"Oh bloody hell, you're not blaming them are you?" I asked indignantly.

"Well it weren't me. Anyway, whose side are you on? You sound like the police."

"Never...I'm only putting to you what I know the prosecutor will put to you at court. To that extent you will be prepared for it. If I didn't put it to you you'd say I hadn't done my job properly."

"Never."

"What about the windscreen washers?" I asked.

"Didn't need 'em, it was raining."

"So we accept they were empty?" I continued.

"Never, they must 'ave bin leaking, they were alright when I set off."

"You mean you inspected it before you set off?"

"Definitely," said Nob, sitting back in his chair.

"If you don't mind me saying, I think you've got too many ready answers and the court are just not going to wear it. For a start, you've got to admit driving with defective tyres because that is a fact."

"Alright, I'll 'ave that but I'm not 'avin' the rest of it," said Nob pathetically.

"Oh well, all I can do is to tell you the strengths and the weaknesses of your case and the weaknesses are very great."

"What about the strengths?" he enquired.

I paused and took a deep breath. "There aren't any." I couldn't help saying it even though I knew it would not foster that inner belief in my abilities that I wished to achieve by rapport with all my clientele. We were always taught that fighting hopeless cases gave you a reputation as a hopeless advocate. This was a classic case for doing a deal with the prosecution and trying to get some of the charges dropped in return for guilty pleas to others but Nob was having none of it.

I escorted him to the office door, after having got his agreement that certain matters just could not be defended and promised him that I would do what I could. His van was parked on double yellow lines outside my office but I couldn't really expect him to park legally; it would not have been in his nature! I followed him out to wave him off and watched in wonder as he drove off in the offending van with the words "Nob's Nobs" emblazoned on the side panels.

I eventually got to the court where Big George greeted me. His case of disorder was in the list and was to be dealt with that day. I expected, "Oh, wonderful you're here, my hero," or "I am so relieved you have arrived," or even, "Thank you for risking life, limb and ulcers by chasing around South Yorkshire just to look after me." Unfortunately I had expected rather a lot.

"Where the bleedin' 'ell 'ave you bin. They've called me in twice but you weren't 'ere."

"Correct," I replied. "I was just chasing round South Yorkshire, trying to help everybody and giving myself ulcers in the process."

"Fuck that," said George impatiently, "just get me in there and get me out."

I went into Court One to find the room empty but for Keith Copley the court clerk.

"Morning Keith, waiting for me?"

Keith lifted his head wearily.

"It's your friend the Lord Chief Justice sitting; we've been waiting for half an hour and he's not pleased."

"Charming. What a good start that is."

"You'll have to apologise, he's really annoyed," continued Keith.

"Well he sits while one o'clock, we're quids in yet."

"Yes, but he wanted to leave early."

"What's the point of doing a court if you've got to leave early?"

"I know, but you know what he's like."

I knew that my main critic of all the magistrates was the Lord Chief Justice and he would love the opportunity to give me a telling-off, so I had to grin and bear it. Answering back would not be tolerated and both he and I knew it, so I had not underestimated the position.

The magistrates entered the court but at least the telling-off was in the absence of any of the clients. I took it like a man and apologised profusely, with all my fingers crossed behind my back, but I put it in my little black book.

My "little black book" is the volume in which I make a mental list of all good turns and bad ones. Some of the contents are kept for years and only used when absolutely necessary. The Lord Chief Justice featured regularly amongst its pages but my turn would come sooner or later.

The prosecutor was none other than Herbert Casson, the prosecutor with a stutter. He was a temperamental person given to black moods when he could be less than cooperative and helpful but when something upset him he would stutter slightly and remarkably at just the wrong moment. The problem usually occurred at the most inopportune moments and today was to be no different.

Three of my remaining cases were dealt with without incident and I couldn't help being amazed at the speed with which they were completed. We then came to George's sentencing hearing.

Harry Fenton was a well-known shoplifter now in his late fifties and very much in his decline. Harry had been caught in Woolworth stealing Clodagh Rodgers C.D.'s but the store detective 'clocked' him. He had pleaded guilty to one offence and not guilty to the other.

Herbert opened his case with gusto getting carried away in the process until...

"The store detective followed him as he switched aisles then when he was out of her sight for a second or two the detective heard the defendant 'drop one – he dropped one...'"

"Well, the crude person," I said to myself.

"...dropped one of the C.D.'s on the floor."

"Oh, not such a crude person after all."

Crude or not Harry got twenty-eight days for his trouble.

"What do we do with the case he pleaded not guilty to?" asked the Chairman of the Magistrates.

"Oh, Mr Casson dropped one," I replied with a straight face…dropped the other charge," I continued with a straight face.

Mr Casson did not disagree.

Keith passed the Probation Service reports up to the Bench and the prosecutor outlined his case. The Lord Chief looked unhappy with the opening and appeared to take a serious view. When the Prosecutor had finished, he addressed me.

"Do you want us to read the reports first Mr Smith?"

"Yes please Sir, if you would. There is a recommendation in the report for a Probation Order and to attend a course on anger management. I will be asking you to follow the recommendation. If not, I'm afraid I will have to address you at length."

"Will you now?" said the Lord Chief defiantly.

He knew as well as I did that I would mitigate, go on and on and on, and he could not do a thing about it. In short, if he didn't follow the recommendation he was going to be late!

"We'll retire to consider the report," said the Lord Chief and the Magistrates filed out one by one.

George whistled across the room to attract my attention.

"Ey up Steve, 'ow about thee saying summat for me first?"

I left my seat to speak to him.

"They are reading the report first then I'll address them, OK?"

"So long as tha does," said George. "It looks a bit one-sided to me."

"You would say that George, wouldn't you?"

"Tha what?"

"Never mind," I said, losing patience.

The bell rang some ten minutes later, calling the court clerk into the retiring room.

"He wants me," said Keith.

"He wants summat," said George under his breath.

"So do you George," I said to myself, "and it looks very much as though you are going to get it."

"Why are they sending for 'im?" asked George.

"They'll want a cup of tea I should think and they'll want their bets putting on at the bookies," I said jokingly.

"Never!" said George, missing the point. "You mean to tell me they're putting bets on during my case – sod me!"

Keith then returned.

"I think it's disgraceful," said George belligerently.

"I beg your pardon?" said Keith.

"Well I mean, putting bets on when my case is on. I don't mind a bet but there's a time and a place".

Just then the Bench returned, which deflected Keith's attention away from George's conversation.

"All stand!" shouted Keith.

In walked the magistrates and I remained standing, waiting for the nod to start. The Lord Chief was clearly anxious to leave for whatever meeting he had to attend and so he spoke first.

"We've looked at the report Mr Smith and whilst this is a serious case, we are prepared to follow the recommendation of the Probation Order and impose a condition to attend an anger management course."

I was shocked and didn't expect such an easy ride. I had nothing to add but George looked bewildered.

"Stand up Mr ...," said the magistrate.

"Hang on!" said George, "my solicitor ain't said nowt yet!"

"It's alright George, the magistrate is going to put you on probation," I said, whispering the news into his ear.

"What, no jail?"

"Yes that's right, no jail."

"Bloody 'ell," said George as the realisation dawned on him and all of a sudden he became almost human again.

The Magistrate read out the sentence and told George to keep out of trouble in the future.

George was delighted and as he walked out of the court he turned towards the magistrates. "Thank you Your Honour. Oh ... and I 'ope your 'orse wins."

It was the magistrates' turn to look perplexed as George gave the thumbs up sign and simulated the movements of a jockey pulling on the reins of a horse before disappearing out of the door.

Chapter 11

HEALTH PROBLEMS

It can be very cold in April, especially at Easter. We had a few days off work and the air of expectancy was exciting to say the least. At six o'clock on Thursday night when the office is closed, you have Good Friday, Saturday, Sunday, Easter Monday and Tuesday to relax and enjoy yourself, pursuing whatever hobby or weird characteristic of your personality that you wish to pursue, providing of course you have a locum or an agent to do the Easter courts. I was no different from everyone else, although I had a similar thought pattern to various of my ne'er do well accomplices in the noble art of increasing your waistline, causing ulcers and shortening your lifespan. In short, I speak of eating and boozing.

I was becoming very accomplished in this noble art and whilst the pressures of the business were building upon me, I found blessed release in the company of my erstwhile companions. I became a considerable favourite with local restraunteurs and landlords whilst increasing my unpopularity with my family. Nevertheless I believed that we were at the height of our powers although I'd not quite become a workaholic; that was something that destiny and necessity would lead me to later.

I propounded the adage of work hard and play hard and felt that having flogged myself to death during the day, putting up with all sorts of weird and wonderful personnel, it was my basic entitlement to be able to trip the light fantastic afterwards.

It was about that time that I'd begun to have certain health problems. It started off one afternoon when I was eating a sandwich quickly because, as usual, I had to be at court at a quarter to two and I'd only got five minutes for lunch. I noticed that it was particularly difficult to swallow and it felt very much as if there was a constriction at the base of my throat. I had to take a long drink to free the discomfort.

It didn't happen again for two or three weeks so I wasn't too perturbed and just passed it off as some kind of inflammation but when it started again I began to feel nauseous in the mornings. Wilf passed it off as morning sickness and I passed him off as an ignorant git but I had a strange feeling about this condition. We're all supposed to be psychic although the scientists will say it's merely being intuitive but I had a strange feeling that all was not well and so I decided to take advantage of the health scheme I had paid into and have a "well man's investigation".

It was a full examination which took place in Leeds and consisted of the usual checks, for which I had to give samples of just about everything that I could produce and even submitted myself to the degradation of the dreaded rubber glove. I lied completely about the amount of units of alcohol I consumed but it appeared that with the exception of being overweight, I was given a clean bill of health.

I mentioned the difficulty I had with swallowing and the doctor felt that it was some kind of inflammation, which had probably been aggravated by central heating. In fairness, he had not completed any x-rays or examination of the gullet but if the condition persisted he suggested that I went back. I was content, probably because he'd told me something that I wanted to hear and for the next week I did not have any problems.

The following weekend it started again doubtless precipitated by one of our famous monthly soirées. The nausea got worse and I was physically ill every morning and then one Wednesday evening I played football and when I came off I was ill again. It's interesting how the mind tries to find excuses for ailments and I put it down to the combination of being involved in a hard match and having had too many late nights but the following day I felt distinctly worse.

Each day I was finding I'd got cases that I had to do and couldn't pass on to anyone else and my days off were becoming more and more limited. We had worked hard to build up goodwill but there was a price to pay.

One Friday morning I was dealing with Nob's case. It had been a very fraught morning and I had a bad start which meant that it perpetuated itself during the day and every time I tried to get a case on there was a queue. Inevitably, when I got to the front of the queue the other courts had finished their work and were waiting for me, causing everyone to shout for me at once. Normally I was able to cope with the pressures but on this occasion I just felt as though I did not want to be there. I dealt with the cases to the best of my ability and was fighting Nob's corner when a dreadful feeling of nausea overcame me. I lost the colour from my cheeks and one of the Court Clerks commented upon how ill I looked. It didn't fill me with great enthusiasm to be told that I had gone "grey" but I knew something was wrong.

The magistrate gave Nob a fair old ticking-off and with a hefty fine, a flea behind his ear and a fond farewell to his licence. He left the court, chuntering about how ridiculous the penalty was. He seemed to have forgotten that he had been driving a death trap but he just would not accept it; after all, they were only traffic offences and what was the point of giving a "working lad" heavy fines. The term "working lad" confused me somewhat because although he was a man of endeavour, he'd never had a job or paid any tax.

"That'll make an ′ole in my dole money," said Nob.

I suppose he did have a point because in an earlier case a man who had fractured his girlfriend's nose had got a smaller fine but in Rotherham road traffic offences are treated seriously!

When I came out of court I went into the rathole solicitors' room and sat down. I had a cup of tea, which burned my throat and I couldn't finish it and then I started to cough. I put my handkerchief to my mouth and looked in horror when I took it away. I was haemorrhaging and realised that the difficulties I'd had with swallowing and nausea were related to this condition.

One of my colleagues, Jon Ford, is the son of a doctor and he telephoned his father for advice. He told me to go the hospital straightaway and check in with the Accident and Emergency Department. I took his advice.

When I told the lady on the desk what was wrong she put me in a chair and called medical staff immediately. The speed with which I was attended worried me, particularly when they took me to a ward in a wheelchair. I explained to the nurse that I had an afternoon court to deal with and consequently wouldn't be able to stay for long. She just laughed. I was taken to a ward and given a pair of government issue pyjamas, which I left neatly folded on the bed. The staff didn't seem to grasp the point that I wasn't able to stay because I'd got four cases in the afternoon list. One very large lady in a dark blue uniform told me with a gruff voice,

"You're going nowhere Mr Smith."

I sat by the side of the bed on a chair in a daze and looked across the small ward and saw a large man in bed, groaning; to his left a man sitting up in bed reading a newspaper which was upside down and to his right a man in pyjamas sitting on a chair at the side of the bed. To my immediate left was a man wearing a facemask plugged into the wall, which I later found out was a nebuliser used to combat breathing difficulties. The bed on my right was occupied by a man who was sitting looking into space and talking to himself. All I could think was, "What the bloody hell am I doing in here?"

The staff kept looking in on me and making sure that everything was alright and in fairness, they were fantastic. Despite being so very busy they could not do enough for me but whilst I must have appeared ungrateful, all I wanted to do was to leave.

Then it occurred to me that I'd got appointments up to six o'clock, which increased my agitation so I decided that I would wait for a doctor to come, see what he had to say and then I would leave; but they had other ideas.

I had to make contact with the office and home to let everybody know where I was, even though I thought it was one of those annoyances that hopefully would go away and later that night, or at the very latest the following morning, I would be able to leave. How wrong I was.

It must have been a great shock to my family and my firm to find me in Ward D3 in Rotherham District General Hospital. My belief in my indestructibility had been severely shaken. With the exception of coughs, colds, croup, perforated eardrum, in-growing toenails and piles I hadn't ailed a thing, certainly nothing serious and here I was about to have all manner of tests carried out to find out what was causing the haemorrhage.

Eddie, in the next bed to me, had taken off his nebuliser. He was a retired miner suffering from pneumoconiosis, emphysema and bronchial problems. He was in a bad way and he knew it. He had caught a cold which turned to a cough, then to bronchitis and eventually to pneumonia, which led to him being rushed into hospital with a collapsed lung. He had been in an oxygen tent all week. This was his first day back on the general ward and despite the fact that he was unwell, he was in reasonably high spirits. He was one of those people who was always laughing and joking and his personality was infectious. He noticed I was looking lonely and forlorn and whilst contemplating my fate the sister came in and brought a glass of water and some tablets.

"You need to take these," she said, "they'll just calm you down."

"I am calm," I said.

"You won't be when you get bed-bathed. Get them taken," she said smiling.

As she was walking away I tried a bit of repartee.

"I'll only take them if you're doing the bath."

"Oh," she said, "I'm not, it's big Hilda, she's in charge of baths tonight and she's twice your size."

I laughed because I thought she was joking. She laughed because she knew she wasn't.

She'd told me that the tablets were a form of mild sedative because the following day I was going to have a gastroscopy, which left me wondering what a gastroscopy was. She came back shortly afterwards to see to Fred across the ward, who seemed to be in a great deal of pain and as she was tending to him Eddie leaned across and spoke to me.

"He's been at it for two days, moaning and groaning, poor bleeder. They reckon to have given him something but it's not worked fully. He doesn't know where he is but he's still moaning and groaning. Last night he was terrible and that crackpot across, well…he's a brick short of a wall he is. He thought I was a priest last night. I think he's lost it a bit. He's harmless, but he's a bloody nuisance."

As we were speaking an elderly lady in a nightshirt appeared in the doorway and shouted,

"Hello boys."

We looked up to see who it was. I didn't recognise her but she seemed to think she knew us. The sister turned away and scolded her.

"Ruby, what are you doing down here? Get back to your ward. I've told you before about coming down here."

"But I like it here."

"Go on, off you go, back up to your ward."

"Oh sister, can't I stop for half an hour."

"No, you certainly can't. These gentlemen don't like it so off you get back to your own bed."

"That's not fair," she said, continuing her protest.

"It's not raining either," said Sister. "Off you go."

Eddie turned to me and spoke out of the corner of his mouth.

"She's a crackerjack an' all; got in bed with me last night, silly old bugger frightened me to death. Had to put the nebuliser back on as I couldn't get my breath."

I was beginning to think I was surrounded by very strange people as Eddie continued.

"Why did she get into bed with you?" I asked.

"She was just wandering about and I think she'd got disorientated. She probably thought it was as good a place as any. She didn't do ought," he said thoughtfully, "…but there again, neither did I."

141

He burst out laughing and then he began to cough…and cough…and cough. Something told me that this was going to be an interesting stay.

My tablets arrived shortly afterwards together with a small plastic cup of something that looked like washing-up liquid. I drank it and took the tablets and the nurse came in to collect the empties. She told me to put my pyjamas on and get into bed.

"They're not my pyjamas," I said.

"They're not anybody's pyjamas until now…now they're yours so get them on and get into bed."

"But I don't know who had them on last," I said.

"I shouldn't worry, he'll not want them back where he's gone."

I was immediately instilled with confidence.

"They've been washed and they're spotlessly clean, so get them on."

"Can I have a shower first?"

"You what?" she exclaimed.

"I never get into bed unless I've had a shower."

"Get those pyjamas on and get into bed. Stop being trouble."

Whilst I appreciated that she was acting in my best interests, having hitherto been relatively healthy, apart from the odd visit to hospital for minor bumps and bruises, I wasn't used to being spoken to like that.

"I'm not actually complaining but it is a bit of a culture shock and when you've been used to satisfying your own particular quirks, as in my case a shower before I retire, I find it very difficult to break from that tradition," I said politely.

The nurse did not reply. I decided to adopt a different approach.

"Nurse."

"What now?"

"Thank you for looking after my best interests…."

"What are you after?"

"Would it be such a hindrance if I just nipped down the corridor to the shower. I'll certainly be able to sleep better. It's a psychosomatic thing really I suppose when one is used to having a shower before one goes to bed…."

She interrupted me.

"You've got five minutes and no more and if you are any longer we'll come and turn the water off."

I was delighted. I never thought I'd be so pleased to be allowed a shower, so I took my things and entered shower cubicle number two, which was in a row of three, all with plastic shower curtains. I undressed, got inside and turned on the water, which was freezing cold. The shock to my system caused me to gasp.

"B...l....o...o...d...y h...e...l...l!"

I twisted the dial to the right and the water began to get warm and then warmer and warmer and warmer, then hot and then scalding. I had no option but to step outside of the shower and in doing so noticed a lady mopping up water in the corner. I jumped back into the shower to protect my modesty to find that having twisted the dial too far it was bitterly cold again. By this time the cleaner was outside my cubicle and I was perched precariously on the ledges of the shower, trying to dodge the cold water.

Eventually I managed to find a happy medium and was standing enjoying my shower when the curtain opened and a hand reached in. A voice said.

"Got any spare soap in there mate?"

I was standing there in the buff with this hand inside the shower and I didn't know whether to shake it, chop it off or trap it against the wall. I took the bar of soap and put it in the hand, which was withdrawn with the comment,

"Cheers mate."

"Charming," I thought to myself, "now what do I do?"

Having no soap left I tried to make do with what little was on the surface of my body. It didn't matter because that shower was all I needed.

I came out of the shower to find that my pyjamas had gone. Someone must have thought that they'd been left there so they'd been taken away.

"B...l....o...o...d...y h...e...l...l!"

Just then the nurse shouted down by the cubicles.

"Mr Smith, your five minutes are up, get back to the ward!"

"Somebody's nicked my pyjamas," I shouted but she had gone by then and obviously hadn't heard what I'd said.

I reached for the towel and found that someone had nicked that as well and all that was available was a foot-square flannel.

"I bet the bastard that took my soap got my towel as well!"

Feeling frustrated I shouted down the rest of the cubicles,

"Has anybody just picked up a towel?"

There was no reply.

"Bloody hell," I thought to myself and picked up the flannel, doing my very best to get dry with it. I was standing with the shower curtain partly open waiting for some unsuspecting shower-person to come and deposit their towel so that I could return the compliment but to no avail.

The cleaner put a small tablecloth-like object on the chair and when her back was turned I reached out and swiped it. It was approximately eighteen inches long by six inches wide and doubled as a floor cloth. Fortunately it was pristine and was better than the flannel. If I put the widest part to my rear it didn't quite meet at the front and if I did it the other way, part of my backside was exposed. I took a deep breath and decided to make a bolt for the ward, which was only a few steps away. I'd covered my modesty at the front and thought that if something had got to be exposed it would be the back bit.

I stretched out of the shower and looked around the corner to see if the corridor was clear so that I could make good my escape. Unfortunately two old ladies had just walked out of the office and were walking towards the shower area. I leaned back waiting for them to pass and then became aware of a middle-aged lady with a vacuum cleaner to my left. She looked at me with some measure of disdain. It wasn't until I realised that I was standing in front of an electricity socket that I realised what the problem was. She held the plug towards me, flicking it from one hand to the other and all I could think of to say was,

"Where do you think you are you going to put that?"

Her eyes widened and she grimaced.

"You're in the way of the socket," she said firmly.

"Oh, I see," I said, "I'm ever so sorry, I thought...."

"Never mind," she said.

She handed me the plug and I bent down to push it into the socket, exposing my entire backside in the process.

"Charming," she said, "shouldn't you be in bed?"

"Yes, I would if I could only get out of this shower area and avoid people nicking my soap, my towel and my 'jamas and asking me to plug hoovers into walls."

"I only asked," she said, completely unfazed by the sight of my private areas.

"You ought not to be standing about like that," she said as she turned and walked away.

I clenched my fist and pretended to throw a blow at her. I peered round the corner once again to see if the coast was clear, only to hear the sound of a vacuum cleaner somewhere behind me.

"I do the corners first," she said defiantly.

"I'll do you," I thought to myself and ventured out into the corridor. There I was, armed with a small piece of material in front to protect my modesty and my arse hanging out at the back. I attempted in my naïvety to walk nonchalantly back to my ward as though it was quite normal to walk about in that state, whistling as I went so as not to draw attention to myself.

Just as I was about to reach my little annexe, the old ladies I'd seen before plus another walked towards me. As they drew close they stopped and looked at me in amazement.

"Good evening ladies," was all I could think of to say.

They mumbled some form of reply and as I walked past them all three of them turned to look at me.

"You ought not to be walking about like that dear," said one of them.

"Somebody might get the wrong impression," said another.

"It's downright disgusting if you ask me, blatant exhibitionism," said the third.

I was not only embarrassed but rather upset at the suggestion that I was some kind of pervert wandering round the hospital wing determined to expose myself but before I could speak the aforementioned cleaner walked past and spoke.

"So it's you that's pinched it, is it?" and she reached out and snatched the piece of material from me. The old ladies looked at each other in horror.

"Oh my goodness me."

I then had to suffer the degradation of being led back to the ward by a nurse who realised that things were getting all too much for me.

Chapter 12

EVERYONE SHOULD TRY A GASTROSCOPY AND DINGLEBERRY GETS ILL

That night I couldn't sleep and neither could Eddie. The chap opposite was moaning and groaning, clearly in discomfort, so he couldn't sleep either and the looney in the next bed was having a long and detailed conversation with himself. I was sitting up in bed reviewing the situation when I caught Eddie's eye. I tutted and looked to the ceiling and he did the same and then we both cracked out laughing.

"Who would have thought we'd have ended up like this?" said Eddie.

"You tell me, I should have been in court this afternoon and I've got God knows how many jobs to do tomorrow morning," I replied.

"Somebody else will do it, it'll take care of itself, none of us are indispensable."

"Yes I know, but I really have got an awful lot of things to sort out."

"You will have tomorrow when you get that camera down...bloody 'ell, I once had that done you know, in fact they might give you a double-ender."

"What's a double-ender?" I asked suspiciously.

"Well a double-ender is when they shove a camera down your throat and then one up the jacksie. The one down your throat's called a gastroscopy and the one up your back passage is called an endoscopy, but then it would be wouldn't it?"

"Charming. What would they want to do that for if I've got problems with my throat?"

"Well they don't know what it is do they? The idea of having these things is to find out what's wrong."

The prospect of having a "double-ender" left me with something less than a zest for life.

"Are they painful?" I asked.

It's not so much that they're painful, it's just that they're so bloody uncomfortable. If you can image shoving two fingers down the back of your throat and leaving them there for about five minutes, that's what it's like. The camera up the jacksie...well...if you can imagine shoving a...."

I interrupted him.

"I can't imagine it and I don't want to imagine it, besides with a bit of luck they might not get me for that."

"Oh I think they will. There's one thing about this hospital, they're very thorough and they care about the patients. If Bardhan's doing it, he's the greatest and he'll make sure that you're alright."

I thought for a minute.

"Eddie?"

"What?"

"You say you've had the throat and the jacksie?"

"Yes, more than once I can tell you."

"Well have you got any advice you can give me about how I should cope with it or any advice at all really?"

"Yes, I have," said Eddie thoughtfully.

"What's that then?" I asked.

Eddie thought for a minute and looked at me quite seriously and said anxiously.

"When you get inside, right?"

"Right."

"When you get inside, ask the doctor if you're having both."

"Right, I understand, yes, then what?"

"Then ask him if he'll do your throat first."

I looked straight forward and nodded in agreement until I realised what he'd said.

"Do you mean they use the same equipment?" I asked, fearing the worst.

Eddie started to laugh.

"You rotten bugger," I said, "winding me up like that."

"Of course they use a different camera, you dickhead."

My preconceived image of having two surgical appliances placed at either end had filled me full of dread. I thought about the matter again and laughed once more.

"You can have the jab if you like."

"Oh not again."

"No, not that sort of jab, you can have the injection...you know the knock-out...the valium."

"You mean an anaesthetic."

"Ah, an anaesthetic. It knocks you out for a full day and you don't feel a thing. Apparently it's as good as the Columbian marching powder!"

"Did you have an anaesthetic?"

"No, I can't do with that sort of thing with my chest and besides I can't do with being knocked out all day, so I like to just have the spray in the back of the throat and get it over with, it's not that bad."

"What's the spray in the back of the throat?"

"Well they spray this numbing-type agent into the back of your throat. It's supposed to make it easier when the pipe goes down."

"When the pipe goes down?" I asked.

"Yes, it's like a miniature camera on the end of a piece of tube but don't be frightened, it's very thin."

"Don't tell me any more," I said despondently.

"Look, don't worry about it. The main thing to remember is when you're laid on that bed you have to relax and try and breath regularly."

"How do you relax and breath regularly when you're having a pipe shoved down your gullet?" I asked.

"Oh you'll see, you'll get used to it. You'll do a bit of gypping you know, just as if you're being sick but that's the idea of not letting you eat anything the day before. All that comes up is a bit of bile and...."

I stopped him in his tracks.

"Don't tell me any more, I think I'll just look forward to it without knowing all the grisly facts."

"Fair dos," said Eddie.

"...and then we'll walk down the park and buy some flowers and we might even be able to pick some wild flowers from the orchard," said the loony in the next bed.

"What's he on about," asked Eddie. "Ey up, chuff nut, give it a rest, this lad's having the camera down in the morning and he needs to get some sleep."

The loony looked across at him and waved, referred to him as "Headmaster" and continued his little conversation with himself.

The man in the bed groaned once more as he tried to turn over onto his other side.

Just then Eddie started to cough again and he was soon in distress. He pointed to the nebuliser on his bedside drawers so I jumped out of bed and in panic pulled the nebuliser towards him. I place it over his nose.

"How's that? Are you alright, are you alright?" I asked.

Eddie looked up at the ceiling and looked at me and with a very wheezy croaky voice tried to speak but I could not make out what he was saying. I was panicking.

"Look, keep calm, you're alright, just take some very deep breaths."

Eddie tried again to say something but I couldn't make it out.

"What is it Eddie? What is it?"

He garbled some words yet again and pointed to the nebuliser.

"What is it, what can I do, I'll get the nurse, I'll get the nurse," I said in panic.

He pointed again quite dramatically towards the nebuliser. He took the mask off his face and slowly and quietly he said,

"Turn...the...fucker...on."

I saw the lead which led to a plug and a socket in the wall. It had been replaced in the power supply by my cassette player. I promptly unplugged it, replaced it with the plug from the nebuliser and turned it on.

"Thank you...bastard," croaked Eddie.

I gave him the thumbs up sign and he gave me two fingers. I suppose I had asked for that.

The machine started and systematically a form of grey mist percolated its way into the nebuliser. Eddie seemed a little more at ease and the blind panic subsided. He looked at me, nodded and held his thumb in the upward position. I sat back in my bed and took a deep breath. I looked at my letter of instruction about the gastroscopy, which told me that the following morning at seven thirty I would be taken down to the theatre....

I stopped.

"The theatre...? Bloody hell, it's an operation...."

I turned to Eddie for encouragement but he was sitting and trying to remain calm with his eyes firmly shut.

Just then a nurse peered into the quadrangle where we were all laid. To the right of me I had the loony, who had begun an argument with himself about the wild flowers he had been picking. My friend across the way appeared to be suffering substantially from whatever ailment he had got as he moaned and groaned vociferously, whilst Eddie on the other hand had his nebuliser working at full rate as he fought for his breath.

"Why aren't you asleep?" asked the nurse.

I looked at her dejectedly and then looked at the others around me, as if to say "you've got to be bloody joking," but I didn't want to upset her. In any event I didn't want the bed bath either, so I stupidly said that I wasn't tired.

"Well I'm sorry," she said, "I can't give you anything for that because you're having the endoscopy tomorrow aren't you?"

"No, it's the gastroscopy I'm having and as far as I know that's all. I hope I've avoided the double-ender."

"You've avoided the what?" she asked.

"The double-ender."

"The double-ender?" she said incredulously.

"Yes, they do your throat and then the other place."

"Who's been winding you up?" she said. "They never do those on the same day. Yours is just the gastroscopy," she said, looking at my notes at the foot of the bed.

"But I was told that they might do both to check everything."

"You don't need both, you're just having the gastroscopy and whoever's told you that wants his legs slapped."

I nodded in contemplation.

"Nurse?"

"Yes."

"Would it be alright if I beat Eddie about the head with a bed pan?"

"I beg your pardon?"

"Oh it's alright, I was just thinking aloud. Tell me, is the gastroscopy particularly awful?"

"Yes," she said, filling me with confidence. "It's very unpleasant but it doesn't hurt and it doesn't last very long but if you breathe deeply and try to remain relaxed you shouldn't have any problem. Look," she said, "I'd get you a cup of tea but you can't have anything to eat or drink before your treatment."

"Oh that's alright," I said, "I wasn't hungry anyway."

"Good," she said. Anyway, do try and get some sleep, you'll be alright in the morning."

I just nodded and smiled and she turned to walk away and to check on her other patients. She comforted the groaner across and calmed down the loony at the side of me. She reassured us and then checked on Eddie. She adjusted his nebuliser, pushed his hair to one side and with a reassuring smile and a squeeze of the hand, turned to go. I watched her depart and then looked back at Eddie. He took off his nebuliser and threw a croaky whisper in my direction.

"She's a lovely kid, heart of gold."

"They've got to have to do this job haven't they Eddie? We'd be in a sorry way without them."

"Ey kid," said Eddie, "you're right there. Anyway, if I were you I'd get some kip, big day for you tomorrow," and with that he laid back, replaced his mask and closed his eyes.

"Eddie?"

"What now?" he asked as he begrudgingly lifted his mask.

"I wish they'd give the loony at the side of me a double-ender."
Eddie replaced his nebuliser yet again and chuckled away to himself.

I found it difficult to find sleep and the last time I looked at the clock it was five in the morning but then at five past six Nurse Nightingale woke me.

"Time to get you ready Mr Smith," she said.

For one moment I actually thought I'd dreamt the previous day but I came back to earth with a bump and the reality of the situation hit me straight between the eyes. I was placed in a smock-type garment and asked if I wanted the anaesthetic. I declined with great bravado, remembering that Eddie had told me that the jab was for puffs.

Eddie was awake and a little better than the previous night. Perhaps it was the nebuliser which had had a stabilising effect.

"You look a bit better this morning Eddie," I said.

"Ey," he said, "I feel much better for having had a wash and a shave...not be long now then."

"What won't? I asked.

"The double-ender."

"Oh bollocks Eddie," I said, "I'm not having a double-ender, I'm just having the gastroscopy."

"Ey," said Eddie, "you just wait until they put that rubber glove on, that's the first clue."

I shook my head and smiled. My friend across was fast asleep as was the loony who'd talked himself into exhaustion throughout the night.

Just then the auxiliary brought in the breakfast. Eddie was having bacon, egg and tomatoes with some toast and I must admit it looked wonderful.

"Shame you can't have any of this," said Eddie. "Never mind, when you've had the gastro you'll not want anything anyway."

"Thanks Eddie," I said, shrugging my shoulders, "You do know how to put a bloke at ease."

He laughed and tucked into his bacon and egg. He slowly but deliberately placed tasty morsels on the end of his fork and then with great extravagance began to eat. As he did so, he was making noises of satisfaction and gratification. I looked away in disgust.

"What are you like with your enemies Eddie?" I asked.

He laughed but in doing so he began to cough repeatedly and violently, so much so that the nurse came running into the room, took away the breakfast tray and closed the curtains.

"Poor old Eddie," I thought to myself.

The coughing and spluttering went on for some minutes and then I heard rather frantic gasping for breath and the sound of the nebuliser once again.

A nurse I'd not seen before came in. She was wearing a uniform with a white smock and one of those funny caps that they wear to hide their hair.

"I've got to take you down now Mr Smith," she said and a porter brought in a wheelchair.

"I can walk, I'm perfectly alright," I said.

"No sorry, you've got to go down in the wheelchair, it's the rules. By the way, have you had a movement?"

"Have I had a what?" I asked.

"A movement."

I was perplexed.

"She means a crap," shouted Eddie demonstratively. "You will do when you get down there."

"I'm alright thank you," I said, finding it difficult to discuss my personal arrangements.

I got into the wheelchair and was pushed from the room along the corridor. Just as I was leaving, the curtains were pushed back from Eddie's bed. I looked across at him and he looked at me and he held his thumb in an upward position. This time I gave him two fingers and he laughed. He looked terribly ill. Within a minute or two I was on a bright corridor leading to the Gastroscopy Unit.

"Had one of these before?" asked the porter.

"No, never," I said, "It's my first time."

"No problem," he said, "It'll be over in a jif, you'll not feel a thing."

He was sympathetic, he was caring and he was doing his level best to put me at my ease but he had lied.

I entered the Gastroscopy Unit and there I saw the great Doctor Bardhan wearing his theatre garb. He pulled the glasses from his eyes and perched them precariously on the top of his head. A plaster across his nose kept his glasses in place.

"Now then Stephen, do you want medication?" he asked gently.

"No thanks doc, I'll manage without if that's OK?"

"Certainly, but what I'm going to do is to spray a little of this substance onto the back of your throat to make it easier for you to swallow the camera. It won't take long, it'll be over very quickly."

I was immediately at ease.

"Just lay on the table there if you will," he continued.

I laid on the table with my head on the pillow which had been covered with a clean cloth. His assistant took a roll of soft paper tissue and placed it in my hand. I lay on my side with my knees slightly forward. The good doctor turned to face me with a long tube-like object. I gulped. All I could think was "Oh my goodness – or words to that effect!" He explained the procedure once again and said that there was nothing to worry about as he was very experienced, having previously worked for Dyno rod. I couldn't help smiling and whilst I expected he used the same line for all his patients, the humour was most welcome.

One nurse held my legs and a male nurse stood behind me. Another was at my head. I was encircled by staff and it became quite apparent to me that if a time arose whereby I did not want to have the treatment, I wouldn't be able to change my mind.

A pot-type object was placed in my mouth with a hole through the centre. This object, said the nurse, was to keep my mouth wide open so that the camera could be administered through the hole in the middle and down into my throat. It was said in such a matter of fact way that the enormity of what was to happen didn't really register with me. Another squirt of the magic potion onto the back of my throat left it numb.

"Right, let's begin," said the doctor. "This won't take very long and I promise you it won't hurt."

He was right there, it didn't hurt but as Eddie had told me the night before, if you imagine placing two fingers down the back of your throat and holding them there for a considerable period, that's exactly what it was like. I felt the object pass down my gullet and into the far reaches of my stomach.

"There's a screen just above your head," said the doctor, "and you can actually see what the camera is photographing."

I closed my eyes firmly shut and I gulped for air and gypped repeatedly. The last thing I wanted was to see it.

"Just calm yourself," said the nurse quietly, "and breathe deeply and slowly."

I took her advice and for a moment the gypping stopped to return spasmodically as the discomfort got the better of me. They were right, it didn't hurt but then vomiting doesn't usually.

It was a sensation quite unlike any other I had experienced. For those who have endured the event you will know exactly what I mean. For the uninitiated, it is like having four feet of innertubing rammed down your gullet and twiddled about so that it bangs to and fro against the inner part of the pelvis.

Fortunately for me I was in the care of the expert hands of Dr Bardhan, probably the greatest exponent of the noble art of gastroscopyism. But for him and his wonderful staff the exercise would have been intolerable.

After what seemed an eternity, the doctor said those wonderful words,

"Right, coming out now Stephen, that's the end of it."

He had dictated something during the "operation" to his staff who were busily taking notes but I couldn't follow what was being said and what's more, I wasn't interested. All I wanted was to get out of there as soon as possible. The camera was being withdrawn and I felt it travel every inch of the way. My eyes and nose had run repeatedly and finally, when the camera was removed, I breathed a sigh of relief. My eyes were red and I was unable to speak. Fresh blood stained the tissue that I'd held against my mouth. I sat on the side of the bed as I felt the aftermath of the doctor's work.

"Well done," said the nurse earnestly, "now that wasn't bad was it?"

"No," I thought to myself, "bung me back on the table and let's have another go – I enjoy a laugh."

I smiled, seeing the funny side of it and she smiled, thinking I meant it.

"You've got refluxasophagitus," said the doctor. "It means that the acid in your system is coming back up your gullet and has ulcerated the sides quite badly and so we'll need to place you on a course of treatment and some antibiotics. I'm afraid you will have to be kept in under observation for about a week or so.

My heart sank.

"During that week I'm afraid you will have to come back down here and we'll see if that initial treatment has removed the swelling and the inflammation."

"You mean I have to have another one of these?" I croaked.

"Yes," said Doctor Bardhan, "but you did ever so well and next time you'll find it will be a lot easier because you'll know how to cope. We've also taken a biopsy, which we will send to the lab for checks."

The very word biopsy sent a shiver down my spine. For the first time in my life I was genuinely ill.

The week progressed quickly, during which time I had a further gastroscopy and some wonderful nights of humour with the boys in annexe D. I must say that of all the things I've done and witnessed, I had more fun that week with those fellows than anywhere else. The staff were wonderful and I couldn't fault the care and treatment that I was given. I had, of course, a number of visits from my family and friends and one particular afternoon Pagey and Jarvis came to see me. Typically Pagey couldn't keep things to himself and whilst picking up various items, he unplugged Eddie's nebuliser. He then plugged it in again and put in on himself, just to see what it was like. He ended up coughing and spluttering all over the place and the nurse came in, seized it off him and put it back on Eddie's unit. The bedpan was the next to be passed around. There then followed an hilarious three-way conversation between Pagey, the loony in the next bed and me. I don't know who was worse, the loony or Pagey, but by the end of the conversation all three of us were getting on famously.

When my meal came Pagey ate half of it and then most of my fruit but he left me a bottle of Guinness and a small bottle of whisky, which the staff took off me immediately. He promised to come again but I hoped that I would be released before he did.

Towards the end of the week Doctor Bardhan cleared me to leave and armed with boxes of tablets and other items, I said my farewells to the gang at the hospital. I was told to go directly home where I would remain for the next fortnight, although I promised Eddie I would call back and see him. Unfortunately I am not good at taking advice.

The following morning I was at the office. The calls had mounted up and there were all sorts of problems on all sorts of fronts. One call in particular had upset me. It transpired that Dingleberry, better known as Mrs Holroyd, had suffered a heart attack and she was resident in the Intensive Care Unit at Rotherham District General Hospital.

A couple of days later, I dealt with the morning court and then went to the hospital because I'd been told that she'd been asking for me. So much for sick leave!

After only three or four days of being discharged from the hospital I was back again but this time as a visitor. I went to the Coronary Care Unit and spoke to the sister in charge of the ward. I explained the reason for my visit and told her of my reluctance to bother the ward at that time. Nevertheless, she fully understood and took me to a small ante-room off the main ward. I went inside and saw Dingleberry, who was plugged into an amazing array of gadgetry all leading to various machines, which were making odd sounding noises. She looked really ill but then she'd just suffered a major heart attack, so I couldn't really expect anything else.

The sister had told me that despite considerable damage to the heart, she was comfortable but it was too early to say whether she would make a recovery or not. Apparently the main difficulty was the next twenty-four hours.

Dingleberry looked and sounded very tired and yet her first concern was for her husband.

"How's George, Mr Smith?"

"He's fine," I said, "he's fine. Apparently Social Services are visiting every day and taking him his meals. I will call on my way back and make sure he's OK."

"He won't be able to stay there Mr Smith," she said in little more than a whisper. "You see, he can't look after himself. The problem is the dementia you see and yet there's still an awful lot he does remember. I just don't know what I'm going to do, where is he going to go?"

Dingleberry began to get upset, so I immediately tried to put her at ease.

"I'll sort it out, Mrs Holroyd, you can rely on me. I'll make sure that everything is OK."

"Oh, would you Mr Smith?" she said, "Oh really, would you?"

"I've told you I will, I'll take care of it this very afternoon. I know some of the people at Social Services and when I explain the problem to them, would you mind…if we got him a place…in a home?"

I thought the mention of such a place would upset her.

"There's not much more I can do is there?" she said pathetically, "but I can't leave him on his own. The specialist tells me that even if I do get out of here, I won't be able to run a big house like ours, so I want you to take steps to sell…."

I interrupted her.

"There's no need to sell that at this stage; you could make a full recovery. It's too early to be taking steps like that surely?"

"No, it's not Mr Smith, you above all should know. I'm not adopting a defeatist attitude but I've got to be prepared you see. It's just got to be done. If I do get out of here I could probably go to the same home, if we could find one that we both liked and then we could perhaps still be together. At least I'd have the security of somebody looking after us."

I was moved by her realism and her desire to put her husband first. I promised her that I would do what I could and would visit her

156

again a week later. I was much saddened by what had taken place because they had no children or family on whom they could call to look after them and I felt very much the isolation that she must have to endure. I was resolved to try to sort out their problems.

On my way out of the Coronary Care Unit I decided to call into my former ward and see the gang and probably have a quick laugh with Eddie. I bought some magazines and chocolates from the newsstand and made my way up the two flights of steps to the ward. I decided I would walk in and shout, "stand by your beds", as though one of the specialists was about to call to see them. Eddie would like that and then he would tell me to chuff off or even words that were stronger.

I rehearsed my little speech on the way to the ward. As I turned the corner I saw the loony sitting at the side of his bed, having a conversation and the man who'd been in such terrible pain, actually sitting up in bed reading a paper. At the far end there was a new face.

As I rounded the corner Eddie's bed came into view.

"Stand by your...."

"That's odd," I thought to myself, "Eddie must have gone for a bath or a shower or something."

The loony greeted me with the words, "Hello Doctor," and I smiled and nodded and went across to Eddie's bed. His locker was open and empty and the bed was rolled down with the sheets gone.

I turned to the man outside who was reading his magazine,

"Where's Eddie?" I asked, dreading the answer.

"Haven't you heard old son?" said the man.

"Haven't I heard what?"

"Oh, poor old Eddie bought it last night. He had one of his coughing fits and the poor bugger's heart stopped. It was like Sheffield station in here but in fairness they did everything they could. They were at him for ages and ages but the poor old bugger's heart gave out."

I didn't answer and I didn't ask any questions. Eddie was dead; that was all that anyone could tell me. The whys and wherefores seemed irrelevant. The man lifted back his magazine and continued to read, leaving me standing in the middle of the ward, almost like a spare part. The loony came up to me and spoke.

"I'm feeling much better now doctor."

I looked at him, almost in a daze. He watched me expectantly as I just looked around the room.

"Oh yes, that's alright Mr Keown, you're doing well. You get back into bed and just have a minute."

"Yes, OK doctor, if that's what you advise."

"Yes, that's what I advise," I said.

I walked to the end of the ward and looked back. The gallstone man was reading his magazine and the loony continued to smile at me and wave. Everyone else was busy doing something else. I just shook my head and left. I gave the magazine and chocolates to an old chap in a wheelchair who was being wheeled somewhere or other. He looked really pleased.

I didn't know Eddie's address and I didn't know who to write to but I got the details from the Sister and when I got back to the office I dictated a letter to his widow, telling her what a comfort her husband had been to me during my week in hospital. Somehow the letter seemed totally inadequate.

I also made a number of telephone calls and finally got the assistance of the department which was dealing with Mrs Holroyd's problem. I also phoned a friend of mine at the local Alzheimer's Society and got them on board.

Fortunately for them, Batsoid and Dingleberry were very well off and could afford to go into the nicest of homes. Within two days I had all the brochures and I took them to the hospital and found Dingleberry sitting up in bed. She looked much better and I told her so.

"I feel much better Mr Smith," she said, "much better. They've told me that I'm doing so well they're going to start working towards letting me go home. Of course I won't be able to go back to home and they tell me I'll always have to have someone to look after me but at least I can get out and be with George to see that he's alright."

I nodded and smiled in approval and showed her the various brochures and leaflets of the homes that I'd been given. There was one home in a beautiful area, not too far from the Peak District. It was expensive but they could afford it and she asked me if I would make all the enquiries and try to resolve it for her.

Within two days I had arranged to see a small flatlet within the grounds, overlooking a beautiful array of rosebeds. The home overlooked a beautiful valley and the conservatory enjoyed the most spectacular of views. It took nearly three weeks to organise everything, something of a record they told me but the main problem was in Mrs Holroyd being well enough to go.

I visited Batsoid in the home where he'd been living in the short term and I noticed that his condition had worsened. He was completely irrational and rather distressed. It was awful to see someone of his calibre or indeed of any calibre, in that distressed state and there was some concern as to whether or not his condition had deteriorated so much that he wouldn't be allowed in the flatlet.

The following weekend I travelled to the Peak District and to Sunningdale Retirement Home. They had fantastic facilities; it was more like a five-star hotel than a home. It was spotlessly clean and everywhere was the smell of polish and air freshener.

I had a very long conversation with the Matron, who had seen Batsoid for an assessment. She shook her head as I implored with her to allow them to be together, suggesting that when his wife was around he was much better and less of a problem because whilst the dementia had progressed at rather an alarming rate, when he was with her it didn't present a problem to anybody. For a time I realised that I was banging my head against a brick wall and then quite by chance his distinguished war career came into the conversation.

It transpired that the Matron's father had served in the same theatre of war as Batsoid and whilst not in the same regiment, he too had been in North Africa. He had been mentioned in dispatches for bravery and understandably she spoke of him with great pride. I listened as she touched upon every facet of their life together, from her childhood until his death some two or three years before. She told me what a blessing it was when he died, for his body had been ravaged by cancer and his final months were so very distressing for them both. She spoke of the happy years when, as a child they would play together, usually at soldiers because it brought back memories from his years with the Army.

She spoke with great love and affection and we were building up a considerable rapport. She had turned from a hard-nosed professional into a thoughtful, caring and thoroughly likeable person.

I saw a glimmer of hope as the Matron's resolve was beginning to weaken. I told her about the Holroyd's background and how devoted they were and what a sin it would be if they had to be parted, particularly as they had no family and I even suggested it would be the end of Dingleberry if I had to be the bearer of bad tidings. The Matron looked out over the view in contemplation.

"What an absolutely magnificent view," I said, changing the subject.

"That's nothing, you want to see it from the conservatory," she said.

"Are they forsythia bushes over there in the corner?" I said noting an extremely thick and luscious hedge.

"Yes," she said, "how observant. I didn't realise you were a gardener."

"Oh I have my moments," I said, "and the roses, they look magnificent. Are they all hybrid teas?"

"Yes, we've got sixty bushes in that particular bed. That's where we get most of our cut flowers from and then to the right is a seat overlooking...."

She hesitated.

"My father spent his last days here...I was able to look after him...he became a resident you know...I could see him every day." Her voice tailed off to a whisper.

"He was a very lucky man," I said, noting the mantelpiece full of photographs. There was a very old black and white picture of a very attractive woman, who I assumed was her mother and then there were a number of photographs of her father, in uniform and then as an old man. One had been taken by the rosebed where he appeared to be pruning the roses.

"My father planted that bed," she said thoughtfully. "That's the one job I reserve for myself in the garden. I always make sure it's weeded, fed and nurtured. I suppose it's something of a tribute."

"It's marvelous to think that you've got something like that to look at, as a memory I mean," I said.

"I sit there quite often with a cup of tea during one of my very few breaks. He spent four years here, until...."

"How old was he Matron?" I asked.

"Oh, he was old, he was eighty-five but until the last year he kept pretty fit and it worked well for both of us. I was able to see to him every day and...you see with this job I don't get an awful lot of time and I managed to combine the two. In many ways we were very lucky."

"Families should always stay together if they can," I said stealing a glance across at her.

She stopped, looked at me and smiled.

"You're a very crafty chap," she said continuing to smile.

"Whatever do you mean?" I asked.

"You know very well what I mean," she said and then she was silent for what seemed an eternity. "If I were to allow the Holroyds to stay, if Mr Holroyd presented a problem, we wouldn't be able to deal with him, you know that don't you?" she said firmly.

"I appreciate that but I think you'll find that with Mrs Holroyd, there won't be a problem."

"But if anything happens to her...?" She paused, waiting for an answer.

"Well if anything happens to her, it won't particularly matter then. Mr Holroyd will be on his own whether he's here or anywhere else for that matter and with all respect to him, without her he won't be bothered where he stays."

Matron said nothing and continue to stare through the window at the rose garden. After another long pause she spoke again, hesitantly at first.

"It would have to be on trial," she said as she turned and shuffled the papers on her desk. "I couldn't give any guarantees at all."

"Brilliant Matron," I said, "brilliant. You're an absolute toff."

"I'm soft," she said, retaining her matronly pose.

"I don't think it's being soft Matron," I said, "I think it's being kind, thoughtful and generous."

"That will do. Now you're taking the mickey."

I laughed, walked towards her and kissed her on the cheek.

"That's for being a star."

I opened the door to leave and then paused and turned.

"Thank you Matron," I said. "You'll make two really nice people very happy."

She looked at me and smiled and nodded. She cleared her throat and went back to being a matron again.

"Well thank you Mr Smith, we'll keep in touch and doubtless you will let me know when the hospital are able to discharge Mrs Holroyd."

She turned and looked back across the rose garden. I wondered what she was thinking at that instant. I closed the door, walked to the end of the corridor, punched and air and shouted,

"YES!"

An old lady who was walking along the corridor with the aid of a stick, pointed it at me.

"You'd better take your tablets, behaving like that. If you want someone to take you to the toilet, ask one of the staff."

I immediately stood to attention and moved to one side so that she could walk past. As she drew near she turned and looked at me.

"I don't know, they'll let anybody in these days."

I nodded and spoke back respectfully.

"Good morning madam,"

She tutted and walked away, pointing to the mens lavatory. When she had gone the smile was restored to my face and with a spring in my step I walked towards the car park.

Within the hour I was back in Rotherham and at the close of the day's business I set off for the hospital. I got to Dingleberry's room, knocked on the door and walked in.

"Great news, I've got great..."

The room was empty and all the machinery to which Dingleberry had been hooked up was standing idle in the corner. I turned and ran to the Sister's office and found her writing on some documents.

"Sister, Sister, what's happened to Mrs Holroyd? Where...?"

She looked at me quizzically and I realised that she was not the sister I'd dealt with before.

"Who are you?" she asked authoritatively.

"I'm sorry, I'm Steve Smith, the solicitor acting for..."

"Just wait a minute, slow down," she said, "who are you again?"

I took a deep breath and regained my composure, unhappy at being spoken to as if I were some irreverent schoolboy.

"I'm Steve Smith, the solicitor for Mrs Holroyd and Mrs Holroyd has a husband who suffers from dementia and I've been out trying to organise a home. I've gone back into her room and she's not there and....What has happened?"

The Sister picked up a sheet of paper which had a number of notes scribbled on it.

"Oh Mrs Holroyd, yes. Sister Truman left me a note."

"Is she...?"

"Is she what dear?" she asked, softening her disposition somewhat.

"Is she...dead?" I asked solemnly.

The Sister looked at me confused."

"Don't be ridiculous, we've moved her onto the General Ward, she's doing really well. Didn't you see the notice on the door?"

"No, I didn't see it. Why, what was it?"

"There was a note just saying where she'd gone to but it must have come off. She's on the main ward. You go past the room to the end of the corridor and turn left. You'll find her in a small anteroom which she shares with another lady. She's doing very well."

She picked up her papers and looked at her watch.

"You'll find her in very good spirits. Now, if you wouldn't mind, I've got things to do."

"Oh yes, of course, thank you...yes...thank you...thank you very much...I'll go and see her."

"Yes, well off you go then," she said firmly, "and then come and see me afterwards. There's some mention of her moving out to a home when she's considered to be fit enough."

"Yes of course, it's Sunningdale in the Peak District."

"Very nice. Well if you don't mind Mr Smith, I've got things to do."

"Yes, thank you, I'm sorry to be…yes…thank you."

I followed her instructions and went to the end of the corridor and turned left. Eventually I found a small anteroom with two occupants. The door was open and Dingleberry was sitting up in bed, reading a magazine and when she saw me her face lit up.

"Mr Smith, how nice of you to call again. Have you got some news?"

I smiled and pulled up a chair.

"Have I got news for you!" I said excitedly. "We've cracked it. Sunningdale are prepared to take you and Mr Holroyd together and just as soon as you get a clean bill of health, you're in. On the same day we do the transfer Mr Holroyd can move in. There's a beautiful flatlet and the views, you would not believe the views. Do you know, there's the most fantastic rose garden and the Matron's father lived there and…"

I realised I'd begun to gabble.

There were tears in Dingleberry's eyes, which she tried to conceal.

"It's these blasted tablets," she said, "they make my eyes water."

I smiled and nodded reassuringly.

"All we need to do now is to get you well enough for the transfer. Mr Holroyd is depending upon you, so I don't want you to let him down."

"I won't," she said smiling, "I've done everything that they've told me to do but I'm finding the diet a little hard to deal with, you see no more scones and butter for me."

"It's a small price to pay," I said.

"Yes, I suppose it is. And George, have you seen him?"

"Yes I have and he's fine. I think once you get there he'll be back to his old self."

Dingleberry sighed and laid back in the bed.

"Thank the Lord," she said. "I can't tell you what a relief that is. Now I'm really going to get better."

"Right, well get on with it then and let's have you in the Peak District. I'll come up and visit you if you like?"

"You'd be more than welcome," she said. "Meat and potato pie might be a thing of the past but I'm sure we'll be able to fix you up with some nice fruit and yoghurt."

I attempted to smile and Dingleberry laughed.

"Enjoy it while you can Mr Smith; I did."

There was something prophetic in that statement.

We talked for about another twenty minutes and when our business was done I turned to leave.

"Thank you," she said. "I hope that one day I'll be able to do something for you."

"You already have, Mrs Holroyd, you already have."

"What do you mean?"

"You've taught me about families and about how they should stick together and how time is precious and we shouldn't waste a minute of it."

She smiled and I returned the compliment and left.

It took five weeks before Mrs Holroyd was fit to travel. I saw George once or twice in that time and his condition had deteriorated, but the day came for them to move in. I drove Mrs Holroyd to the home and George met her at the gates as he had moved in two days before. He recognised her as she got out of the car.

"And where do you think you've been?" asked George. "I've been waiting for you for ages."

"Have you George," she said smiling. "Well I think it's time that we had a cup of tea."

"Good," said George, "and then to the dining room. Its meat and potato pie today."

He looked across at me and winked.

"Well, carry on," he said and with that he turned and gently taking his wife's arm, he took her through the large oak door.

I accepted the invitation for a cup of tea and carried their bags to the one-bedroom flatlet. It overlooked the rose garden and the view into the valley. The roses had just begun to flower. Matron was right; it was a beautiful garden, with such a glorious view.

They enjoyed two more summers together but then George Holroyd died suddenly. His wife, whom I knew affectionately as Dingleberry, died shortly afterwards – just as the roses had finished flowering.

Chapter 13

BARRY MANILOW AT WINDERMERE

The down side of our profession is that you do have to deal with some pretty awful people, charged with some really dreadful offences and I've often said that you witness human nature at its very worst. I would hope that the reader would forgive me for becoming something of a cynic but at the risk of being negative, if you never trust anybody and you always expect the worst, you never get disappointed, or so it seemed to me at that time. But every so often my faith in human nature was restored as it was in the case of Eric Barnard.

Eric was a former miner who, like many others, fell foul of pit closures in the 1980s and found himself unemployed. He took up a job working for one of the better security firms and whilst he worked twelve hour shifts on an alternative days and nights basis, he was reasonably happy because he was working. He told me how the strike and unemployment had affected him, describing them as the worst days of his life.

Eric was the salt of the earth; a hard-worker, honest and a good family man. Not somebody you would expect to see before a criminal court. He was very well thought of in his local community and did a lot for the old people of his village, who treated him as though he was a member of their families. He would collect shopping and when his shift times allowed it, he took old people to hospital, doctor's appointments and tended their gardens. He was something of a hero in his mining community. Eric was in his mid-fifties and still extremely fit, apart from a "slightly dicky chest", a legacy from thirty years in the pit. He was over six feet tall and as strong as an ox. He was still handsome, with a firm square jaw and bright blue eyes, which sparkled when he laughed. He was of the old school and when he was out and about he wore a tie. With his impeccable manners he was a shining example for the people of his village.

He'd only had one previous brush with the law when he was seventeen and had been fined for drinking under age. Apart from that case he was "squeaky clean". He was not the sort of man you would expect to find in my diary, unless he wanted to make a will or buy a house, so it was with some surprise that I found that he faced two charges of assault.

I was attending the Cross Keys one lunchtime for a hot roast pork sandwich and a sherbet dip when I was approached by Barry Bealby, otherwise known as Baz. Baz was an interesting character who'd spent the majority of his adult life in prison for things that he claimed he hadn't done. He was the unluckiest man in the world because he had twelve previous convictions and according to him he was innocent of them all. Quite how there could be twelve miscarriages of justice in one person's life was beyond me but Baz was philosophical and said that he "put it all down to experience".

His forte was commercial burglaries and the removal of office equipment. He worked with a Sheffield "fence" (handler of stolen goods) and together they earned a reasonable income whilst he was at liberty. He was a small-time Mr Fixit, committing many of his offences to order, that is to say that someone would tell him what they wanted and he would go and steal it.

This particular afternoon he was in something of a buoyant mood and after a full week's work, primarily on the night shift, he had decided to have a few days off to enjoy the proceeds of his nefarious activities.

One of his old schoolfriends was Brian Barnard and Baz had been called upon to advise him on the plight of his father Eric who, at the age of fifty-two, had got himself into trouble for the first time. Baz introduced me to Brian and apologised for disturbing my dinner break but said he wanted me to give his mate some advice.

He was a young man in his early twenties, well-dressed with a fondness for aftershave. He was very well-mannered and spoke about a family problem, which had placed the household in trauma.

His father, Eric Barnard, was to appear at the police station to answer questions about an assault which was said to have taken place two or three nights before. The simple facts were that Eric had been in his local chip shop at about eleven thirty at night when two local yobs came in. They were both drunk and looking for trouble and were abusive to the lady who was serving. Eric was unimpressed by this behaviour and although he didn't want to get involved, there came a time when he thought that enough was enough and he told them so. He in turn was abused and threatened and whilst he was more than their equal, he decided that discretion was the better part of valour and having been served, he left. He was abused again and some vinegar was thrown down the back of his new overcoat. Eric was very angry but with strength of character and purpose he turned and walked away. It seems that the two yobs had followed him to his home and extracted their revenge by damaging Eric's car. There was an incident during which the two young men were injured and the police had become involved.

I gave Brian my card and told him to tell his father to contact me, saying that I would be prepared to go to the police station with him when he was interviewed. The appointment had been fixed for later that week and with a bit of reorganisation in the office I was able to attend the interview. I met Eric in the office shortly before we were due to travel to the police station and we discussed the case at length. We set off for the local nick, arriving five minutes early and some ten minutes later a burly police officer from CID appeared at the reception desk and called out our names. We walked into the doorway of the reception area to be greeted by DC Robertshaw of the South Yorkshire Police stationed at Maltby.

Eric was wearing a smart sports coat and cavalry-twill trousers with a cream shirt and tie. I was wearing my pin-stripe trousers, black jacket and carried a briefcase and a new file.

"Which of you is Mr Smith, the solicitor?" he asked.

"That would be me," I said, stating the obvious.

With that DC Robertshaw turned to Eric and spoke.

"Eric Barnard, I am arresting you on suspicion of assault occasioning actual bodily harm. You are not obliged to say anything unless you wish to do so but whatever you say will be taken down and used in evidence."

Eric froze.

We were escorted into the charge office, the scene of very many memories for me. We were second in line behind a middle-aged lady who had been charged with prostitution.

"We won't be long," whispered the police officer, "just as soon as they've dealt with this town hall steps merchant."

I just nodded in agreement.

When the "town hall steps merchant" was charged she turned, saw me and winked.

"Hello cheeky," she said to me.

I smiled and felt her tweek my backside. I did not react.

"Good evening Mr Smith," said the custody sergeant.

"Good evening Sergeant."

"What brings you to my humble abode?" he asked sarcastically.

"I'm acting on behalf of Mr Barnard who is with me. He's going to be interviewed about two assaults."

"Very good," said the sergeant who then set about filling in various forms and checking that my client was neither a drug addict, a terrorist, suicidal or likely to self-mutilate. I confirmed that he was none of those things and after he had been given his rights we went into a small interview room which would have housed a dwarf comfortably but two police officers, a solicitor and his client was another matter. There was no ventilation and whilst there was a fan in the room, this was never used because it would interfere with the tape-recording process. Quite why they kept it in there I will never know.

The police officer made the introductions.

"Right Eric, have you been interviewed on tape before?"

"No, I've not been in a police station before," said Eric meekly.

"Right, well I've got to read some words to you and I'll do it off this idiot board," he said, trying to make Eric feel at ease. It didn't work. "I'll then ask you some questions which will be recorded and at the end of the interview I'll explain how you can get copies of the tapes. Are you OK then?"

Eric just nodded.

"My name is DC Patrick Robertshaw and I'm an officer of the South Yorkshire Police situated at Rotherham. For voice identification my colleague is PC Turnbull, South Yorkshire Police. What is your name please?"

"Eric Barnard."

"And your date of birth?"

Twenty-seventh of April, nineteen twenty-eight."

"And you are here with your solicitor. Will you identify yourself for the tape please?"

I did so. The other formalities were then completed.

"Right Eric, we're here to ask you about two incidents on Thursday last when it's alleged that you committed two assaults, is that right?"

I interrupted.

"Which question do you want him to answer? Is he here to be interviewed or has he committed two assaults?"

The officer breathed deeply and shrugged his shoulders.

"I'll try again then," he said sarcastically. "Is it right you've been arrested in respect of allegations of assault?"

"Yes," said Eric, even more meekly than before.

"Right, tell me your movements last Thursday night."

I thought it best not to clarify whether he meant his physical movements or those of the bowel.

Eric took a deep breath and said, "Well I went down to the chip shop at the end of our road and there was something of an altercation with two youths. I left the chip shop and got home and not long after they were either damaging or trying to break into my car. I went out to try to stop them and they squared up to me. One of them tried to punch me so I just hit him back and then I hit the other one. Then they ran off and I called the police."

"Right, let's just take that stage by stage. You say you'd been to the chip shop on the night in question?"

"Yes, I had."

"It might seem something of an obvious question, but what did you go for?"

The blasé way in which the officer approached the interview annoyed me a little. I wanted to say that this is a man of perfectly good character who had to deal with some violent yobs, the sort who were not fit to lace his boots. He has no previous convictions, he's very upset and he doesn't like being in a police station being asked why he clouted two yobos who'd damged his car. But then the interview was on tape and I thought that my petulance would not have helped the situation.

"I went for some fish and chips for me and my wife."

"Ok then, so what time was this?"

"About half past eleven."

"OK. When you got into the chip shop who was there?"

"There was the lady behind the counter and I think it's her brother who does the actual cooking and then there were these two lads."

"What was your state of mind?" asked the officer.

"I don't think I know what you mean."

"Well, it's obvious isn't it? What was your state of mind? Were you happy, sad, mad, angry, in a mood, what?" asked the officer pointedly.

"I was alright. I was in quite a good mood really."

"Right."

I decided to intervene.

"You've not asked Mr Barnard what mood or state these two yobs were in," I said, "perhaps you'd like to comment about that Mr Barnard."

"Well, yes, if you must," said the officer reluctantly.

"Well they'd been drinking definately. I wouldn't say they were drunk but they were definately affected. I would say they were boisterous, yes that's right, boisterous. They were talking loudly and swearing."

"Swearing?"

"Yes, swearing. F's and B's and things like that. I looked at the lady behind the counter and she didn't like it. I didn't say anything at first but when she put their fish and chips in a sort of parcel in the paper, one of them said, 'put more f.....ng scraps on'. I thought enough was enough. I wouldn't let anybody speak to my wife like that and I certainly wasn't going to let them speak to her in that way, so I told them, 'come on lads, pack it in, there's no need for language like that in here, this lady is only doing her job'."

"What happened then?"

"One of them said, 'What's it got to do with you?' "

"What did you say to that?"

"I said I didn't think it was right that they should go in there and use language like that."

"What did the woman say, or the man for that matter?"

"The woman was clearly upset about it and the man was in the back, I think he must have gone for something, so he didn't hear it. That's why I interrupted."

"Well it had got nothing to do with you had it?"

"No, I suppose it hadn't."

"Then why get involved?"

"Well I wish I hadn't now but at the time it just seemed the right thing to do."

"Yes but it was your attitude to the lads that started all this."

I interrupted again.

"Are you saying that he shouldn't interrupt if two yobs are being vulgar and rude?" I asked.

"I don't want to have an argument with you Mr Smith, I'm simply doing my job and asking the questions. It's for him to answer, not you."

"I understand that perfectly well officer but I don't think you'd have been very pleased if it had been your wife."

"It wasn't my wife sir and I'm just doing my job."

"Yes, and not terribly well," I thought to myself, gritting my teeth. I felt something of an argument coming on.

"Anyway, you told them off in no uncertain terms?"

I interrupted again.

"No, I don't think he said that. I think he said he didn't feel it was right that they should speak to a lady in such a disgusting manner, yob or not."

The officer grunted in disapproval.

"So what happened then?"

"Then they turned on me and started calling me names."

"What sort of names?"

"All sorts of rude and vulgar names and they told me that I should mind my own f......ing business."

"Well you had got involved hadn't you?"

"Yes, I had got involved," said Eric, "but I wish now that I hadn't. I probably should have left them to continue their abuse but unfortunately I'm not like that. I don't like to see ladies being referred to in that way."

"Good for you Eric," I thought to myself, "That's just the way to deal with it."

"What happened then?" asked the officer.

"I got served, during which time they were continuing with their chuntering. I set off and walked home."

I remembered that Eric had told me that as he left one of them attempted to block his way and so I prompted him.

"Before we go on officer, I would like to ask something."

"Of course," said the officer, looking up to the ceiling as a sign of his contempt.

"You say that you then left, is that right Eric?"

"Yes, that's right."

"Did anything happen as you were leaving."

"Oh yes, of course," said Eric.

The officer looked to the ceiling again.

"One of them blocked my way."

"Yes and....?"

The officer scrutinised the ceiling again, this time for longer than before.

"He shouldered me as I walked out."

"Yes, thank you. Carry on officer," I said.

"Where did you go then?" continued DC Robertshaw.

"I walked home."

"Then what?"

"I went in the house and my wife had already set the table so she served out the meal."

"Yes. Then?"

"There was the sound of breaking glass so I went to the window and saw these two youths at my car. I recognised one of them definitely as being in the chip shop so I ran out, I'd still got my slippers on."

"What did you do when you got outside?" asked the officer.

"I'd never seen anything like it. They were as bold as brass and they didn't even try to run away. When I went out to them, they just turned and squared up to me. That stopped me in my tracks."

"So you ran out to have a go at them?" said the officer.

I had to interrupt again.

"What makes you think that he had to have a go at them?" I asked, "he didn't say that did he?"

"Well I'm just asking if that's what he did."

"No you're not, you put it to him as a general proposition, as though that was what he was going to do. I'm sorry but I think the proper question is to ask him what he was going to do and not to assume anything.

The officer looked at the ceiling yet again.

"Alright," he said grudgingly, "what did you do then?"

"There was a set-to."

"What do you mean, a set-to?"

"We hit each other."

"Let me just ask you, what did you run up to them for?"

"Well it was an automatic reaction. They were damaging my car and I didn't know what I was going to do."

"Surely you had formed some intention. You don't just run up to somebody with nothing in mind."

"I suppose I was going to try to stop them."

"Exactly. How were you going to do that?"

"I was just going to…stop them."

"Yes, you would have got involved in a fight, which is exactly what you did."

"I didn't actually go up to fight them but when I got there they set on me."

"Well what would you expect if somebody runs at you like you did?"

I interrupted again.

"Are you saying that this man was not entitled to protect his property?"

"I'm saying Mr Smith that he is not entitled to take the law into his own hands, which is what he did."

"I would respectfully disagree with you officer. I think he's entitled to protect his property. There's no evidence to say what he was going to do when he got there. He hadn't considered it. He has just said he thought they would have run away.

"Now who's putting words into his mouth?" said the officer.

"Well let's just ask him and see."

"Oh we will now that you've told him what to say. Well…what did you intend to do then?" asked the officer.

"Well first I would have tried to stop them from damaging my car. I wasn't looking for an argument, not with two of them, I'm in my fifties and they were both young men."

"Alright then," said the officer, "so you got up to them."

"Yes, that's right."

"Tell me exactly what happened then?"

"They squared up to me and moved towards me and I thought they were going to hit me. You remember there were two of them so I hit out."

"Did they actually hit you?" asked the officer.

"I'm not sure," said Eric. "I was actually quite frightened and it happened so quickly it's difficult to remember exactly everything that took place."

"Oh do try," said the officer patronisingly.

"I just don't know…I can't answer that question…I just don't know."

Eric was beginning to get distressed and the continual questioning was wearing him down. After all he wasn't a criminal and had never been in that situation before and I thought the officer had forgotten just how stressful those experiences were.

"Alright then," said the officer, "tell me what you remember doing."

"Well, I just hit out as a natural reaction. I hit one and then I must have hit the other, although to be honest I can't remember doing so."

I interrupted again.

"Why did you hit them Eric?"

"Because they were going to hit me and there were two of them."

"Thank you…yes officer, any more questions?"

"So you don't know whether they hit you or not?"

"I could lie," said Eric, "but that's not my way. I honestly can't remember if they did or not."

"Well I suggest to you that they didn't hit you at all."

"I wouldn't argue with you Sergeant," said Eric.

"So therefore you had absolutely no need to hit either one of them and certainly not both."

"I thought I did."

173

"Well that's a matter for the court isn't it?" said the officer sharply.

"Will it go to court?" asked Eric.

"I should think so," said the officer. "The two lads received quite serious injuries. One of them has a fracture of the jaw and whilst it's not needed to be wired it's still a serious injury. The other has a broken nose."

"So to sum it all up then, you saw the two lads who you had had a confrontation with earlier and you went out to sort them out."

"No, that's not the case," I said. "You seem to have forgotten what Mr Barnard said in the early part of the interview. That's not a fair summary."

"Well that's how we look at the case Mr Smith and we'll ask the CPS to confirm what the charges should be. Well, unless anyone has anything else to add I'm going to switch off the tape."

With that the officer turned and switched off the tape and started to fill in certain paperwork.

"I take it you'll have prosecuted the two youths for damaging Mr Barnard's car?" I asked pointedly.

"A file is being prepared in respect of that matter and will be sent to the CPS in the ordinary way for them to decide what to do. It's not my decision Sir, it will have to be left to the CPS," said the officer.

"Well let me make one thing clear," I said. "If you don't prosecute them, we will by way of a private summons, so one way or another they will end up in court for criminal damage."

"I've no doubt you will do as you think best," said the officer, who then turned to Eric and asked him to select a tape, which he would use as the master copy. Eric sat meekly and signed the appropriate forms where the officer indicated he should do so.

"I'm going to bail you to come back to the police station Mr Barnard," said the officer, "when we will know what proceedings, if any, will be taken. Do you want any more time with your client Mr Smith?"

"No thank you, let's just get him bailed straightaway, I don't see any point in hanging around here."

We left and went to the charge office and within fifteen minutes Eric was released. We got outside and he was visibly shaking.

"I'm sorry Mr Smith but I'm not used to this sort of thing. The police don't seem to believe me do they?"

"It's not what the police think Eric," I said, "it's the court, if it gets that far."

"Do you think they'll take me to court?" asked Eric.

"Well, it's a matter for the CPS thankfully. I would hope that when they look at the case they will see there's no case to answer but the strangest things happen in criminal cases. I shouldn't worry about it, just leave it until we're back at the police station and we'll sort it out."

"Don't worry about it?" I repeated to myself silently. What sort of advice was that? Here was a man of good character, respectful of authority and the police in particular. He suffered the degradation of being interviewed about an assault upon two yobs who, quite frankly, deserved it.

The main problem with the case was that he had actually run out to them and the officer had a point when he said that Eric wasn't running out to help them smash the car so he must have had some other objective in mind. On the other hand he was entitled to defend his property. However the law of self-defence is not always fair and misses the point that sometimes judgements have to be made in a split second.

I was worried that if he was prosecuted the court might think that he was some form of vigilante who took the law into his own hands and that annoyed me because it had the effect of giving yobs carte blanche to go about their dishonest and disorderly behaviour without rebuke. That just couldn't be right.

Eric thanked me for my help at the police station and for "sticking up for him" during the interview. I told him it was all part of the job and that I would see him again at the police station just in case there was to be a further interview.

When I got back to the office I dictated a letter to the police to make representations about the damage to Eric's car, saying that I would have expected that proceedings be brought against the two youths who had caused it. Then I wrote to Eric, confirming what had happened and giving him every assurance that I was firmly and squarely on his side.

On my way back to the office I had passed the travel agents and had picked up a brochure for the Lake District. The Lake District always appealed to me and yet I was well into my thirties before I ever visited it. I was captivated by the scenery and in particular Windermere itself. I would visit the Old England Hotel in Bowness and if it was warm enough would sit outside on the verandah with an orange juice or some other drink, watching the yachts sail by and the mighty ski-pulling cabin cruisers saunter into the restricted speed area of Windermere harbour.

On one Sunday visit, I'd gone for a sail with a long queue of passengers on one of the large boats called the *Swan* which plies the lake. It had a licensed bar downstairs so I treated myself to a drink and sat at the front of the boat with the wind in my face. I observed every nook and cranny of the water's edge as the old vessel steamed serenely towards Ambleside. I looked out over the water as my wife and daughter sat shivering, protesting that it was far too cold to sit outside at the front of the boat. They left me to muse upon my wanderings and it occurred to me what a great weekend it would be if Goody and gang could get leave of absence from their homes and join me in a weekend of temperance!

When I got back on the Sunday night I rang Goody, Jarvis, Wilf and Pagey and put the idea to each of them. It was well received and I was left to organise the event for a weekend just after Easter. It's true it would be very cold but I was sure that the odd half pint of beer would warm us up and make for a superb weekend.

On the Monday morning I made all the arrangements. We were going to stay the weekend in a pleasant little cottage just outside Bowness in a row of seven overlooking the lake. My planning was thwarted by a telephone call from DC Robertshaw who called to say that when Eric Barnard went back to answer his bail he would be charged with two offences of assault occasioning actual bodily harm. I was less than pleased and I told the officer exactly what I thought about the charges, only to be told that it wasn't his decision and he was only doing his job. I did not believe him.

He told me that the two youths had not been charged with criminal damage because they had been interviewed and had said that the headlight was damaged during the scuffle and if anything it was caused by Eric's reckless challenge. He said that on the basis that the only evidence against them was Eric's statement the CPS thought it was insufficient to prosecute them for criminal damage. I was appalled. I had no alternative but to telephone and give him the news.

The following night at exactly five thirty Eric called at my office to meet me so that we could walk the short distance to the police station and collect his charges. It was an understatement to say that I was disappointed.

"What will happen to me Mr Smith?" he asked.

"We're pleading not guilty Eric," I said. "You can rest assured that we will fight this case to the death."

My positive attitude did nothing for his demeanor and no matter how I tried, his head had begun to sag and the first signs of defeat were etched across his face.

"Just because they've charged you it doesn't mean to say you'll be found guilty. I've dealt with very many cases like this and the defendant ended up winning.

"The defendant," said Eric, "that's what I am...a defendant...I never thought I'd end up in this state."

I decided to give him a good jolt.

"It's no good crying over spilt milk Eric," I said, "this case has got to be fought. You've got to pull yourself together and you've got to face it. I do not believe for one minute that you're the sort of man who will fall over and play dead. If you've got half the bottle I suspect you've got, you'll help me to fight this allegation and if God's good we will win it."

He nodded and smiled and I think he appreciated the reaction.

"Will it go in the newspapers," he asked.

"I hope so," I said, "it'll be a good advert for me when we win it."

He laughed and the ice had been broken.

We set off for the police station and were waiting in the interview room when I was approached by a rather motley-looking fellow who was doing his best to restrain the oddest looking animal I'd ever seen. It was huge and was having problems with its bowels.

"'ere, dus tha want to 'old this?" asked the man.

"No thank you very much," I said, "I'm OK as I am. I'm going in for an interview in a minute."

"I need somebody to take charge of this. I found it on my allotment, eating all my veg. There was no-one in at the RSPCA so I brought it 'ere."

"What is it?" I asked.

"It's one of them them Vietnamese pot-bellied pigs. They're loveable really."

"Quite so," I said as it brushed past me and layered the side of my trousers with tincture of Vietnamese pot-bellied pig waste.

"Shall I just tie it up and leave it 'ere?"

"You'd better not do that, it might get away again. I should wait for the receptionist to come and she'll advise you on what to do."

"I think it wants a drink."

"Well there's a toilet in there, there might be something for you to put some water in."

"Oh good, just hold this while I get some water."

"Not bloody likely," I said. "You'll bugger off and leave me holding it and I've got an interview to do. I don't want to make light of your problems but I didn't come here to adopt that bugger."

"Neither did I. I can't just leave it to eat my entire allotment."

"Quite...."

Just then I was rescued by the receptionist.

"Mr Smith and Mr Barnard, can you ..."

By this time the pig had heard her dulcet tones and had stood up on its back legs, with its front legs on the counter facing her as she was speaking.

"What the f...?"

"It's a Vietnamese pot-bellied pig," I told her "and I think he's lost."

She looked at me and looked back at the pig.

"Has it got a nametag on?" she asked.

"Has it got a nametag on?" I repeated. "I think it's very unlikely. I don't think pigs have nametags do they but please feel free to look, preferably when we're gone. Anyway, if you'd be kind enough to let us in, we've got an interview to do."

She pressed the switch to allow the door to open and we walked inside. I couldn't resist the quip, "Best of luck with the pig."

We were greeted by DC Robertshaw who appeared to be much happier than on our first meeting. We were taken into a small ante-room and offered a seat.

"I've got the charges here," said the officer, "and I'll take you into the charge office, we'll get you charged and you can go. There's no need to arrest you and fill all those forms in. If you'd like to come with me?"

We followed him to the charge office and who should be there but my old friend Sergeant Whitehouse. He was grumpier than usual.

"Yes?" he said, gripping the side of the counter.

"This gentleman is to be charged," said DC Robertshaw.

"Which gentleman? Mr Smith or this other chap?"

"The other chap of course," said Sergeant Robertshaw, missing the joke.

"Very good, what are the charges?"

He handed him two pink charge sheets, which were identical apart from the names of the persons assaulted. Sergeant Whitehouse went through his ritual and then charged Eric with the offences. Even though he'd been told what would happen and even though he knew what would take place, he was very alarmed to be there facing those charges.

"Has your client anything to say Mr Smith?" asked Sergeant Whitehouse.

"Yes, I think he'll be saying not guilty to both charges Sergeant."

"Very good. Is that what you're saying Mr Barnard?"

"Yes, that's right," he said.

"Very good," said Sergeant Whitehouse, "that's not guilty then. You'll be at court on the twenty-fourth and I'm releasing you upon unconditional bail. If you don't turn up on that date you'll be committing an offence which is punishable by a fine or imprisonment. Do you want the charge sheets Mr Smith?" he asked, offering them to me.

"Yes, thank you."

I took the charge sheets and we waited for the sergeant to press the button which would free us from the charge office. As we were leaving the phone rang and Sergeant Whitehouse picked up the receiver.

"Sergeant Whitehouse charge office speaking...you've got a what?...a Vietnamese what...? And what the hell do you expect me to do with it? I don't want it in here."

I turned before closing the door and waved at Sergeant Whitehouse, giving him the thumbs-up sign. He just looked at me and sneered.

When we got to the reception area we were fully expecting to see that huge member of the animal kingdom but he appeared to have gone. However, he had left his trademark all over the reception floor so we both trod warily until we got to the exit. As we passed the car park we saw two police officers desperately trying to push the animal away from the open door of their motor vehicle. It had one of the officers trapped against the side of the panel and the other was doing his best to pull its shoulder. I waved and walked past.

"Nice looking pig that," I announced.

When we got back to the office we discussed our next move and Eric left in the certain knowledge that in just over a fortnight's time he would be making his first appearance in a criminal court on two charges of assault.

I rang Goody and told him about the cottage I had booked for us in Windermere. We were going to set off after work on the Friday, stay two nights and return on the Sunday afternoon.

Sure enough, on the Friday I had finished my court list by one o'clock and my appointments by four. I tidied up a bit of dictation and then switched off my phone. My experience was that if I answered a call on my way out I would live to regret it. I went to pick up Jarvis from his home and met Wilf and Pagey there. The three of us then picked up Goody and off we went, straight down the M62 to the M61 and the road into Windermere.

The journey was enjoyable, with great banter en route and when we got onto the road into Windermere we passed a rather quaint old-looking public house and feeling the need to make a call of nature, or rather that's what he said, Pagey called for the car to stop and we all went inside. A couple of drinks later we were back on our way down the twisting, winding road to Windermere.

It was still light as we rounded the bend that gave us the most welcome view of the lake. The evening sun reflected on the water; it was a wonderful sight. Pagey was fast asleep in the back of the car and missed it completely.

Eventually we arrived at Windermere itself and visited the local supermarket for some provisions. I bought some bacon and Goody bought some bread and eggs. Jarvis bought some tinned stuff and sausage and Pagey bought a bottle of whisky, some mixers and twelve cans of lager. We set off for the cottage and parked our car in the space provided.

I was sharing a room with Goody, which was not the smartest thing to do because Goody snores like a pig and breaks wind a little too regularly for my liking. Wilf shared with Jarvis and Pagey got a room on his own. It was far too risky sharing with Pagey, you never knew what he was going to get up to, whether he would put something in your bed or otherwise mess you about. He was dangerous and completely unreliable. Jarvis said that he was mentally unstable and I think he was probably right.

We showered and then set off for an evening stroll to the Porthole restaurant. Gianni Bierton is the owner and he and his wife Judy have delighted diners for years with their fabulous cuisine. He was delighted to see us and showed us to our table.

As the evening wore on we had more and more to drink and after a sumptuous meal the coffee was served. I noticed that Wilf had become a little worse for wear. He was staring at a couple sitting minding their own business in the corner. The man was much older than the woman. They were holding hands, oblivious to other diners, and there was a hint of romance in the air. It looked very much to me as if this was an illicit meeting and we all thought that he was the boss of a firm and she was the secretary.

She was a very pretty girl and the man was extremely smart, wearing an expensive suit but his most notable feature was an extremely big nose, which Pagey referred to constantly in our conversation as "the ski-slope".

"Have you seen the size of that bloke's hooter?" whispered Pagey.

"How on earth does he carry that about without bowing his head," said Wilf.

There were other sorts of remarks and comments and we all laughed but we were far enough away so that they couldn't hear us. Wilf was fascinated by the size of the man's nose.

"I've never seen a conk that big," he said.

We thought we'd played out all the humour in respect of 'Mr de Bergerac' but for some reason Wilf had formed a fascination for the appendage. I asked him to stop staring and get on with his coffee but he persisted.

"I'll tell you who he looks like," said Wilf, tapping the table as the realisation came to him.

"Who's that?" asked Jarvis.

"Barry Manilow," said Wilf

"It's who?" I asked.

"Barry Manilow, that's who it is."

Wilf was convinced that our guest was none other than the great American singer. He was nothing like him and the only point of similarity was the giant hooter. I asked Wilf to concentrate on the coffee and leave Barry Manilow out of it but when Wilf had a bee in his bonnet he wouldn't let it go.

"I'm sure it's Barry Manilow," he said.

"It's not Barry Manilow," I replied. "He doesn't even look like him so leave it at that and let the man enjoy his meal."

"I bet that's his daughter," said Wilf, "and she must have her mother's nose."

I shook my head in despair.

"Yes, I'm satisfied, it's Barry Manilow."

We all attempted to persuade Wilf to concentrate on his coffee and a nice liqueur before leaving because we were worried that he might find the urge to go and ask him for his autograph. I could just imagine the situation if, as he was whispering sweet nothings into his girlfriend's ear, Wilf arrived and announced,

"I've got all your records Barry."

I shuddered to think of the possibilities.

A waitress came with a smiling friendly face and asked Barry if he required anything else. She was dismissed in a most arrogant fashion, causing Barry's girlfriend to laugh. Suddenly I lost all respect for them. I hated that sort of attitude.

Then Wilf decided it was time to pay a call of nature. We all warned him not to say anything and Wilf reluctantly agreed. He rose to his feet with some measure of difficulty and then strode towards the door leading to the toilets. In doing so he had to pass Mr Manilow and his girlfriend. We all looked on eagerly to see whether or not Wilf would keep his word and sure enough he did. Not one mention of Barry Manilow until he'd just walked past their table and he struck up with the song, 'At the copa copacabana.........'.

Everyone in the restaurant looked on in amazement as this inebriated troubadour danced samba-like through the doorway and up to the toilets, tripping over a wine case on route. Gianni approached us with his effervescent smile and we complimented him on a superb meal. He presented us all with a liqueur of our choice and when Wilf returned to the fold, we prepared to leave. After we'd paid the bill Gianni asked us to wait in the foyer and he went to fetch his car. He was good enough to give us a lift back to the cottage, which was only one or two miles away but nevertheless it was a nice thought. Barry Manilow sneered as we left.

As we walked down the sliproad to where the cottages were situated we decided to take a look at the lake and we walked down the little track that led to the moorings, which belonged to the properties. It was a very picturesque little spot which looked out over a wide area of the lake. Cinders had been placed along this track over a period of years, to make it more comfortable to walk. There was a railing at one side and a wall at the other. The wall led to a large property and the railing onto an open field. The little cinder track was on a gradient and it wound its way down to the lakeside.

Having put the world to rights at the water's edge, we decided to return to the cottage when all of a sudden we heard the sound of an owl hooting in the distance. Wilf was a very keen ornithologist and his ears pricked up when he heard the sound.

"That's a barn owl," he said thoughtfully.

"Very good," said Pagey, "that's made my night that."

"Let's go and have a look at it," said Wilf.

"It's one thirty in the morning, I don't think we're going to be able to find a barn owl in this light do you?" I added.

"Come on, where's your spirit of adventure," said Wilf.

He then climbed onto the metal railing and jumped into the field. What he hadn't realised was that the field, being on an incline, collected all the water at the bottom. This meant that the bottom of the field was waterlogged whereas the top of the field was fairly dry. In addition all the silt and mud would collect at the bottom of the field and form a sort of bog, which was not evident until you jumped into it. The field housed a herd of cattle and manure had been collected and dumped at the bottom and left to coagulate over a period of time. The result was obvious. When Wilf landed from the height of about three feet, he continued to sink, albeit slowly.

"What the f....?"

As Wilf began to slip into the mire we all laughed. Well, you would when one of your friends was about to die a terrible death. We waited until we heard the magic words, "H...e...l...p m...e..." before contemplating our next action.

By that time Wilf was up to his knees in silt of the most odious kind.

"He's sinking," said Pagey.

"He's sinking quickly as well," said Jarvis.

"How long do you think it will be before it covers him?" I asked.

Wilford was beginning to get distressed. It was the reaction that you get when someone feels the joke has gone on long enough but Wilford was not one for pleading or slight protest.

"Get me out of this f...ing cesspit you b...s!"

Pagey of course was the ultimate stirrer.

"If you don't ask us nicely we won't lift you out."

Wilford called him another unpleasant name, by which time he was up to his waist in the thick, black sludge.

I began to get a little concerned because I realised that if we couldn't pull him out of that he might actually drown. I made the point to Jarvis who just started laughing.

"Oh well Wilf, there is it. It looks like you're stuck with it. Not only that, I'm not coming in after you as I'll never get out," I replied, laughing, "and that will teach you a lesson for having upset Barry Manilow."

It was then that we noticed that Wilf was getting extremely agitated, so joke over we leaned across and began to pull him out. It was not easy. Eventually we managed to free him minus his shoes, which are presently somewhere at the bottom of a bog in Windermere. When we got him out he was in an appalling mess. He was black from just below his ribcage down and covered in the most offensive-smelling substance. It appeared that cows had been kept in that field for many years and all the slurry had tended to collect at the bottom where Wilf had been standing.

Pagey laughed like a drain as he'd never seen anything like it and he insisted on taking Wilf's photograph. Wilf was so relieved to be released from the cesspit that he began to see the funny side. We walked back to the cottage and as we walked along the path to it I fumbled for the keys.

"Come on," said Wilf, "I'm freezing."

"Yes, come on," said Pagey, "I fancy a drink."

Wilf was still leaking with the offensive mixture and we told him that we were not prepared to let him into the house wearing those clothes, so he would have to leave them outside. Wilf saw the point and so he removed his trousers, which were stuck to him like glue. In doing so he removed his underwear as well and he also took off his socks. His jumper had been tinged with the material as well so off that came but we allowed him to wear his T-shirt. Just then the door to the adjoining cottage opened and the occupier and his wife peered round the door.

"What on earth's going on?" they asked, just as I managed to open our door.

"We've found this naked tramp outside," said Pagey, "and we're going to give him a bath and something to eat. Would you care to join us?"

The door slammed shut and Wilf went inside and straight into the bath. When he came out we toasted him in a royal fashion and some time later, I can't remember when, we all went to bed. Because the cottage was only small, I had to share the settee/fold up bed in the front room, the door of which led straight to the path outside. We changed and got into bed and I didn't realise another thing until I was woken the next morning by a knock on the door. It was the postwoman.

I got out of bed and in so doing pulled all the bedclothes off Goody, who was laid there in his birthday suit, grasping a Chinese sculpture which normally lived in the fireplace, as though it were a doll. I put a tracksuit on and opened the door.

"I'm sorry to bother you," said the postwoman, "but there is a Recorded Delivery for the occupier and it's got to be signed for."

"Well we're only renting the cottage for the weekend, I think that must be for the owner."

"Well it does say the occupier, so if you'd like to sign for it...."

In my confused state I agreed and asked her inside, forgetting of course that Goody was laid on the settee like the proverbial beached whale. The postwoman looked away in horror and seized the signed document from my grasp. Just then Goody was woken by the noise. I took the liberty of introducing the two of them, very much to Goody's horror.

"It was the postwoman that came in with a letter but she saw you and decided not to stay."

"Oh bollocks," said Goody, and turned over and went back to sleep.

I didn't open the letter and simply left it on the kitchen table for the owner on the Monday but I set about making arrangements for breakfast. We'd bought some bacon, eggs and sausage and we had tins of beans and were going to have a royal feast. I felt a little under the weather but I thought a fry-up would do me a power of good. I put the food into two large frying pans and began to cook. Just then Pagey wandered in. To say he looked rough was an understatement. He lit a cigarette and started to cough.

"What are you doing old bean?" he asked.

"I'm doing the breakfast," I said.

"Oh well done."

"Look Pagey, can you look after the breakfast while I dive in the shower?"

"Certainly old man, leave it to me."

I went into the shower and then woke the two sleeping beauties next door. When I went into the room Pagey was busy tickling Goody's ear with a feather in an attempt to amuse himself. I laughed and then turned to the kitchen area which adjoined the living room and found the frying pan on fire.

"Pagey you idiot, you've let the pan catch fire."

"Oh bloody hell," said Pagey, "throw it outside."

With that Pagey seized the pan and ran through the door and threw it on the grass outside. Unfortunately the couple next door were just about to go for a morning walk and witnessed what had taken place. They stood back openmouthed and stared at Pagey.

"Bit too well done for me I'm afraid," said Pagey, "so we thought we'd let the birds have it." He smiled and walked inside and the couple looked at the grass to see two frying pans burning merrily.

"Fire, fire," shouted Goody through the smoke.

"It's alright old bean," said Pagey, "I've sorted it and I've saved you all."

He lit up a cigar and sat on the kitchen chair and began to laugh loudly. We opened all the windows and managed to get rid of the pungent smell of burnt bacon. We sat around the kitchen table discussing what to do. Everyone was hungry and so we decided to set off into Windermere and find the nearest café and have a nicely-cooked breakfast.

We found a suitable establishment and sat round a table. We placed our order and we were drinking tea from some massive mugs when I noticed a couple sitting in the corner out of the corner of my eye. I realised it was Barry Manilow and his girlfriend from the night before. I nudged Wilf and nodded in their direction. Wilf didn't recognise them and put his head back into his mug of tea. I nodded to Pagey and did the same with him and he looked across and immediately his face broke into a wide grin.

"It's Barry Manilow," he said, laughing.

"It certainly is," I said. "I think on this occasion we can leave him to it."

Pagey prodded Jarvis and pointed across and just then the man looked up and spotted us. He looked at the ceiling, drank his tea and he and his child bride left rather hurriedly. I looked at Pagey and we both simultaneously broke into song.

"At the copa...copacabana...."

We all laughed, much to the complete amazement of everyone else in the place.

We had had an absolutely fabulous weekend, which cost a fortune, increased my weight by a few pounds and left me with every intention of getting home and seeking an early night.

When I got home my wife asked me if I'd had a pleasant time.

"Oh yes, very quiet you know but pleasant nevertheless. We met Barry Manilow..."

"Oh, that's nice," she interrupted whilst continuing with her ironing.

"....Wilf nearly drowned in a sea of cow muck whilst trying to catch an owl..."

"Oh good," as she wrestled with a recalcetrant shirt collar.

"...Goody flashed to the post woman..."

"Yes, of course."

"...Wilf exposed himself to the next door neighbours and Pagey nearly set the cottage on fire."

"Lovely, I'm glad you enjoyed it."

I don't think for a minute that she believed a word I had said.

Chapter 14

AND THEN THERE WAS DONOVAN

I got to a point whereby I was running from one court to another and it was proving far too much for me. The work was extremely hard and I was no longer managing to get to the lunchtime leisure sessions because I was so busy and time didn't permit it. I told Wilf that it was impossible for me to continue in that way and I needed another advocate to help me. Wilf agreed and so I placed an advert in the local paper and a weekly legal newspaper.

I had some peculiar replies. One was from a woman who'd worked in a flower shop and fancied having a go at being a solicitor, another from someone who'd just completed a prison sentence and thought he knew all about criminal law, and another was from a Frenchman who'd been trained in China and couldn't speak any English. One application came from someone with the name Kevin O'Donovan. His CV looked pretty impressive so I sent him an appointment for an interview.

He came in to see me and we hit it off straightaway. He had a good working knowledge of courts and particularly matrimonial work, which would leave me free to concentrate on the criminal cases. He told me that he was the son of a doctor and his mother had also worked in the medical profession. On a personal note he valued camaraderie and liked nothing more than a drink with his friends. That swung it! In the words of the Honourable Jack Heptonstall, "he'll do for me cocker."

Kevin served his notice period with his old firm and within five weeks he made his first appearance in the office. The girls like him and appreciated his rather eccentric style but he took his work seriously and because he was single and a free spirit, he was always out and about enjoying himself. He had inherited his Irish charm from his parents, quite where he inherited his eccentricity I'd no idea.

I took him out for a meal one night to introduce him to my group of friends and he made the mistake of trying to keep pace with the likes of Jarvis and Pagey. The net result was that at about ten thirty that night he was wobbling a bit; in short, he was plastered. He lived near Chesterfield and so driving home was completely out of the question and so he decided that he would stay in the office overnight. I told him to switch on the heating and make himself comfortable and we left him about midnight to wander down to the office.

I went to work early the following morning because I had a big court list and when I arrived, Vera, our cleaner, was busy vacuuming the rooms. My office door was open and I heard her chuntering in one of the other rooms.

"Who's rolled this carpet up...I ask yer...who would do a thing like that?"

I went to see what the problem was and Vera pointed to a large rug which had been rolled up underneath the radiator. She bent down and took one end and lifted it, unrolling the eight feet square rug. As it rolled towards me, a body in bright blue underpants and nothing else, rolled out at my feet. A bleary-eyed Kevin O'Donovan rubbed his eyes and rose to his feet.

"What the f...?"said Vera.

"What the f...?" I replied.

"What the f...?" said Kevin. "I couldn't find the heating switch and it was freezing last night, so the only thing I could think of was to roll up in this carpet," he said shivering.

Vera and I looked at each other.

"My God, it was freezing," continued Kevin as though nothing unusual had happened.

I looked at Vera and she returned the stare as I passed him his trousers, which had been laid over a chair in the room and we beat a hasty retreat. I checked the heating and found that Kevin had turned if off instead of on.

Within the hour I was ready to set off for court and Kevin joined me in my office. He seemed most put out that he should have been seen in that condition by our cleaner.

"It was an awful shock for me," said Kevin.

"It was a bloody awful shock for me as well. I'm not used to such sights as you in your underwear," I replied.

"Look...we won't be telling anybody about this?" asked Kevin pathetically.

"Of course not Kevin, I wouldn't dream of it."

That lunchtime I was recounting the story at the Cross Keys to the gathered throng when Kevin walked in and ordered a large glass of mineral water.

"Hey, that's good about the rug," said Pagey.

"Yes, that's a corker," said Jarvis.

"I would like to have seen the look on that cleaner's face," said Tim Johnson from the Bradford and Bingley.

"I bet you looked a right arse," said Wilf.

Having been bombarded with comments from all the group, Kevin hung his head in shame and embarrassment.

"Don't worry Kevin, it won't go out of these four walls I can assure you."

That afternoon Kevin had to attend Sheffield Magistrates' Court and deal with one of our regulars and when he walked into court there was a gathering of Sheffield solicitors, all of whom burst into laughter. Word had spread.

In our fairly close-knit community, you can't do anything without the jungle drums knowing and passing it on, so Kevin learned a salutory lesson that day.

He made a considerable difference to my lifestyle in that I could share the Saturday morning courts and free myself of matrimonial cases, which were a thorn in my side. Kevin also got on very well with the clients and was able to take on board all their complaints, worries and matrimonial disputes. As a single man he found it difficult to understand how people could be madly in love one minute and hate each other the next but the worst thing of all was how the children were often used as pawns in the game. A detached attitude was best to deal with these cases but I felt somewhat incapable of disassociating myself from the characters and the children, so I palmed off the matrimonial section onto Kevin and I concentrated on the rest

The real immediate worry was Eric Barnard's case. He was a likeable, honest and hard-working man who deserved a lot more than an appearance in the local criminal court, charged with assaulting two yobs. I had adjourned Eric's case for eight weeks so that all the witnesses could be called and the court could finally decide whether they found him guilty or not.

Time was flying by so quickly, I hardly ever had time to sit and reflect as each day brought a new crisis. I was trying to suit everybody all of the time and my inability to say "no" was getting me into considerable trouble. However, I soldiered on with my self-imposed death wish, fostered by insecurity, which left me little room for movement. I had endured a major health scare but the thought of having to take any time off work was unthinkable but then I had the monthly gastroscopy to look forward to, which did curb my enthusiasm for the mad-cap evenings out with the gang.

189

I had also grown several more layers of skin and a stainless steel protector in between my shoulder blades, which became a necessary part of my everyday equipment. Over the years I'd seen a number of lawyers who had an abrasive edge and could never understand their attitude but as the years wore on I found myself becoming more and more like them.

Eric's trial could not have come at a more inconvenient time. I had a number of clients who'd been arrested in a police operation centering on a car ringing gang. A small group of personnel had been stealing cars to order. They had an arrangement with a local garage who had been coopted onto the payroll, where the cars were resprayed and the licence numbers changed before being shipped out for the European market. The group were well organised, carrying out the operation with clinical efficiency. However, one minor error alerted the police and the stolen vehicle squad pounced. Five of the gang of seven were arrested and I was called upon to represent three of them. That number was reduced to two because ethics decreed that I could not act for them all because a conflict had arisen within the group. The police were understandably keen to get on with their interviews but this caused a problem for me because Eric's trial had been set for the full day and attending the police station was out of the question.

I had a choice; I either dealt with the trial or dealt with the prisoners. I had no wish to give up either case because I believed in Eric's innocence and the other case meant many weeks of guaranteed work. To be perfectly frank, I was torn between a moral duty and my own welfare. In such a situation most lawyers try to cut themselves in half and deal with both but it is not always possible and on this occasion a choice had to be made.

I had side-stepped the police and persuaded them to interview the defendants whom I didn't represent first and that left me free in the morning at least to do the trial. I could visit the cells at lunchtime and placate my clients and be ready straight after the trial for the interviews. My afternoon appointments would have to be re-arranged or someone else in the office would have to see them and if my trial finished in time I was quids in, if not….

Just after eight a.m. I had all the balls on my desk, ready to be thrown into the air in the hope that I would be back in time to catch them when they came down. I went to court early and had a long conversation with Eric, doing my best to tell him what to expect in cross-examination. I was psyched up and, if truth be known, I was ready for a hard-fought trial. In many ways this is the best attitude to approach a contested matter, particularly if you've got to have a go at the witnesses in cross-examination and the fact that my life was going to be an absolute misery, added that certain venom that would be required for going about a case like Eric's.

I had taken him into court to acclimatise him to the atmosphere when the clerk came in with his papers and sets of books and laboriously placed them on the bench in front of him.

"Is this going to take long?" he asked dispiritedly.

"Probably," I replied, "knowing my luck but I've got to be finished for one o'clock if at all possible."

"Why, what have you got on?" asked the clerk.

"I'm in that big car ringing job which the police have lovingly referred to as Operation Whippet."

"How many have you got," asked the clerk.

"Well I had three but I've got two now and if I don't get there this afternoon, I won't have any and then I get the free one way ticket to Shitville."

"Who's prosecuting your trial?"

"I haven't a clue," I said, "nobody's turned up yet but I do need to speak to them before the trial starts. There are certain issues that we've got to resolve. Who have we got? It's not the Lord Chief Justice is it?"

"No, he's on holiday but we've got a visiting stipendiary magistrate and he is anxious to get on with it."

I was disappointed. I preferred a lay Bench for this case because I thought they would be more sympathetic to Eric for what he had endured.

The Prosecutor came into court at 9.56am, as harassed as I was and before I could say anything he said those magic words.

"We have a problem."

I closed my eyes and looked to Heaven for inspiration.

"Well of course there would be," I said sarcastically.

"We seem to have a problem with our witnesses."

"Not as much as they are going to get when they get in the witness box," I said with my patience being tested to the full.

"I've only got one complainant. The other and his witness haven't turned up yet, so we'll have to wait for a while."

I was livid. All I needed was one slight delay to completely ruin my day and here it was.

"Well whilst I know it's not a problem for you, I've got an important interview to do this afternoon which will last for ever and the last thing I want is this trial to be delayed," I said defiantly.

"There's not much I can do about it. I've sent the officers out to try and find the witnesses so I'm going to ask the court to put the case back for half an hour."

"Bloody charming...bloody charming, it always happens to me...why is it always my case that turns to shit?" I asked in annoyance.

"Dare I say you shouldn't take so much on?" said the prosecutor, smiling.

"Dare I say you can go and commit an unnatural offence with a horse?" I replied.

There was something about the courtroom banter that never ceased to amuse but conversely when you're under great pressure there is a tendency to get up tight and sometimes it shows. Some people burst out into anger, some people burst into tears, some people burst into song and some people try to burst your nose!

I've always been taught that when faced with matters of great stress to sit down, straight-backed, take a very deep breath, close your eyes and think of nice sweet-smelling flowers. My experience led me to do just that. I sat down, took a very deep breath, closed my eyes and thought of nice sweet-smelling flowers. After ten seconds I got up and attempted to wring the prosecutor's neck.

Eric on the other hand was a bag of nerves. I left the court and found him sitting outside in the corridor on his own. He was wearing his best suit, with a freshly starched shirt. His shoes were polished so that you could see the reflection of your face. He was sitting with his head bowed and I saw that his hands were trembling.

"There's been a bit of a delay Eric," I said, wearing a plastic grin and trying not to distress him, "but it's nothing to worry about, nothing we can't handle, so I'll buy you a cup of tea and we'll run things through once more before we go in."

"What's the matter?" he asked anxiously.

"Well, a couple of the witnesses haven't turned up and the court have agreed to an adjournment, just for the police to try to see where they are. Don't worry, we'll resolve it. Come with me and we'll try a pot of WRVS Special," I said trying to sound as though I hadn't a care in the world.

Eric followed me to the tea room but en route we met the archetypal neanderthal man sitting with his legs outstretched. He had blocked the majority of the corridor and I was unable to walk round him.

"Excuse me please," I said politely.

"Tha what?" came the reply.

"I'm just trying to get past to go into the tearoom. Sorry to be a nuisance but would you be kind enough to move a little?"

"Supposing I don't want to move?"

"Ah," I thought to myself, "a stand-off situation."

"Well I wouldn't want to trip over you and you come into contact with me because I'm riddled with scabies and I can't get treated for it until tonight because of the tablets I've taken for the gastroenteritis. I'll sit down next to you and tell you about it because I don't think people realise just how highly contagious it is. It's marvelous if you want to lose a bit of weight but it's not the best way to do it and the discomfort is unbelievable. Then of course it can lead to haemorrhoids, which are an abomination. To be perfectly frank with you, the inserting of Anasol into the anal canal when suffering from that malady is probably one of the most unpleasant and painful things that you have to do. In fact, somewhere in my pocket I've got one of the bloody things, so I can show you just how big they are."

Before I could go on any further Neanderthal had got up and moved. I thanked him and went into the tearoom and asked for a tea with two sugars. I was given a polystyrene cup of oxtail soup, which was quite pleasant but I would have preferred tea.

"What have you got Eric?" I asked.

"Coffee," he said.

"Oh you've done well, that's what you asked for."

"No it isn't," he said, "I asked for tea as well." He smiled and the tension was broken for the moment.

The usher called me back into Court one and upon entering I saw early neanderthal man standing in the doorway. He moved quickly out of my way and I thanked him as I scratched my shoulder quite fiercely.

"It's a bloody nuisance, this scabies," I said.

He moved further away and I could have sworn I saw him scratching.

When I entered the court the prosecutor had some news for me.

"We're one witness short, the other one's turned up now but the remaining one is missing, so I'm going to ask for an adjournment."

I took another deep breath and counted to ten.

"I'm afraid I've got to oppose that application and ask that the case go on. We have been waiting for four months for this matter to be dealt with, my client has no previous convictions whatsoever and whilst your witnesses are well used to attending court, I think it's in the interests of justice to proceed."

I sat back and opened my file and felt quite proud of myself, having kept my cool under great pressure.

"Well, I'm applying for an adjournment, no matter what you say."

"Please feel free to do so," I said, "but I'm going to object."

"Well it's not my fault," said the prosecutor.

"I know it's not," I said calmy, "neither is it mine and it's certainly not my client's, so I'm going to ask the court to order that the case should proceed."

"But I'm one witness down."

I took a deep breath and bit my lip.

"Yes, you've already told me that four times. I understand it completely, I have full and perfect hearing and I heard you last time, so you don't have to repeat it again or tell me again in any way, shape or form because I fully and completely understand the position that you are in and where you're coming from. Just for the avoidance of doubt, I am opposing it, OK?" I said as my voice reached a crescendo.

"I think he's against you," interjected the court clerk smiling.

"Oh very well," said the prosecutor, "I can't understand why you're getting so het up."

I didn't reply.

Eric was called into court and took his place by the defendant's seat. The stipendiary magistrate then walked in, bowed ceremoniously and sat down.

"Call the case please Mr Clerk," said the stipendiary, officiously.

"It's the case of Eric Barnard, Sir. He has been charged with two assaults occasioning actual bodily harm and the case has been ruled suitable for summary disposal. Mr Barnard has pleaded not guilty and the case is listed for trial. The case is prosecuted by Mr Appleby and the defendant is represented by Mr Smith."

"Very good," said the stipendiary, "are we in a position to start?"

The prosecutor stood up.

"I'm sorry sir, there is a difficulty and I wonder if the defendant might be seated?"

"Sit down please Mr Barnard," said the stipendiary. "Yes, carry on."

"My case involves the calling of three civilian witnesses. There are the two complainants and a witness in corroboration. Unfortunately, whilst the complainants have attended, the corroborating witness has not. I've caused enquiries to be made and that witness cannot be found."

"Have the police been out to try and find him?" asked the stipendiary.

"Yes indeed they have sir but unfortunately he is not at home and there was no one there. In those circumstances I am obliged to ask the court for an adjournment, so that all the witnesses can attend on the next occasion."

The stipendiary took a deep breath; he was not particularly impressed with the application. He was one of the new breed who don't like adjournments and like to make progress to keep the statistics up to scratch.

"Yes, what do you say Mr Smith?" he asked.

I got to my feet.

"I oppose the application for an adjournment sir. This case is four months old already. Whilst it's the first listing for trial we have had a pre-trial review and this date was selected to suit the prosecution's convenience, not mine. In fact, your learned clerk's notes should show that I didn't want to have this trial date but as it is it has now been fixed for some time, my client has attended and has taken a day off work to be here. Not that my convenience is of any importance but I've made special arrangements to be available for this trial. We've no information about the whereabouts of the witness, save to say that he's not at home and we might have this problem next time."

"Well I could always adjourn the case and order the costs to be paid by the prosecution," said the stipendiary.

"Well you could sir but it's not about the costs, it's about the interests of justice. My client has no previous convictions whatsoever and it would be intolerable for him to have to wait any longer. We have no explanation from the witness, no sick note, no confirmation of his whereabouts whatsoever, so on that basis I would ask you to order that the case should proceed."

My opponent had nothing further to add and so the stipendiary magistrate asked to speak to his clerk. There was a whispered conversation and then he made his announcement.

"In view of all the circumstances, I'm going to ask that this case proceed."

All of a sudden, I liked him.

The prosecutor was slightly flustered and he read out his statement of facts. He put the case on the basis that the two complainants were walking past Eric's car, with the result that Eric went out and set about them, causing injuries. He then called his first witness. David Lansdell was eighteen years old at the time and I'd found out that he was well experienced in visits to the court. I'd asked the prosecution to provide me with his criminal record and just before he came into the witness box the prosecutor gave me a copy to consider. I noticed that he had two previous convictions; one for interfering with a motor vehicle and another for theft of property, interestingly enough, from a motor car. He was going to have some explaining to do.

The other, Mark Markwell, had been to court a number of times; once for burglary, damage, theft, once for interference with a motor vehicle and twice for taking without consent etcetera. He had got more to worry about than his colleague.

Lansdell came into the witness box with a swagger. He was chewing gum and he had to be warned by the stipendiary magistrate to remove it.

"That's a good start," I thought to myself.

The prosecutor began his questions, establishing his identity and minor preliminary matters. He was not a good witness and he came over as a sneering, arrogant, rude ignoramus. I was going to have a lot of fun with him.

"What happened when you got to the car in question?" asked the prosecutor.

"What do yer mean?"

"Did something happen when you got to the car?" said the prosecutor firmly.

"I didn't do owt."

"I don't think you understand the question," said the prosecutor, trying to give him a hint. "Just tell me what happened when you got to the car."

"I just told yer, I didn't do owt and then this bloke came and cracked me."

"Let's take it stage by stage," said the prosecutor. "What were you doing when the man who you said cracked you, appeared on the scene?"

"Nowt."

"When did you first see the man?"

"When he came running up his drive. He never stopped, he just ran at me and lunged at me."

"What did he lunge with?" asked the prosecutor.

"His fist of course, what do yer think he lunged at me with?"

I was getting to like this witness.

"What part of his anatomy was in contact with you?" asked the prosecutor slowly.

"What part of his anatomy?"

The stipendiary was losing patience and he interrupted.

"Did the man touch you?"

"Did 'e what?"

"Did the man touch you," he asked fiercely.

"Well of course 'e touched me. He 'ad to touch me to crack me didn't 'e?"

"What did he 'crack you' with?" asked the stipendiary, losing his patience.

"His fist of course, what else?"

"That's all I asked you. If you would just concentrate on the question and give me a proper answer....."

The witness mumbled something under his breath and the stipendiary disregarded it.

"Did you do anything to provoke the assault?"

"Tha what?"

"Did you do anything to cause the man to hit you?"

"No. He cracked me for nowt."

"How many times?"

"How many times what?"

"How many times did he hit you," said the prosecutor indignantly.

"Five or six," came the reply.

By then the prosecutor had almost given up the ghost, so he told the Bench he'd no further questions and sat down.

"Mr Smith, would you care to cross-examine?"

"Oh yes please sir," I said.

I stood up, straightened my jacket and my tie and looked the youth firmly in the eye.

"What were you doing on that road?"

"What do yer mean?"

"You know very well what I mean. You're not deaf are you?"

This comment provoked a response from the stipendiary magistrate.

"There's no need for that Mr Smith."

"I apologise sir. I'll try it another way. Why were you on that road?"

"I've as much right to be on that road as anybody else."

The stipendiary interfered.

"You've been asked what you were doing on that road. Why were you there? You know very well what that means. Give the court an answer."

"We were going 'ome."

"You were going home?"

"That's what I said."

"Were you walking up the street or down the street; in other words, were you going up the hill or down it?"

"Going up it."

"Looking at the street plan I've got in my file," I said, producing the document quite dramatically, "if you were going up the hill you were going towards the traffic lights, is that right?"

"Yea."

"That's going in the opposite direction to Eastwood where you live."

"It were a short cut."

"A shortcut, where to?"

"To get 'ome."

"Here is a copy of the plan, it's been increased in size on the photocopier...."

The stipendiary interrupted me.

"Have you got a copy for the court?"

"I have indeed sir, it's been increased in size by about a hundred per cent by our new office all-purpose photocopier," I said, handing him two copies of the plan.

The stipendiary did not enter into the spirit of my light-hearted approach.

"I have marked the road in yellow sir and there is a red arrow which points towards Eastwood, which you will see to the right of your plan. The green arrow shows the direction up the hill, which is the direction that the defendant claims to have intended to walk. As you will see, he's walking in entirely the opposite direction."

The stipendiary looked intrigued.

"Pick up that plan young man and show me the shortcut," I continued.

The witness was clearly taken aback by the presence of a plan and he seemed to study it carefully. I thought he was trying to find a way out of his predicament.

"You know the area do you?"

"No," came the reply.

"You don't know the area?"

"No, not really, no and I wasn't really sure which way to go."

"You mean to tell me that you live in Eastwood, which is a matter of half a mile away and you don't know which way to go?"

"Not really."

"Where do you get the shortcut from then if you don't know the area?"

"Well I thought it was a shortcut, I just assumed it would be."

"Oh I see, you assumed it would be a shortcut."

"Well I wasn't in a rush, so what did it matter?"

"It doesn't matter at all, except to say that you said that you had taken a shortcut to get home."

"Well I was going 'ome anyway."

"So why did you stop outside this particular house?"

"I didn't stop outside the house."

"Well you did because you said earlier in your evidence you saw a man looking at you through the window."

"Yea, so what?"

"Well you said that the man looked through the window, is that right? Then he opened the front door and looked out, is that right?"

"Yea, so?"

"And then he walked up the drive towards you?"

"Yea, so what?"

"Well if you were walking home, how come you saw all these things?"

"I don't know what yer mean."

"You do know what I mean. You must have been standing at that house."

"'ow do yer work that out?"

"Well it's obvious. You must have been standing at that house for some time because you saw the man look through the window, correct?"

"Yea."

"You then saw the door open, correct?"

"Well, yes."

"You then saw the man look out in your direction, specifically looking at you?"

"Yes."

"And then you saw him walk up the drive."

He didn't answer.

"All that takes time. If you were walking past the house, by the time he'd got outside and begun to walk up the drive, you'd have walked past wouldn't you?"

"I were only walking slowly."

"Well what were you doing? Which direction were you looking?"

"There are two questions in one there Mr Smith. Do you want to pick which one you want to ask him?" said the stipendiary sharply. I didn't like him again!

"Of course sir," I said. "Let me put it another way. Were you actually walking when all this was going on or were you standing still?"

"I were walking."

"Well you must have been walking extremely slowly not to have gone past the house by the time that this man had walked up the drive."

"Well I were just...like...taking my time."

"Alright, what did he say to you?"

"He said, come 'ere."

"And what did you do?"

"I didn't do anything, I just stayed there."

"Why?"

"I was frightened."

"Why were you frightened?"

"I thought he was going to cause trouble."

"Why on earth would he want to cause trouble with you?"

"I thought he didn't want us standing there."

"But you just told me that you weren't standing there, you were walking past the house."

"Well you know what I mean."

"No, I don't know what you mean. Try and explain it to me."

"Look, we were walking past 'ouse and this bloke came out and 'ad a go at me, alreight?"

"No, it's not alright, you're telling me a different story; you're changing it when I've caught you out and then you go on to something else."

"You 'aven't caught me out."

"Look..."

The stipendiary magistrate interrupted me again.

"I think it's for me to decide as to his credibility or otherwise Mr Smith."

Whilst he had a point, I don't think he should have interrupted me there because I was establishing that this youth had changed his story and was telling lies. However, I chose not to argue with the stipendiary because I knew he wouldn't back down, so I persevered.

"What was the attitude of the man?"

"I don't know what you mean."

"I think you do. I want to know what was his manner, how was he behaving?"

"Well, he were up for it weren't he? He wanted a fight."

"When did you work that out?"

"Reight from the start, when he came outside."

"Well you told me earlier he didn't say anything."

"Well it weren't what 'e said, it were the way 'e was."

"Well explain to me what you mean."

"I don't know what you mean."

"Of course you know what I mean. You are saying to me that he was aggressive when he came outside, I'm asking you in what way?"

"He was shouting and bawling like, looking for trouble."

"And then what?"

"And then he came out the gate, walked up to me and punched me."

"Can I ask you this. If he came out the house and was extremely aggressive, why didn't you run away?"

"What for, it's not his street."

"No, I appreciate that, but you were telling me that he was aggressive, looking for trouble and he came out towards you. Did you want trouble?"

"No."

"Well why didn't you disappear then?"

"I was shocked."

"Alright, what were you doing when the man came out of the house?"

"I've told you, I were walking past."

"You'd damaged his car."

"I hadn't."

"You'd damaged his car. Were you trying to get in it?"

"No, I weren't."

"Well you've done it before haven't you?"

"I don't know what yer mean."

"Oh I think you do. You see I've got your criminal record here and according to this, that's your specialty isn't it?"

The prosecutor stood up.

"I object to that sir. I don't think that he can be accused of having a specialty with only two previous convictions."

"Well they're both for offences concerning motor vehicles sir," I countered.

"Well, I suppose the word "specialty" is not appropriate for a man with just two previous convictions, but I note that they are convictions nevertheless Mr Smith. Please continue."

"You see I have to suggest to you that the reason he came out in what you describe as an aggressive manner, was that you'd smashed the headlight of his car."

"No, that's not right."

"Then would you kindly explain to me why you think he came outside in an aggressive manner?"

The prosecutor objected again.

"I don't think he can speak for what is in someone else's mind sir."

"Quite right," said the stipendiary. "I think he has a point there Mr Smith."

"Well, I hear what you say sir but my point is, if this witness says that the man was aggressive when he came out of the house, and that aggression was aimed towards him, that would tend to suggest that the witness had done something to have caused that aggression and I think I'm entitled to ask about that."

"Well ask it in another way then," said the stipendiary.

"You're saying you'd done nothing to deserve this."

"Yes."

"So if you'd done nothing, you didn't deserve for this man to treat you in this way, is that right?"

"Correct."

"Well answer this. You're saying that for no reason whatsoever, this man came out, was aggressive to you, shouted at you and punched you."

"Yes."

"Well do you know that this man has a long and distinguished work record and has never been in any form of trouble before?"

"No."

"I suggest to you that no decent honourable man like this would act in that way unless someone had provoked him and what's more, I suggest that you had broken the headlight of the car."

"No."

"What was your mate doing when you got punched?"

"'e tried to get 'im off me and stood in between us. He tried to defend me."

"And what happened to him?"

"He got cracked as well."

"How did he get cracked?"

"'e fisted 'im or nutted 'im, I'm not sure."

"Was that after he struck you?"

"No."

"How did the incident finish?"

"I managed to get away and ran up the street."

"And what about your friend?"

"'e ran with me."

"What did the man do?"

"'e chased us."

"Why did you report this to the police?"

"'cos he cracked me."

"Wasn't it because you'd damaged his car and he'd caught you, so you wanted to get the first word in?"

He didn't reply but just stared at me.

"I'll take that as a yes then shall I?" and I sat down. The stipendiary magistrate glared at me.

The prosecutor called his second witness. He was an entirely different proposition. He was smartly turned-out with a neat haircut, clean and tidy and he spoke in a loud, clear and decisive voice. I knew then that this witness wasn't going to be as easy as the first.

He gave his account to the Prosecutor quite clearly. In fact, he was almost glib. I couldn't help thinking that this lad knew the ropes and he'd been in the witness box before. Of course he had a lengthy criminal record, so I'd got that to play with if nothing else.

The prosecutor took him through his evidence and then I stood up to cross-examine. I noticed half a smile on the witness's lips. I seized my opportunity with both hands.

"Is something amusing you Mr Markwell?"

"No."

"Well why are you smiling at me?"

"I wasn't smiling."

"No, probably not. You were grinning weren't you?"

"I wasn't grinning."

The stipendiary must have seen it because he interjected.

"I want you to take this seriously Mr Markwell. This is a court and these are important proceedings. Please carry on Mr Smith."

"What were you doing outside this man's house?"

"We were just walking past."

"Well tell me, at what stage did you first see this man?"

"Well we saw somebody looking out of the window, so we stopped to see who it was."

"Oh, you stopped did you?"

"Oh yes."

"Well I suggest to you that you didn't stop, that you were walking straight past."

"Oh no, that's definitely not right. We stopped and we had a look. I remember saying that there was something funny about the bloke staring at us."

"And then what happened?"

"Well he looked at us and then he came to the door and looked at us again."

"Did you recognise him?"

"No."

"Then why didn't you just walk on?"

"Well, he continued to look at us and we thought it was funny."

"So what did the man do then?"

"Well, he then walked down the driveway."

"And?"

"He came up to us."

"What did you do?"

"I didn't do anything, I just stood there."

"Well what did the man come out for so far as you were concerned?"

"I haven't a clue."

"So go on; what did you do then?"

"Well, he opened the gate and came straight up to us."

"So let me see if I've got this right. He looks through the window and you stopped to look at him, yes?"

"Yes."

"Then he walked straight down the drive towards you and through the gate, yes?"

"Yes."

"And you are still there?"

"Yes, of course."

"What were you doing?"

"We were just looking at him, wondering what his game was."

I didn't want to ask him if he was aggressive because if I'd have done so it would have tipped him off and put the words into his mouth.

"And then what did he do?"

"He punched my mate Dave."

"What did you do?"

"I just stood there in amazement, I couldn't believe it."

"What do you mean, you couldn't believe it?"

"I couldn't believe that this bloke could just appear and take a swing at Dave."

"So you just stood back in amazement?"

"Yea, that's right."

"And then what?"

"He fisted or nutted him, I'm not sure which, but he hit him anyway."

"Was it a strong blow?"

"Yea, a real strong blow."

"Strong enough to knock him down?"

"Oh yea."

"So he was knocked down?"

"Yea, I think so."

"And what was your reaction to this?"

"I was shocked, I couldn't believe it. I just stood there in amazement."

"You hadn't been damaging his car had you?"

"Definitely not and not smashed the light or owt?"

"How did you know the lights had been smashed?"

"Er, the bobby told me...He told me that the man said that we'd smashed his car up."

"No, he didn't say that you'd smashed the car up, he said that you'd smashed the headlight on the car"

"At any rate, it's not right."

"Well how did the incident finish?"

"Well, I helped my mate away but he was really groggy."

"Really groggy? What was the man doing?"

"He ran back into the house."

"Did you hit the man?"

"Definitely not."

I knew that he hadn't hit Eric but I wanted to wrongfoot him and let him think that was what we were suggesting. I anticipated that he would then try to distance himself from Eric and perhaps give a different account to that of his mate. I wasn't to be disappointed.

"I didn't give him a chance. I just helped my mate and we scarpered double quick."

"Let me suggest to you what I think happened. You had a run-in with this man at the chip shop didn't you?"

"No."

"Yes you did. You mentioned in your statement to the police...." I paused, took up a copy and read from the statement.

"It was the same man who we'd had the argument with in the chip shop," I said quoting from the statement.

"Oh yes, I'm sorry, I forgot that. I hadn't remembered about the man...yea that's right."

"Yes and you followed him home didn't you, so that you could cause damage to his car?"

"No I didn't."

"Well you went past his house and you damaged his car."

"No I didn't, we were on our way to see one of our mates who lives up that way."

"You were visiting a mate were you?"

"Yes."

"What's his name and address?"

"I'm not sure, it wasn't my mate it was Dave's mate and he was taking me to see where he lived."

I couldn't resist my next question.

"Did you take a shortcut to get there?"

"No," he said quizzically.

"Very well. So tell me what happened? Did you get to your mate's house?"

"No, when we got to the bottom of the street, Dave wanted to go home because he was dizzy and in a lot of pain."

"Let me just ask you about the blow that was inflicted upon you. How was it delivered?"

"With his fist."

"Can I ask you, at what stage was that blow delivered?"

"Well, he cracked my mate and knocked him down, or half knocked him down, I can't remember, and then he just turned on me."

"So he'd finished the assault on your mate then?"

"Oh yes, he'd finished that and then he started on me. I was still shocked."

"So it wouldn't be right to say that as he hit the other lad, he hit you as well in the general mêlée."

"No definitely not."

"Are you sure you're not mistaken?"

"No, definitely not, I know what happened."

"Well supposing my client was to say that that's how it happened, would he be lying?"

"Yes."

"And so would anyone else who saw it that way?"

"Definitely."

"I see."

I paused to allow the stipendiary magistrate to make a note because he'd spotted the point.

"Oh, there's just one other thing I wanted to ask."

"Yea?"

"What did you say to the man when he came out of his house?"

"I don't know what you mean."

"What did you say to him when he opened the door? Remember, he'd been looking through the window and then he opened the door. What did you say to him?"

"I didn't say anything to him."

"And what about your mate?"

"He didn't say anything to him."

"And what about the man, what did he say?"

"He didn't say anything either."

"Are you sure about that?"

"Yes, I'm sure about it. He never opened his mouth."

"I see. Thank you for that. Well I'm going to suggest to you that you followed this man. You'd every intention of doing something at his house when you got there and the car was conveniently placed."

"No, I wouldn't do anything like that."

"What do you mean when you say you wouldn't do anything like that?"

"Well I wouldn't have damaged his car."

"But you had a reason to. So far as you were concerned, this man had had this argument with you in the chip shop and you were annoyed about it weren't you?"

"No I wasn't, I wasn't annoyed at all."

"You were, that's why you went up to his house. It's a lie that you were going to see some friend."

"No, we were."

"Of course your friend would tell us exactly the same story, about visiting this so-called friend, would he?"

He paused for a minute and I think he realised what I was after. There was no answer so I just stood and looked at him and the silence was incredible.

"Well?"

He was panicking and I saw the glimmer of a bead of sweat running down the side of his face.

"Very well, if you don't want to answer. You then walked up to the house and saw his car and you thought you'd take it out on that."

"That's not true."

"Yes it is and that's why he came out isn't it? I suggest to you that he came out and he was shouting, he was very annoyed."

"Not at all, he didn't say anything."

"You said that you wouldn't have done anything like that didn't you?"

"Yes."

"Well that's very odd because I have your criminal record here. Let's just have a look at it."

In a very flamboyant way I flicked over each of the pages.

"Let's look at this; criminal damage. Can you remember what you damaged?"

"No."

"Well you got fined one hundred pounds for it and ordered to pay compensation of...oh yes, here it is...compensation of three hundred and fifty pounds. Wouldn't be a car would it by any chance?"

"I can't remember."

"You can't remember it; that's odd, it's only three years ago. Let's see if we can find one that you do remember. Here's one look...theft from a motor vehicle...what do you say about that one?"

There was a long pause. Just when I thought he was going to answer, I interrupted him.

"Well if you can't answer that, let me ask you about this other one, three months later; taking without consent, a motor vehicle. Can you remember that or has that conveniently been lost in your memory?"

The prosecutor tutted.

The stipendiary did not object to my line of questioning.

"And what about this...oh, yes let me put this to you...interfering with a motor vehicle and another charge of theft of petrol. Would that have been syphoning from a car perhaps?"

The youth took a deep breath and looked up to the ceiling, tutting.

"You don't have to tutt at me young man, I asked you a simple question, or all of a sudden has your memory gone again?"

"Alright, so I've got some convictions but I'm being honest about this."

"Well you weren't honest on these occasions were you. Let's be fair, there's a lot on this record."

He didn't answer.

"Look, I don't want to embarrass you by reading them all out, not only that I don't think we have the time...."

The stipendiary glared at me again.

I looked away from him and stared at the witness.

"Are you a violent man Mr Markwell?"

"No."

"Well that's very odd because only four months ago you were before this court for assault occasioning actual bodily harm. Who was that on may I ask?"

"It was a fight."

"Yes, I accept that but what I want to know is who was it perpetrated on?"

"Look, what's all this got to do with whether I've...?"

The stipendiary interrupted.

"Just answer the question."

"Yes, I've been done for assault."

"So you're not adverse to getting involved in a bit of fisty-cuffs if you need to then?"

"I don't like fighting."

"Well you did on this occasion because you got sent to prison for three months, so it couldn't have been a very minor incident could it?"

"Well the sentence were unfair. I should never have got sent down for that."

"No, but you did. Are you saying that the court got it wrong?"

"Yes, they did."

I felt very tempted to ask him if it was the stipendiary magistrate from this case that had sentenced him but I didn't want to take any more liberties.

"Can I just ask you one other thing? Were you both at this same incident, you and your friend?"

"What do you mean?"

"Well you see, you're telling different stories."

I started to highlight the differences and as I did so the witness began to shift from one leg to the other. His body language indicated extreme discomfort as he knew he'd been caught out. He had no answers for any of the remaining questions and he could not conceal his anger until, on my final question, he banged his fist down hard on the witness box; so much so that the stipendiary magistrate cautioned him about his conduct. I saw little point in going on any further and so I sat down.

Throughout this, Eric's face never moved even when the witness had been caught out. He was calm, very quiet and kept his dignity.

The evidence of the police officers was read out because we agreed it and at the conclusion of the prosecution case, I called Eric to give evidence. I took him through his evidence stage by stage and then the prosecutor cross-examined him. Eric did extremely well in cross-examination, so much so that I didn't interrupt, even though I had just cause on more than one occasion. It seemed to me that the answers that Eric was giving were sensible and reasonable.

At the conclusion of his evidence I addressed the stipendiary magistrate, waxing lyrical about the rights of the common man to defend himself or his property and then concentrated on highlighting the differences between the two versions. He retired at the end of my address to consider the matter and prepare his judgement and so Eric and I went back to the WRVS room for a cup of soup tea.

"What do you think then, Mr Smith?" asked Eric.

"It's always difficult to say Eric. My problem is that I'm pretty close to this case and because I actually believe in your defence I can't see any fault in it and so in a way I won't have a rational and unbiased point of view."

"That's why I instructed you Mr Smith," he said. "If you believe in a case you give it all you've got."

"Flattery will get you everywhere," I said, smiling. "Now, you can buy the teas."

Eric's hands trembled as he held the cup in its saucer and being embarrassed he moved the cup into his other hand. The cup continued to tremble and in embarrassment Eric put it down on the counter and tried to change the subject.

"What will they do to me if I'm found guilty?" he asked.

"Let's consider that, if and when he finds you guilty Eric."

"Yes, but you know what I mean. I just want to know what's likely to happen. I won't go to prison will I?"

"Is that what you've been worrying about all these weeks; whether you'll go to prison or not?"

"Well to be honest with you...yes."

"I promise you won't go to prison," I said, with my fingers firmly crossed behind my back. I felt so very sorry for him.

After about ten minutes we were called into the courtroom and the stipendiary magistrate started to pass his judgement.

"This is a case of alleged street violence of an unprovoked nature. The evidence can be said to fall into two versions. The prosecution would have me believe that this was a completely unprovoked attack and the prosecution witnesses were at pains to point this out. They gave their accounts of the night in question, maintaining as they did that they had done nothing to justify being assaulted."

I began to worry because the tone of the summing-up seemed to be going in favour of the prosecution.

"The defendant gave evidence and said…"

"What is going on?" I thought to myself, "he's not pointed out once that the prosecution witnesses told entirely different stories. They made so many mistakes and not only that, they clearly lied on more than one issue, particularly about the direction they were going, so what the hell is he doing, why hasn't he spotted it?" I was panicking inwardly.

"…The defendant said that he had been abused in the chip shop, walked home and had been followed by the two men in question, who then caused damage to his car. He admitted going outside and confronting the men and he admitted that he delivered blows, although in fairness he reacted in self-defence. However…."

"What does he mean, however?" I asked myself. "Is he going to say that he doesn't believe us and he's going to believe the two toe-rags that were lying through their back teeth."

I shuffled in my seat in an attempt to seek comfort.

"…It's my duty to see if there is evidence to convict of assault and to do that I have to be sure, beyond reasonable doubt, that that assault was committed. The defence say self-defence, the prosecution say unprovoked attack…."

"For God's sake get on with it," I thought. "Tell us we're guilty if you must but just get it over with."

"…I have been asked to take into account the criminal records of the parties. On the one hand the first witness has two previous convictions, ironically for offences involving motor vehicles but the second witness has a positive string of offences and consequently if there is a doubt in a case I must acquit and so Mr Barnard," he turned to him, "I find you not guilty of both charges of assault and you are free to go."

There was a sharp intake of breath from Eric and from me.

"I always liked that stipendiary," I thought to myself. "What a really nice bloke and how quickly he'd seized upon the salient facts."

"Is there any application for costs?"

"Oh yes of course sir, I'm sorry, I'd actually forgotten that. We are not legally aided and if the court would favour me with such an application I would be most grateful."

Having been given the decision, the least I could do was to ingratiate myself in Uriah Heap fashion, but what the hell – we'd won.

Eric was still standing, looking into space, as though he hadn't really taken in what the stipendiary magistrate had said, so I leaned across to him and whispered.

"It's over Eric, you can go…Eric…it's over, you can go…Eric."

Just then Eric fell back into the dock. He had collapsed. The stipendiary magistrate retired from the courtroom and the clerk called one of his colleagues, who was proficient in first aid. For one awful moment I thought that the stress of the occasion had caused Eric to suffer a stroke.

After some minutes of attention from the first aid officer Eric came round; thankfully he had only fainted. We took him into the rathole solicitors' room and I fetched him a glass of water.

"Do you want me to call an ambulance?" I asked.

"No, don't do that," said Eric, "I'm alright, I was just a bit overcome. I didn't really understand what was happening and it just got the better of me and then all the lights went out."

"Well I think you just ought to wait here for a few minutes so that we can see you're alright."

"No Mr Smith, I'm alright I assure you but I do need to phone my wife and let her know what's going on."

"Just sit here for a moment and I'll phone your wife and tell her what's happening. Will you be alright while I'm gone?"

"Yes, certainly," he said, breathing deeply.

I passed the news onto his wife and I could hear her burst into tears on the other end of the line. I told her that her husband was ready to be collected and then I went back to see Eric.

"Have you spoken to her?" he asked.

"Yes, certainly, I've given her the result and she's absolutely delighted."

"Thank God," said Eric, "I couldn't have stood it if I'd got a conviction against my name. That's the last time I'll ever do anything like that."

"But you don't have to reproach yourself," I said, "You didn't do anything, you acted in self-defence...they were yobs and they damaged your car...."

Eric didn't answer.

"But Eric, we're in the right...they lied...their stories weren't the same and they made all sorts of mistakes. You heard what the stipendiary said, their evidence wasn't believable."

"Yes I know Mr Smith but...well you see it's...I know it's over but I'll still have to live with it."

"I don't think I know what you mean, you've got to live with it. You haven't done anything wrong. After all, they tried to attack you and you defended yourself."

Eric's head dropped and again he didn't answer.

"That's right Eric, isn't it?" I asked.

"Is it really over now Mr Smith? Is that the end of the case, no matter what?"

"Well yes, of course it is. You can't be tried twice for the same crime," I said. "Why, whatever is the matter?"

"Can I tell you something in confidence," he said.

"Yes, of course, what is it?" I asked suspiciously.

"I did it."

My eyes opened wide. I couldn't really believe what I was hearing.

"What...you mean...they were telling the truth?"

"Yes, I did beat them both up; I wasn't defending myself. I belted one then the other, they were frightened to death. I came back after they'd limped away and pretended to look at the light and when no one was looking I put it through myself.

"You've committed perjury Eric."

"Yes I know, that's what makes it all the more difficult but I couldn't have a conviction; my family, my friends, everything. You understand don't you? After all, they're only yobs and they deserve to be beaten. We ought to make a stand. People are sick and tired of being abused in public. They deserved all they got."

I was speechless.

Eric finished his tea and thanked me for all my work and effort. His wife picked him up from outside the courthouse and they drove off. I was left thinking that the police officer in the case had got it right all along and I had got it so very wrong. Whichever way you look at it, albeit inadvertently, I had been party to an injustice, or had I?

Chapter 15

HE SHOULD NEVER HAVE HAD
PAGEY AS BEST MAN

Roger Blake-Johns went to a private school with my old friend
Sean Page and despite that they remained good friends. Roger had
joined the family business of cabinet makers and Sean had gone
into the insurance profession and both of them have done
reasonably well.

There is an unusual bond between public school boys! I think they
are taught to "look after one's chums" and more power to their
elbow for that. It is an ideology which always had a considerable
appeal for me but if you accept the good you also have to accept the
bad as Roger was to find out.

Sean or Pagey as we always refer to him, was and is a character.
Tall and quite distinguished-looking he has a certain carriage which
is knocked into public schoolboys before puberty. He's balding now
and has put on a lot of weight but he's still as barmy as ever and at
the time of Rogers wedding, he was on his very best form.

Roger was marrying relatively late at thirty years old, or whatever
he was, but women had tended to avoid him for his "silly arse" or
schoolboy behaviour and personality and so he had concentrated
upon enjoying male company until he met Josephine Tilletson, ten
years his senior, well-educated, well-connected but rather plain,
prim and proper. Her father was at the same public school and
consequently their paths seemed destined to cross sooner or later.

Josephine had no sense of humour, hated childish pranks and was
teetotal. She spoke with a finishing school accent enhanced by a
rather peculiar deep baritone voice, so inappropriate for a woman.
She was a snob with an unpleasant disposition but for some odd
reason Roger liked her.

Josephine had chosen to marry in the village in which she had
been brought up and where her grandparents and parents had
married so she wanted in some way to perpetuate the dynasty. She
took in hand all the arrangements but Roger chose his best man. His
choice was the redoubtable Page. His track record for officiating at
events was not of the best, for he was given to bouts of hard drinking
and irreverent behaviour but he was and is wonderful company,
providing it's not your wedding.

Wilf, Jarvis and I had been invited and we were quite looking forward to the event. Not only that, I wouldn't miss Lord Page's efforts as best man for all the Guinness in Ireland! The stag night was one to remember. We started off at Vitos', my favourite Italian restaurant, at Crookes in Sheffield and from there we went to nearly every pub in Rotherham before a rather harassed taxi driver, Jeff Taylor, picked us up in his converted transit van. We dropped Wilf off first, carrying him gently from the back of the van. We sat him on his garden wall whilst we fetched his coat. By the time we got back to the wall Wilf had gone and we couldn't find him anywhere until our attention was drawn to a great deal of swearing coming from the flower bed over the wall.

"He's here look," shouted Broomy.

"Sod off!" shouted Wilf, or words to that effect.

We helped him up and threw him through his front door. From there on in it was his wife's problem not ours. As we closed the door all I heard was shouting coming from a voice that resembled that of Mrs Wilford.

Bader was next; our esteemed football captain needed no assistance. He fell out of the van and Broomy fell on top of him.

Jeff drove off leaving Broomy three miles from his home, which was not realised until we got to Broomy's house. Jeff opened the door just as Mrs Broom appeared on the doorstep, resplendent in her towelling bathrobe and hair curlers. She was not amused.

"Good evening Mrs Broom," said Jeff smiling inadequately.

She made no reply but glowered at him with her arms folded as he fully opened the back door.

Jeff smiled again and held out his arm as if to introduce a singer from stage left, but nothing happened. His smile turned to a nervous grin and then a blank stare.

"Broomy" shouted Jeff. "Your good lady wife is waiting. Broomy! Broomy!" but there was nobody there. Broomy was walking it from Bader's house, three miles down the road and Jeff had just looked a considerable pillock.

"Well it's good night then Mrs Broom," said an embarrassed Jeff, who then promptly waved and wandered nonchalantly back to his van.

"Bloody 'ell, did you see the look on her face," said Jeff.

"What do you expect?" replied Jarvis. "You turn up unannounced and open a van door, pass the time of night with a grief-stricken beer widow, introduce her husband who then fails to appear and then drive off as though it was normal behaviour."

"I didn't know he'd got out earlier," pleaded Jeff.

"Oh bugger," I said, "just get me home; I'm busting."

We drove off and two miles later Jarvis got out. I got out quickly as Jeff fumbled with his car radio, which blared out in the quiet street. Jeff hadn't realised I had got out and continued to try to find Radio One on his radio. All was silent on the street as Jeff turned off the radio.

Unfortunately when you have to go, you have to go and I had to go so I positioned myself at the rear wheel with my back to the pavement and a high wall. It was the best I could do given the discomfort I was in and after all, there was no one about and I had Jeff's hatchback for protection.

As I was in mid-flow, so to speak, Jeff set off leaving me standing by the causeway looking out across the empty road until a large touring bus went past carrying forty-eight nuns en route to a new convent which had just been opened north of Rotherham. Having committed myself, all I could do was wave. When Jeff realised he had gone without me, he reversed and off we went for my home and another stunning welcome.

The wedding was set for twelve noon on the Saturday morning but unfortunately I had to go to town first for a special lock-up court, which meant that I had to go in my rented morning suit because there wouldn't be time to change.

I got a remarkable reception from Sergeant Whitehouse and Harry Miller, who was in for burgling a bookies' office, thought I was going to a circus. Harry was a bit of a character who specialised in small-time commercial burglaries but he had committed the most original offence I had come across in a long time. He had broken into a bookies' office and had taken nothing. No attempt had been made to open the safe or the cash drawer and he had not been disturbed either.

It was a strange case and finding the motive was impossible, especially when Harry wouldn't make me any the wiser.

"What's the game Harry?" I asked.

"It was just a break that's all. I didn't find anything so I left. I got caught outside."

"But everything was untouched."

"Well...there was nothing there. I thought there might be typewriters and such."

"But there was, it says so in the police summary."

"I didn't see any typewriters; it was dark."

"But you had a torch."

"I still didn't see any," said Harry persistently, who by this time was beginning to get agitated so I left it at that.

Harry got bail, thanked me and told me to enjoy the circus!

It wasn't until five years later I found that Harry had been breaking into the bookies and alterning betting slips into his favour. The locals couldn't work out why he was so successful.

I picked Jarvis up on the way and then on to Bodgers, who was seen off by his wife in the infamous towelling robe. She still wasn't smiling.

We got to Roger's house at just after 11am. The house was in disarray and Roger couldn't find his top hat and Pagey his shoes. We found the hat but not the shoes and all Pagey had was a pair of Dunlop trainers.

"Put black shoe polish on them," said Broomy.

"Don't be daft," replied Pagey, "I'm not stupid."

I looked at Pagey in a black tailcoat jacket and a bright yellow waistcoat with a muffle necktie.

"He already looks stupid," I thought to myself, "so what's the problem with the trainers."

By the time we left for church we all looked resplendent in our morning coats. Whilst we waited Pagey had a cigarette. I had been free of the habit for many years following a bout of bronchitis which ruined my Christmas and I have not smoked since Christmas 1976. I started to work out how many cigarettes I would have smoked since then when Pagey interrupted my thoughts.

"Something went wildly wrong last night old bean," said Pagey dispiritedly.

"What do you mean?" I asked.

"What happened to the Blobber-Booba-Gram?"

"What happened to the what?" I replied.

"The Blobber-Booba-Gram," repeated Pagey.

"And what in goodness names is that?"

"I arranged it last week. She should have turned up last night. It's a bugger that, I paid forty pounds."

"Thank the Lord for that," I said.

"I can't understand it, I gave them all the details, so why didn't she turn up?"

"And what was she going to do?"

"Just walk up to him wherever we were, flash the lot and pose for photos with him."

217

I breathed a sigh of relief.

"She was the best they had and the biggest. Do you know…"

"No, I don't," I interrupted, "and what's more I don't want to hear anything more about it. If her parents get to know…"

"Yes, but what a laugh, what a send-off."

"What a load of bollocks," I replied.

"She's sixty-two," he said thoughtfully.

"That's what you call a real bust," I quipped.

"No, that's her age, her bust is bigger than that," said Pagey seriously. "I just can't understand it. I could have sworn I gave her the right time and place."

I shook my head.

The vicar then interrupted our discussion as he came to the front door having put Roger through his paces.

"How's it going Rog?" asked Pagey.

"I'll be glad when its over," said Roger nervously. "What time is it?"

"Five minutes to three," said Pagey, "and all's well. By the way I'm sure that vicar's a puff."

Roger and I looked at each other. Roger sighed a deep sigh and I looked to the sky for inspiration.

We walked into the pretty church only to be told by a rather effeminate verger that confetti was not allowed as his reverence thought it pagan and discourteous to the church. Pagey thought he was a 'dickhead' and said he hoped he would fall over into a pile of 'rhino shit'!

We waited at the front of the church as it filled with guests representing both sides of the families.

"Their family are very prim and proper you know, regular churchgoers…I'm going to have to go on Sundays," said Roger thoughtfully. "She's in the choir…"

Pagey looked at me.

"She's a warden…"

I looked at Pagey.

"She takes her work for the church very seriously…"

We both looked at him.

"What?" asked Roger noticing us.

Both Pagey and I laughed but sharp disapproving glances from 'her side' caused us to face the front and try to show a little more decorum. This made us laugh even more and we couldn't stop. Even when the music heralded the arrival of the bride we were helpless with laughter but the vicar put a stop to that.

"Dearly beloved," he announced, staring intently at us. "We are gathered here…"

Pagey and I looked across at Josephine and whispered to me, "Rather him than me."

I closed my eyes and ears and concentrated as intently as I could on the altar before me in an endeavour to avoid laughing again.

"…to join together this man and this woman in holy matrimony."

The ceremony proceeded without difficulty and Pagey did his duty admirably, handing over the rings to the right people at the right time then standing back proudly as the vicar announced that the parties had become man and wife.

"Well done you two," I said.

"Poor bugger," said Pagey.

I remained in the church as the bride and groom, parents, best man and bridesmaids went into the vestry to sign all the appropriate papers. When the parties emerged the entire congregation rose to its feet and the customary *'Here Comes the Bride'* was played by an aging but intoxicated organist who'd had one too many prior to the ceremony. The choir sang with great gusto including one very large woman who was remarkably off key and put off the other singers by singing 'Here Comes the Dried'.

As we got outside Pagey removed a large box of confetti from his pocket.

"Oh no you don't," said the verger, "we don't allow that sort of thing here. The church governors would go mad."

"If they haven't already," I said in a whisper.

Charles Leatherhead was the wedding photographer. A small feisty perfectionist who marshalled the wedding guests unsympathetically into the positions required to formulate his pictures. The bride's mother, who was an elderly version of the bride, decided to say a few words on the church step. She was standing next to the bride and groom with her husband to her right and Roger's parents to her left. They were bounded at each end by the vicar and the verger. The congregation were in front of them interspersed amongst the graves in the churchyard as Mrs Tilletson spoke in her deep resonant voice.

"Members of the congregation, my husband and I would like to take this opportunity of thanking everyone for attending this afternoon and for making this event so memorable."

Charlie Leatherhead by this time was filming the event on an extremely large video camera but there was some confusion as he urged Mrs Tilletson to start her speech again after he had rapidly replaced the film in the camera.

" Members of the congregation, my husband and I would like to take this opportunity of thanking everyone for attending this afternoon and for making this event so memorable," said the bride's mother impatiently.

Just then a rather large, elderly lady in a light fawn mackintosh made her way through the graveyard and stood in front of the congregation. I was extremely suspicious about her because it was a very warm day and yet the mackintosh was fastened tightly around her neck. It was a full-length coat but much too small for her. She positioned herself immediately in front of the main group and Mrs Tilletson. Just as Mrs Tilletson's speech finished she threw back the coat to reveal her huge, white body covered only by a red feathery thong. Her enormous bust drooped south almost as far as her naval as she held her arms outstretched and cried,

"Surprise, surprise!"

And we were…we really were.

Chapter 16

A HOST OF GOLDEN DAFFODILS
AND RINGS

The daffodil season was upon us; row after row of golden trumpets leaning towards the sun, forming the proverbial carpet of golden yellow; breathtaking in beauty and simplicity.

I was standing by the churchyard gazing at such a display when a hand touched my arm. Startled, I turned and saw AB standing behind me.

"Good morning Mr Smith," she said politely. "I'm coming to visit you."

"Oh, good morning Mrs Goodyear. I'm sorry, I hadn't seen you, I was lost for a minute."

I thought she had come to see me about Graham Taylor who had just been sentenced to eighteen months imprisonment but strangely enough she never mentioned him.

We shared the view together.

"They are beautiful aren't they?" she said. "You must see the ones at the house. We have a fabulous display every year."

"Yes I must one day. I do like nice gardens."

"Well you had better make it quick Mr Smith because I'm selling up and I would like your firm to deal with it for me."

"Well of course Mrs Goodyear but why are you selling up?"

"It's my age dear, I'm slowing down and it's far too big for me to cope with, even with my daily help. I've decided that the time has come when I ought to be looked after. I want some form of security, you know, the kind of quality sheltered housing where I keep my independence and yet I have always got somebody there. There's a very nice new secure housing area opening and you don't have to buy it, you can rent it, so that will leave me free to move about and go where I please. I want to spend some time with my daughter. She lives in southern Spain and has a very nice place there and my doctor says that the weather and the dry air will do me good. It might even slow down this arthritis," she said, wringing her hands to direct me to the area of pain.

"Well if we can help, we certainly will. When are you going to put it up for sale?"

"It's already arranged. All I need is just to confirm who my solicitors are and then we can get on with it, nice and tidy, you know what I mean."

"Yes of course, what we'll do is get you in to see Steve Wilford and he'll sort it out because he's the conveyancer in our setup."

"Very good."

"How will we start it?" she asked.

"I'll send you a letter and an appointment as soon as I get back to the office."

"That's good, thank you so much for that."

She smiled sweetly and shook my hand firmly. A remarkable grasp I thought for an old lady with arthritis, although I must confess she had youthful eyes and but for her laboured gait and her rather old-fashioned countenance I would have said she could have passed for being a lot younger.

We discussed the benefits of the daffodil family for a moment or two and then I returned to the office, picking up the local newspaper on the way. The front page was dominated by the headline, "Jewellery Thief Strikes Again". A large detached house in one of the most prestigious areas of the town had been burgled and jewellery to the value of twenty thousand pounds had been taken, according to the quote from the CID who were dealing with the case.

About a week later the police were carrying out some routine stop and search procedures and a young man called Ken Chambers was found in possession of a diamond ring. The police were suspicious and they arrested him, taking him to the police station. Some checks were made on the ring, which had been found concealed in a security pocket within his trousers. The police made various checks and found that the ring was from the burglary that I'd seen referred to in the newspaper only a week before. I was called to represent the interests of the young man who had been locked up.

When I arrived at the police station they told me that the ring had been positively identified by the owner of the house as being hers and was part of a large haul of expensive jewellery. The police told me that the owner had absolutely no doubts about identifying the property but then I suppose they wouldn't have because jewellery is such as personal thing. Significantly however, all the rings were extremely small because the owner had very small bony fingers.

Chambers had no previous convictions and had not even previously been cautioned, so he was a bit of an enigma to the police. Detective Sergeant Sutcliffe was leading the enquiry and he was anxious to try to recover as much property as he could. He was an officer in his mid-forties and he had been around the block a few times. He knew his job and he was known for being a very competent and thorough interviewer.

"We need to recover as much of this property as we can, because unfortunately the owner had forgotten to renew her insurance and at the moment she has no cover for any of these items. Plus the fact that some of the rings were of great sentimental value as well as being expensive," he said, staring at me through his dark-brown eyes.

He was reminiscent of the politician Dennis Healy in that he had very bushy eyebrows and a considerable girth. He was small in stature but very stocky. He had a staccato style of speech, using words sparingly as if to use more than was necessary would cost him. Consequently he was very much to the point.

I noticed he had two rings on each hand and a very expensive Omega watch. His trained detective's eye saw me evaluating their worth.

"You into jewellery Mr Smith?" he asked.

"Not at all, but I like watches and that's a rather nice one you've got there. It's an Omega isn't it?"

"Yes, that's very observant of you," said the officer. "You don't know anything about rings as well do you?"

"Afraid not. Out of my range of expertise," I said.

Quite what use he would have been able to have put my knowledge to I'd no idea but policemen have the habit of asking questions and I've often thought that after a while they do it subconsciously. I suppose I'm the same.

The officer explained the case to me, telling me that a detached house had been burgled and interestingly the thief had gone for the jewellery casket and nothing else. Approximately eight rings were taken and oddly enough, a gold gate bracelet had been left. The officer was convinced that this was a professional offence, to order.

"There's no doubt about it, he's gone specifically for rings. I wouldn't be surprised if he's taken the stones out and melted the gold down but I can't prove that at the moment. What we can prove is that young Chambers has been caught with one of the rings and it's definitely from that offence. What we want to know is where he got it from, how long he's had it, why it was concealed in an inlaid pocket and where it was going to."

"Is there anything known about the lad?" I asked.

"I thought you might be able to tell us that because he's nominated you as his solicitor. What can you tell us about him?" he asked pointedly.

"I've never heard of him," I replied.

"Surely not," said the officer. "He specifically asked for you and wouldn't have anybody else."

"That doesn't mean to say I know him does it?"

"I would have disagreed with you there," said the detective sergeant.

I realised that it was going to be one of those interviews! No matter what was said to this policeman he wasn't going to believe it unless it was the answer that he wanted.

"Well I'll have a word with him first if I may and then we'll get the interview done."

"Yes," said the officer, "but we don't want any of this 'no comment' rubbish."

"You've got your job to do Sergeant and I've got mine. It doesn't make you right and me wrong. We'll deal with this matter according to the book."

The sergeant nodded and put his pencil behind his ear. It was quite clear to me that he didn't like all solicitors but then again, I couldn't fault him because neither did I.

I was shown into a cell/interview room and young Ken Chambers was brought in to see me. He was wearing one of the Government issue white jumpsuits, which are supplied when clothing has been taken away for forensic testing. He was in his stockinged feet, his footwear having also been taken from him.

Chambers was extremely nervous. The officer had told me that he'd never been in trouble before, or he'd certainly not been convicted, and he certainly didn't look like the usual run-of-the-mill burglar. He was tall and slim with a badly spotted face and swarthy complexion. His eyes were dark and jaundiced and he looked decidedly under the weather.

"Come in and sit down Kenny. It is Kenny isn't it?"

"No, just Ken," said the young man.

"Now then, what age are you Ken?"

"Twenty-two," he replied in a loud clear voice.

He gave me his other particulars, telling me that he was a single man and lived in a bed-sit flatlet on the outskirts of town. He had no relatives with whom he'd any contact. He had never met his father and his mother had died when he was fourteen years old. He went on to say that he'd spent the majority of his life in care until, in his mid to late teens, he lived with a foster parent. He obtained his own flat when he became twenty-one. He worked in the warehouse of a local supermarket and described himself as 'looking at options'.

"Do you know what the allegation is Ken?" I asked.

"Yes, they're saying I burgled that big house up Moorgate and took some jewellery."

"Yes, that's true but I've got a little bit more news now, which is that the ring that you were found in possession of, has been positively identified as having come from that house and that burglary. The burglary only occurred a matter of a few days before your arrest, so the police will say that they've got recent possession."

"Recent possession?" he asked.

"Yes, recent possession. That means you were in possession of an item stolen from a burglary that only took place a short time before and the inference will be that because only a short time has elapsed since the burglary, that you must in some way be connected with it."

Ken nodded grimly.

"I bought the ring the day before, from someone in a pub."

"Oh, I see. Which pub was that?"

"Can't remember exactly because I'd been on a bender and I can't remember which one it was."

"How much did you pay for it?"

"Forty quid," came the answer.

"Forty quid? That's cheap. That was a diamond ring and according to the police it was worth a thousand pounds at least."

"Well I didn't know it was a real one."

"Who sold it to you?"

"Oh it was a young kid, I can't remember his name and I haven't seen him before."

"Well can you give me a description?"

"No, I can't remember."

"Well, where did he say he'd got it from?"

"He said it was his but he was a bit short of money so he wanted to flog it."

"Was it his ring?"

"Yes."

"Tell me what he was like, this lad."

"Well he was average really. About my age, about the same size really."

"You don't seem too sure about this," I said.

225

"No, it's a bit back and my memory's not very good."

"Did you say he was wearing the ring?"

"Er yes, he was, he just took it off and showed it to me. I had forty pounds on me. He asked me for fifty pounds but he settled for forty pounds."

"The problem is, it is only a small ring. It would only fit a child or small thin person. Looking at you it wouldn't fit."

Ken lowered his head to avoid eye contact and didn't answer.

"I'm not saying this to get at you but the police will ask you these questions. I'm only trying to help."

"Yes, thanks for that, I see what you mean."

He thought for a moment.

"Will they give me bail?" he asked.

"I can't say, I've not discussed it with them. I suppose they will say that they can't make a decision until the interviewing is finished.

"I must get out, I've got something on."

He appeared to be most agitated.

"Well look, just what are you saying?"

"Well…I…er…"

"Why was it in a secret pocket?" I asked.

"Just for safety so I wouldn't lose it."

"What were you going to do with it?"

"Wear it"

"But it's a ladies ring."

There was no answer.

"It wouldn't fit you would it?"

Again there was no answer.

"I'm afraid this won't look very good on tape will it?"

"I don't want to drop anybody in it," he said.

"What do you mean by that. Is there someone else involved?"

"Well…yes…no…not really."

"Look, you are going to be interviewed and you have to give an answer or remain silent, you can't have it both ways."

"Will they charge me?"

"Yes, I think they've got enough to charge you and then what? What will you say if you give evidence?"

"I don't want to give evidence, I want to keep my version as simple as possible."

"Well then you will have to remain silent but if you do you must keep to it. Don't answer the questions you can handle and leave the others. Remember, anything you say can be used in evidence."

We were called into the interview room and the interview began. Ken stuck to his guns despite great pressure from the police and after we had finished he was taken to the charge office. The police told him he was being put before the court the next day because they weren't going to give him bail.

Ken was distraught.

"You can't keep me, I've got things to do. Why are you doing this?"

"We think you will interfere with justice," said the sergeant firmly. "We believe you are in this with someone else and now they will know we are onto them. If we release you, you will tip the others off and that will impede our enquiries."

Try as we might to get the police to let him out, they refused. Ken was staying, whether he liked it or not.

The following day at court Ken was desperate.

"I've got to have bail," he said.

"Yes, I understand that Ken. I think we should be OK but I might need a surety."

"What's a surety?"

"It's someone who will stand bail for you by promising to pay a sum of money if you don't turn up, but…"

"Yes I have someone," he interrupted.

"Just a minute, they will have to be good sureties. They must have some money and be able to prove it. Have you got such a person?"

"Yes, my old foster-mother will stand bail for me, Anne Goodyear."

"Really," I said, taken by surprise. "When did you live with her?"

"I was with her from being fourteen to twenty-one."

"How do you know she will stand surety?" I asked.

"Oh, she will, she'll do anything for me, just ring her."

He gave me the telephone number without hesitation and I rang her.

"Hello Mrs Goodyear, this is Steve Smith, solicitor."

"Oh yes, hello Mr Smith, how nice to hear from you," she said.

"Yes, I'm sorry to bother you but I'm at court."

"Yes?"

"I've got Ken Chambers here."

"Oh dear, what's happened?"

"Well there's quite a coincidence. Ken has been locked up for a burglary involving some property."

"Oh dear, how upsetting."

"Yes, I'm afraid so. I'm sorry to bother you but we need a surety, someone to stand bail. Can you help us?" I asked her.

"Yes, of course."

"Is there any chance you could come to court this morning?"

"Well yes, if I must."

"Well would you bring some identification and some proof that you are able to stand surety with you?"

"What do you mean?"

"Well, something to prove that you have some assets; a bank book will do."

"Alright, what do I have to do?"

"Well if you could stand surety in the sum of five thousand pounds...."

"Yes, I will. Oh, and by the way, could you do me a small favour?"

"Yes, if I can," I replied.

"Well, I want to keep my move a secret at the moment. It might upset a few people if they know I'm going so until Im ready I would rather no one knew."

"Yes, of course," I replied, "don't worry I won't tell anyone and I'll tell Steve Wilford to make sure nothing is passed on to anyone."

"Oh thank you, you are so kind. Well I must go now so I'll see you at the Magistrates court in the morning."

"What a lovely lady," I thought.

The following day Ken Chambers was in court. He was pacing up and down his cell when I arrived.

"Has Mrs Goodyear come?" he blurted out.

"Not as yet," I replied, "but she is coming and she's going to stand as surety."

"She'd better," said Chambers.

I noted a measure of hostility in his voice but perhaps it was just the occasion and with being locked up.

"You ought to be grateful that she's here at all, and more importantly, you ought to be grateful that she's prepared to stand as surety. I 'm sure she's got better things to do in her life than be running around courts chasing after people who've let her down."

I've always believed in being straight with defendants. I didn't want them to run around with the idea that I was either stupid of soft and the majority of them seemed to appreciate it. However there are those that don't like to face the truth and like being told about it even less.

He just grunted and left it at that.

We discussed the bail application and he was decidedly uneasy but then at worst he was looking at a remand in custody and so it was perhaps not surprising that he wasn't falling over with laughter.

We got into court and the magistrates wanted to hear from our surety before deciding on bail, so Mrs Goodyear went in to the witness box and the magistrates were suitably impressed. Ken was given bail subject to conditions, including the five thousand pound surety from Mrs Goodyear.

They waited in the court corridor for me whilst I dealt with my last case. It was Graham Samuels, one of Albert's pals. He had burgled a house at Hooton Roberts, about four or five miles from town. It belonged to one of the hippy fraternity who was known to grow his own cannabis. Harry had seen a small casket about as big as a cigar box on the sideboard in the living room. It had the name 'Charlie' on it. Graham knew that 'Charlie' was a slang term for cocaine. Tempted to try anything once, Graham opened the box and took a portion of the grey powder ash. Depositing it on his thumbnail he then snorted it up his nose and waited for the effect. The effect was an enormous sneeze which, to cut a long story short, led to a citizens arrest by a rather annoyed householder carrying a baseball bat. He was angry enough at being burgled but he couldn't stand by and see the ashes of his recently departed great dane called Charlie being snorted up the burglar's nose. That really did upset him. Graham on the other hand, complained of a lump at the back of his head. I told him there was always a downside to sniffing dog's ashes!

Graham was sent to crown court and got two years imprisonment. I understand that he is now off drugs.

As I was leaving court I remembered that Mrs Goodyear was putting her house up for sale and was contemplating moving out. This troubled me because a surety is required to ensure that the defendant turns up at court and of course she couldn't do that if she was out of the country. I raised the point with her outside. She assured me that it would be some considerable time before she left the area, which satisfied me and then signed the bail forms and shortly afterwards Ken Chambers was released from the cell area and joined us in an interview room.

I found him to be a most surly youth with very little to say in his favour but nevertheless Mrs Goodyear did not differentiate between the various people that she had to look after.

Ken's attitude towards her was not what I expected. Again, the surliness continued and I had to remind him that but for Mrs Goodyear he wouldn't even be on bail.

"That's all right Mr Smith, he's a good boy really," she said smiling as Ken looked at the floor.

"Come on Kenneth, let's go, we'll get a taxi and be on our way. Thank you once again Mr Smith for your kindness."

"Not at all Mrs Goodyear," I replied. "By the way," I said pointedly to Ken, "if you fail to turn up you will be in serious trouble. Not only that, Mrs Goodyear could lose all or part of the five thousand pounds."

"He won't let us down Mr Smith, will you Ken?" she said smiling and nodding in his direction.

There was no reply and I thought it time to conclude the interview.

I watched them from the upstairs window near the rathole interview room and couldn't help noticing that there appeared to be some form of argument going off between the two of them, so much so that I thought I probably ought to interfere but then the taxi arrived and they went out of sight. With that I concentrated on my next case.

At the end of the morning the CID arrived and handed to me a list of additional property which had been omitted from the statement of the person who had been burgled by Ken Chambers. As they had been cleaning up after the burglary they realised that a further ring of great sentimental value to the owner had been stolen. It was a rather magnificent diamond on white gold which had been handed down from one of the unfortunate householder's relatives. It had been made for a child by a rather wealthy family and it was quite distinctive because of its size. The officer told me that the diamond was of a very high quality and worth a considerable sum of money. He asked the prosecutor if he would amend the charge to include this item but the case had been adjourned and so the file was noted for next time. I wasn't given a copy of the amended charge and I simply forgot to tell Ken Chambers that the charge would be amended and another ring would be included. The effect was that Ken thought it hadn't been reported stolen.

The case had been adjourned for eight weeks so that it could be committed to the crown court. As with the other cases it was placed in the diary, an appointment made for a couple of days prior to the next hearing when all the documentation should have been received. There was nothing to do in the meantime and so my mind went elsewhere.

The next morning I had a welcome visit from Jack and Albert, who I'd not seen for some time. Jack had been given some papers by one of the banks in relation to Madge's estate and he didn't know how to fill them in, so he made a special visit to see me.

We completed all the paperwork and Albert told me that he was keeping out of trouble and had started to see Caroline again, despite her father's wishes. He was back working at the animal sanctuary and he was enjoying the work.

"I'll tell thee what," said Jack, "he'll be going to church next."

I laughed and Jack joined in but Albert didn't find it amusing. When we'd finished our business I took them to the front door and as I did so a gentleman in long flowing white robes with garlands about his neck walked past with a small entourage of helpers. Jack and Albert stared at him with some confusion so I decided to put their minds at rest.

"He's a Fakir."

Jack thought for a minute before speaking.

"He must be, walking around in 'jamas like that during the day."

I realised that Jack has misunderstood but I saw little point in explaining it so we shook hands before Jack spoke again.

"By the way, all my kids are turning into puffs."

"How do you work that one out Jack?" I asked.

"Even our Morris has got a job now."

"Really?" I asked, "where at?"

"He's at the Sheffield Road swimming baths."

"Oh, is he really? What doing?

"He's the shithole attendant," said Jack in a most matter of fact way.

"I think you mean the lavatory attendant, don't you?"

"There tha' goes again, correcting me. Tha' knows what I mean. So far as I'm concerned he's the shithole attendant."

"Yes, of course Jack but nevertheless it's a job and full credit to Morris for doing it. I can't compliment him enough."

"I suppose so," said Jack. It's not a bad wage and at least now we get some board off the bugger and as much soap as we can use."

"I bet you don't use much," I thought to myself.

"Our Clorris has got a job as well," said Jack proudly.

"Oh good, I am pleased."

Clorris was the brightest of the family. A nice girl, so unlike the rest of her siblings.

"What's she doing?

"She's a trainee secretary at the clap clinic in Sheffield."

"I think you mean the urinary department."

"Neow," said Jack, "the clap clinic...tha knows clap dunt tha...?

"If you put it that way then yes. What a turn of phrase you have."

A shithole attendant and the clap clinic. What must their conversation have been like at their house during dinnertime?

Jack turned to walk away.

"I'll tell thee what though," said Jack.

"What's that Jack?" I asked.

"The towels are pretty good."

"Oh, bugger off," I said laughing, realising that Jack had to have his little joke, except that I didn't really think he was having a little joke. I'd got visions of towel upon towel hanging on his washing line with the letter RBC (Rotherham Borough Council) emblazoned thereon or even worse, SCC – not Sheffield Council but the Sheffield Clap Clinic!

A week later Wilf told me that a buyer had been found for Mrs Goodyear's house. The purchaser wanted an early completion and did not have a property to sell. He came up with the asking price and so contracts were soon exchanged and a completion date was set for only a fortnight later.

Mrs Goodyear came in to see Wilf to sign the contract and I saw her quite by chance in reception.

"Oh, I'm glad I've seen you Mrs Goodyear, can I bother you for two minutes?"

"Certainly," she said in her usual pleasant manner and held out her hand for a handshake. I noticed she was wearing a very attractive ring with a diamond set in white gold. I had not noted it before.

We went into a small room near Reception and I invited her to sit down.

"If you sell your house we will have to notify the court that you have changed your address."

"What for?" asked Mrs Goodyear.

"Well, you're a surety for Kenneth aren't you, so the court will need to know where you are."

"Oh, of course," she said, "I understand. Well I'm going to stay at a local hotel until I sort out my sheltered housing accommodation."

"Well that will be a bit expensive," I said.

"Not really," she said. "If I'm going to be staying there for about three months or so they will give me preferential terms, so it's not as bad as you might think."

"Trust you to do the appropriate deal," I said gently 'pulling her leg'.

She gave me the particulars of her hotel and I wrote to the court and formally notified them of the details. We had about four weeks to go before Kenneth was in court and so I thought it right to arrange an appointment so that I could go through his papers just before the hearing. Consequently an appointment was sent out and the file was put back into the filing cabinet until I needed to see it again.

On the day of Mrs Goodyear's completion I was in the area of her house. Steve Wilford had a cheque to send to her and other than send it, I decided to drop it in personally. I didn't think that she would mind my visit because she always seemed pleased to see me but despite my best intentions I had forgotten to telephone her to tell her to expect me.

I got to the house and knocked on the door. I heard some movement inside so I realised that someone was at home, although it took quite a time for them to answer the door and I had to bang on the door repeatedly.

Eventually Mrs Goodyear's son, Alan, came to the door. He seemed rather surprised to see me.

"Oh, Mr Smith, we weren't expecting you."

"Yes, that's right. I hope I haven't called at an inopportune time but I was in the area so I brought Mrs Goodyear's cheque."

Alan looked most put out.

"Oh, that's very good of you," he said, "I'm afraid I can't offer you anything, its embarrassing but we were in the process of putting everything away."

"Oh, that's all right," I said, "don't worry about me, I'll just pay my respects to your mum and get on my way."

"Well, it's not really convenient at the moment," he replied.

"I'm awfully sorry," I said, "I hadn't realised. I certainly don't wish to hold you up so I'll move on."

I handed the cheque over and he thanked me most graciously. I turned to leave and in doing so I walked past the entrance to the front room. I couldn't help noticing a selection of jewellery on the coffee table near to the door.

"I shouldn't leave that lot lying about, there's some real rogues out and about," I said laughing.

Alan joined in the amusement and having forced a laugh, hurriedly closed the door.

"Oh, it mother's jewellery. Because she's going to the hotel we're going to put it with the bank so we are getting it ready to take there now."

"Good idea," I said and turned to leave.

"I'm very sorry to seem so inhospitable," said Alan.

"Oh, that's perfectly all right, I understand. I hadn't made an appointment and you weren't expecting me, so it's probably remiss of me to have called without telling you, so there's no harm done."

"Anyway Mr Smith, thank you to you and Mr Wilford for being so kind. Mr Wilford has dealt with this transaction so expertly and so quickly that it's saved us a great deal of stress."

"Well, at A.B.'s request we deducted our charges from the proceeds."

"Oh, that's fine, just like a solicitor."

""Yes, but you've not seen what we've charged!"

We forced another laugh, shook hands and I left.

I had been blocked in by another car and so I had to reverse before setting off and in doing so I thought I saw Mrs Goodyear looking out from the bedroom window. I must have been confused and so I put the car into gear and off I went.

It was two or three weeks later and the day before Ken's case. His appointment was for 4pm but I was delayed at court and returned late. I looked in the visitor's book but Ken had failed to turn up. It was an omen. If he failed to turn up at court Mrs Goodyear might lose the money she had offered as surety.

The following week my worst fears were realised. Kenneth did not turn up but more importantly, neither did Mrs Goodyear. The alarm bells had begun to ring but nothing made any sense. I telephoned the number of Mrs Goodyear's hotel only to be told that she had checked out the day before without leaving a forwarding address. I checked my file to see if Alan Goodyear had left a phone number, but I hadn't written it down. I cursed at my inefficiency.

With the exception of Ken's case the court list was completed by twelve fifteen. I did my best to persuade the court to adjourn the case but they would have none of it and issued a warrant without bail. They also indicated that they would require Mrs Goodyear to attend at court to show cause why her surety in the sum of five thousand pounds should not be forfeited.

When I got back to the office I told Steve Wilford what had happened. The cheque that was made payable to Mrs Goodyear had been cleared. We had no information about where the money had gone because of course Mrs Goodyear's bank would not have disclosed that information. I then mulled over the entire case in my mind, starting with our first meeting at Ranulphs restaurant in Sheffield. I knew she had been a foster parent.

I was reassured that this nice old lady was what she seemed. But then I thought about her failing to go to court. Perhaps she had forgotten, that must be the reason, but then why check out of the hotel and not let me know her forwarding address? After all she was an old lady and she had so many other things on her mind.

But then I thought about the visit to her house and her son's very strange attitude towards me when I called. It was almost as if I was not only unexpected but also unwelcome. But then he was packing to move and so he wouldn't welcome a guest at the time and neither would I so perhaps I was becoming paranoid in my old age. Then I considered the coffee table full of rings, but then she was old and had probably collected them all of her life, even the small white gold one with the large diamond, which she had been wearing when I met her by chance at the office. I had no answer for that one but then Wilf shouted me.

"Are you deaf?" asked Wilf.

"Am I what?" I asked as if raising from a slumber.

"I asked if you would give me a lift."

"What with?" I replied.

"A lift home, you burk!"

I must confess I was only half listening because my mind was working overtime piecing things together bit by bit. I wasn't a detective but something was not quite right and I didn't like what I was coming up with.

"What if.......?"

"Are you on something," asked Wilf.

"Oh, I'm sorry, yes, you wanted a lift. Yes, OK."

I recounted to Wilf what I'd seen and what had happened. He was very understanding but he thought I'd been reading too many books.

"She's obviously got the date wrong, they both have and with flitting and all that..."

"Yes, I'm sure you're right," I said, "but what about the ring?"

"Here we are, drop me off because I'm really late and I'll see you tomorrow," said Wilf almost dismissively.

"But the ring?"

"Yes, I'll give you a ring and see you later." Wilf scurried down the drive, into his house and was gone. I on the other hand had a sleepless night.

The following day I contacted the religious order where Mr Goodyear had been training. They were born again Christians and whilst they were very nice and helpful they couldn't tell me much, although they did recall Mr Goodyear. He had come to them via his foster mother who had taken him in when his parents had disowned him following his constant brushes with the law. He'd adopted her name and for the rest of his youth lived with her. A close perusal of their records showed that he had dropped out of the unit some two years or so before, blaming family responsibilities and what they believed was the death of his foster mother. I was even more confused than before.

The case was beginning to dominate my thoughts and a fortnight later, despite all my enquiries I had not been able to find Mrs Goodyear or her so-called son or Kenneth Chambers for that matter. The court heard an application to estreat the surety and an order was made against Mrs Goodyear in her absence.

Ken had disappeared off the face of the earth and so I put my file back in the cabinet until such time as I would need it again.

One afternoon I visited the block of flats that Mrs Goodyear had talked about. They had never heard of her. They'd no record of any enquiry or any communication from a Mrs Goodyear. Something told me that I had been had.

Chapter 17

MEETING THE JAPANESE EMPIRE

The firm was expanding at a considerable rate, so much so that I began to worry about the inevitable difficulties relating to cash flow. We were taking on new staff at a rate of about one per month but the overdraft was growing too and in retrospect I can understand that the bank was becoming more and more agitated about it. Wilf had the problem of financial administration and left me to carry on in my own sweet way as the front man of the business. It suited us both.

Criminal law became my main area of work, which was restrictive in one sense but it did allow me the odd jaunt out of town and sometimes to the Appeal Court in London, but the majority of my time was spent in the Magistrates' and Crown Courts of Yorkshire.

It was and is demanding work, with an ever-increasing responsibility of time limits playing their parts in our daily working lives. The result was that the "jollies" or fun time was on the decrease as we strove towards the dreaded monthly targets. I never wanted to have to work that way but it was inevitable, as the bank played an evermore inhibitive role in our day to day working life.

The great Jarvis had the responsibility of trying to guide us on the path of solvency; no mean task as things turned out. Some of the clients were still driving me to distraction with their eccentricities, illnesses, peculiarities and behavioural abnormality patterns, which proved to me that a substantial part of the world was either mad or not far off it.

Jack and Albert continued their attempted rehabilitation by their entrepreneurial activities, selling everything they could get hold of from furniture to pig manure. Wherever there was a retail opportunity, they persued it, whether they understood what they were doing or not. At least they were avoiding crime.

Their lives had changed in the aftermath of Madge's death. Each Sunday Jack would make sandwiches and he would have his weekly picnic at Madge's grave. More often than not Albert would join him and they would sit for two hours or more, relating the events of the week towards Madge's gravestone in the belief that she could hear them.

The consuming curse of drugs spread over an ever-widening web of intrigue and deviant commercial activity and more and more of my cases were drug related. Defendants still failed to turn up to court with all sorts of excuses and the ubiquitous sick note found its way onto my desk and into an increasingly cynical courtroom.

Just before Christmas my clients the Dobkin family suffered a highly infectious bout of gastroenteritis, referred to lovingly by Edna Dobkin as the "Eartha Kitts". The youngest, Tyrone, was due to appear at the Juvenile Court but Edna had the "Earthas" and Tyrone had got "lug trouble". In other words, problems concerning the functioning of the inner ear. She wrote to the court with a view to excusing her own and Tyrone's attendance. I've kept the letter because it amused me at the time. I have reproduced it here.

'Dear sir or missis

Our Tyrone can't come to court as the doc as seen him and ee says is ears are in flames. Ive got bowil problems and am never off it so I daren't go away without avin an imediate thingy to and. ope you realise what is like to av bowil probs and will ajurn case to after my bowils is working again which cud be a weak or too.

P.S. Tyrone cunt ere you anyway and only sign words ee nose are rude wons so that's abart it.

Yours suffering,

Edna Dobkin (missis).'

I had visions of seeing poor old Tyrone with his ears on fire and Edna the same somewhere else. I was resolved to speak to her the next time I had a mask and a fire extinguisher.

The court was not sympathetic and despite my pleas, the Magistrates issued a warrant with bail, which meant that the Dobkins would not be arrested unless they failed to attend court next time.

I wrote to Edna and gave her the news. She sent me some mince pies for Christmas with a note saying she had made them whilst she had been confined at home during her illness. I gave them to the emphasemic usher, who coincidentally had the following week off work with the "Earthas!" Serve him right, the miserable old bugger!

There was always a large post comprising of junk mail and begging letters from the nick or complaints about certain barristers who had "got me eighteen months". Ironically the fact that they had offended seemed irrelevant to them and it was definitely the barrister's fault.

"I don't want that wanker again," wrote Gordon Wilks, having just been sentenced to twelve months for burglary.

I thought "the wanker" did pretty well, bearing in mind Gordon's extensive criminal record and the fact that he accepted the inevitability of his return to crime, made his comments seem all the more irrational.

One other letter invited me to a commerce function at the Town Hall. A Japanese delegation was to visit Rotherham to discuss some business opportunity or other and members of the local business fraternity were invited to attend. I wasn't interested until Pagey rang and told me that he and Bodger were going and the thought of Pagey and Bodger greeting the imperial might of the Japanese empire intrigued me. As a result Wilf and I turned up.

It was a lunchtime meeting at the Town Hall and a splendid buffet had been prepared to honour the guests. For some reason we had managed to get into the VIP area and we found ourselves being introduced to one of the delegation. The interpreter was a Japanese lady who spoke the Queen's English better than any of us but mistaking us for Council officials, she invited Pagey and I to meet the chairman of the group.

"I have the honour to introduce you to Fok Woo Yoo," she said turning out of earshot to her boss.

"I say, that's a name and a half – Fok Yoo too," said Pagey.

"No Pagey, that's not what she said so don't embarrass us with any smart-arse comments," I whispered firmly. "She said Fok Woo Yoo, Yoo, not Too.....Yoo.

"That reminds me," said Pagey, "what's the most common owl in Britain," he asked in a stage whisper.

"I don't know," I said dismissively.

"Go on, guess," insisted Pagey.

"Oh, bloody hell...the barn owl," I insisted in the hope that he might go away.

"No," said Pagey smugly.

"Go on then...what is it," I asked losing my patience.

"It's the teat."

"Rubbish," I whispered, "there's no such thing as a teat owl."

"Just then I realised what I had said. Pagey's little joke had given him great amusement at my expense and he laughed out loud as a small Japanese woman walked past him. She thought the joke was on her so she stared at Pagey before walking away. Pagey pretended to karate chop her when her back was turned.

The interpreter turned to us and continued the introduction.

"And you are?" she asked looking directly at Pagey.

"I'm Sean Page darling," said Pagey.

The interpreter whispered into the man's ear. He then turned to Page and with a broad smile said, in a staccato style of speech, "Argh...you...are...a...darling?"

"Yes old bean, I'm a darling."

"Argh...good," he said bowing gracefully. Then he turned to me.

"And...you...are...a...?" he asked expectantly.

"Stephen," I said smiling.

The interpreter started to whisper in his ear but he waved her away arrogantly, believing he had the ability to persevere on his own.

"Argh, you are a Stephen."

"Yes, that's correct," I said nodding.

Just then the magistrate whom the solicitors had nicknamed the Lord Chief Justice walked into the room and moved towards the interpreter. He caught sight of me and I noticed a look of disdain on his face, as if I was some kind of intruder. He saw me look across at him and he nodded reluctantly as he walked in our direction.

The Japanese gentleman saw him and must have believed him to be some kind of dignitary as he was wearing the chain of office of some local federation of which he was a member. He turned to me and asked in pigeon-English, even more staccato than before,

"Argh...he is a...?"

"He," interrupted Pagey mischievously and believing it would go no further, "is a shitbag."

"Argh...so," said the Japanese as he turned to the Lord Chief's direction.

"You arse Pagey," I said, "now what have you done?"

"Well it's that so and so. You know what he's like, bloody shitbag."

Of course it was inevitable that the Lord Chief held out his hand and Mr Yoo responded. I looked on in horror as Mr Yoo spoke.

"Argh...so you are a..."

I turned and made for the buffet before he said anything further and found Bodger at the sandwich display. He had filled his plate in a fashion that resembled a Japanese pagoda and I smiled at the similarity.

"You should have seen his face," Pagey said laughing. "That was the funniest thing I've seen this year – and you are a...," said Pagey imitating Mr Yoo. " ...a shitbag'," he continued.

Unfortunately the last two words were heard by His Worship the Mayor who thought he was referring to him, so I walked away whilst Pagey tried to talk his way out of it.

There was a small presentation and a special welcome and Mr Woo's interpreter replied on his behalf, including a reference to him meeting some people with very strange names. The Lord Chief made a speech in reply, during which Pagey whispered to me,

"I told you he was a shitbag."

I nodded in agreement.

We left after spending about another hour listening to interesting comments about world trade and having had an enjoyable free lunch, leaving Pagey bowing to the Japanese delegation repeatedly and shouting,

"Argh sole."

Chapter 18

KENNETH'S RETURN AND THE
PLOT THICKENS

It was one of those calls I didn't want. I was finishing early, I had something arranged and I was anxious to go but I was daft enough to answer the telephone.

It was the charge office at Rotherham who, I suppose, thought that they were doing me a favour and indeed they were but I could have done without it on that particular night. My interest was soon aroused however when they told me the name of the person under arrest.

"It's a young man called Kenneth Chambers," said Sergeant Brown. "He's been arrested on warrant for failing to appear at court some time ago but the CID also want to interview him about some other offences where they have forensic evidence. It seems he got very careless at the scene of one offence, leaving a footprint at the scene when he jumped out of a window to escape, having disturbed the occupiers. The offence was some time ago but nevertheless it looks like he'll have to have it."

'He'll have to have it' is common parlance for 'he has no option but to plead guilty and admit his wrongdoing whether he likes it or not'.

I could have asked someone else to go and indeed as it turned out I wished I had but I went down to the police station on the understanding that it would take no longer than one hour.

I saw young Chambers in his cell.

"Have you got any fags?" he asked.

Fortunately I had one left from a packet which I used for my cell visits so I gave it to him and he smoked it furiously as though it would be his last.

"You've been arrested on warrant then Ken and I understand they want to talk to you about other offences."

"What shall I do Mr Smith?" he asked.

I noticed that he was much more polite than when I'd seen him before.

"Well I don't think you've any option on this one because they've got footprint that matches your shoe and the forensic boys say that it must be you or someone's gone out in your boots."

"I've blown it anyway, haven't it?" said a down-in-the-mouth Chambers.

"In a word, yes. I always say that if the game's up with no way out it's always best to admit it straightaway and try to get into the court's good books."

He knew I was right and that it was good advice.

"I understand that you've stolen jewellery."

Chambers just shrugged his shoulders.

"I suppose the police will ask you where it's gone because nothing has been recovered"

"I haven't got it," said Chambers.

"Is there any chance of getting it back?" I asked.

"No chance, it's gone. It's too long ago now."

"The police will ask you where."

Chambers thought for a minute before answering.

"Would it do any different to my sentence if I came clean?" he asked.

"If you are open and frank with the court and with the police, you will get something knocked off your sentence but at the end of the day it's a matter for you to decide what you want to do. I can't answer that one for you."

Chambers thought for a moment. It was a decision for him and him only and I wasn't going to influence him either way.

Just then the police rapped on the door and asked if we were ready for the interview. Chambers shrugged his shoulders and nodded his assent and so we left and followed the officers to a pokey little room at the back of the station. There was an air of confidence about the investigating officers for they knew they had the evidence and it was just a question of whether he was going to make it easy for himself or not.

The interview took its normal course with all the various warnings and cautions being made. Kenneth was rather defeatist, so unlike his attitude in the past and he admitted the offence straightaway, telling the police that he had escaped via the downstairs window in a blind panic when he was disturbed. He agreed that the footprint outside was his but as the police pointed out, he really did not have any option.

At the end of the interview the officer asked him about the property.

"Where did the rings go Ken?" asked DC Blenkinsop earnestly.

Chambers thought for what seemed like an eternity before speaking.

"I gave them to my Fence and he's got them."

The police officers' ears pricked up and they looked at him most intently.

"Do you mind telling us who he is?"

Chambers thought for a while and then spoke with considerable venom.

"It's that bastard," he said fiercely.

"Oh yes," said the officer, "which bastard is that?"

It was clear that Ken was wrestling with his conscience as to whether to mention the name or not and then he said it.

"It was Alan Goodyear. Yes, it was that bastard, it was always that bastard, manipulating, throwing his weight about."

It was like watching a film when it gets to the best bit and you are about to find out who had committed the murder. You could have cut the atmosphere with a knife.

"He's had all my gear and I might as well tell you, he's had a lot from other silly buggers who he duped. He was always the favourite one wasn't he, it was always him, Mr Nice Guy, Mr Clever at School, Mr Passed all his Exams. Mrs Goodyear loved him because he was her own and left people like me out.

I couldn't believe what I was hearing as Ken poured out every ounce of hatred from his soul into this vitriolic outburst.

"You mean Alan Goodyear, the so-called vicar?" asked the officer.

He took a deep breath before speaking.

"Yes, it was him. He's had all the gear. They had it at the house and shared it all out, leaving the mugs like me with the rap. They gave me spending money and put me up."

"They?" said the officer.

"Yes, they – him and his bloody mother. She's not what she's cracked up to be and he's not adopted, she's his real mother."

"Are you saying that Mrs Goodyear knew what was going on?" asked the officer making no reference to the relationship which Ken had referred to.

"She must have done."

"Did you discuss it with her?"

"Well…no I didn't but she must have known, she's not stupid."

"You mean you never spoke to her about it herself?"

"Well no I didn't but she must have known."

"What a relief," I thought," and yet why didn't she know and what was all this about Alan being her real son? It was so confusing but I needed to know for my own benefit.

"Did she know?" I wondered. "I thought Alan was at theological college." I couldn't wait for the questions to be asked but the police, understandably, were only interested in the offence and not the side issues.

"Well," said the officer demonstratively closing his file, "we'll have to find Mr Goodyear and speak to him. Where is he Ken?"

"He's not at college that's for sure," he said grinning.

"And he's not a holy Joe." Ken laughed out loud quite nervously.

"What's funny?" asked the officer.

"He'll take some finding. They've gone. Try somewhere in South America," he said smiling again.

"We'll find him," said the officer forcefully.

The police completed the paperwork and Ken was told he would be charged and put before the court the following day. I saw him in his cell afterwards. He appeared contrite.

"I shouldn't have said that," he said regretfully.

"What?"

"Told them about Alan, but I'm on my own, they've left me to it so they deserve to be shopped."

"You say they?"

"Well she must have known."

"Yes, you said that to the officer but you never discussed it with her and stolen property was never mentioned in her presence.

"No, Alan told me."

"Alan told you what," I asked.

"Well, he told me that he had all the money."

"But did you ever discuss it with Mrs Goodyear?"

"No he told me not to, saying that he would deal with it but from time to time if there was ever a really nice ring that was small enough to fit her, she kept it."

I then recalled the diamond ring on white gold which I had seen on Mrs Goodyear's finger when I saw her last.

"From one of those burglaries I think there was a diamond ring with white gold wasn't there, a small one?"

"Yes," said Ken, "but how did you know that? It's not on the list of property the police showed to me."

"No, it came to light afterwards and wasn't processed in time for the court proceedings, although I suppose they'll amend the charge when you get to court."

"Well that explains it," said Ken.

"What do you mean?"

"Well, he was very careful was Alan. He's obviously let her wear that because he thinks they haven't realised it was pinched."

I was confused again.

"But at no time did you ever discuss it with Mrs Goodyear?"

"Well...no."

"Well if she knew all about it, how come you never talked about it to her?"

"Because Alan told me not to. He's very devious you know and violent and I didn't want to get on the wrong side of him. One word from him and I was out."

"Well what's all this about the theological college?" I asked knowing the answer.

"Oh he went there all right but he didn't stick it. He used to set off every morning as though he was going but he never went. He was usually out and about. He had a friend and he had a workshop. They used to melt down the gear and take the stones out. His friend was a bit of a jeweller and he knew how to carry on. They used to make their own rings and flog them on the black market like."

"And who's this so-called friend? No, don't bother, I don't want to know," I said dismissively. "If he looked as though he was going to college, surely that must have been for Mrs Goodyear's benefit?"

"I suppose it was but she must have been suspicious because he never brought any work home or anything like that."

"Perhaps she was just trusting?"

Ken laughed sarcastically.

"Can you tell me then where they are?"

"How the bloody hell would I know."

"What do you think I'm asking you for?" I said angrily.

Ken bowed his head apologetically.

"Well, when the going got a bit too hot for them they buggered off."

"But Mrs Goodyear was going to visit her daughter in Spain."

"I dare say she has. You see the daughter and Alan never got on. I think they were stepbrother and sister to be honest but I don't know much about it, except that Sophie didn't like Alan and the feeling was mutual. I think that's why she went abroad."

"What does she do?"

"I'm not really sure. All I know is that when Mrs Goodyear got divorced Alan went with her and Sophie went with her dad. He's some big-time businessman in Spain. Funnily enough he imports and exports jewelry. That's where Alan got his knowledge. Anyway, why are you asking me these questions? What's it got to do with my court case?"

"I'm just interested, that's all. You see, if you're blaming Mrs Goodyear that puts me in a difficult position because she's also a client of mine and this creates a conflict. We are not allowed to act for you in those circumstances. I'm trying to work out whether you should be represented by somebody else."

"Well maybe I should. If you are for her, you can't be for me."

"Exactly. That's why I'm asking you these questions."

Once more Ken's tone had altered and he had become his usual ignorant self.

"I think it probably would be best Ken if you did see another solicitor."

"Hang on, don't be hasty, where does that leave me? I'm not going to court on my own. I want bail."

"Of course you do," I said, "there are very, very few who want locking up."

"Yea, but I don't deserve that, I've been used."

I felt the compulsion to tell him that the victims of his crimes may have a different view but I didn't bother, it would have been a waste of breath.

"I'll see who the duty solicitor is and he will be able to take over the case from me."

"Well thanks for nothing," said Ken offensively.

I disregarded his comment.

"Oh, there is one thing I'd like to know."

"What's that," asked Ken.

"You really don't know where she's gone?"

"No, I don't. I don't know where Alan is either but I doubt if he's gone to Spain, he wouldn't be welcome there. There was some trouble between the kids when they were younger but I don't know what it was."

"Oh, finally," I said as I turned to leave, "Mrs Goodyear was going to buy one of the flats in the sheltered housing complex. Did you know anything about that?"

"No, she never told me about her personal business. She played her cards close to her chest she did."

"Was Mrs Goodyear frightened of Alan?"

"What's with all the questions? You're not representing me, why should I bother telling you?"

"Because your new solicitor will want as much information as he can get so that he can apply for bail for you. I would think it's in your interests that all the information that can be given is handed over and I wouldn't want to forget anything would I?"

I realised I'd overstepped the mark but Ken was making me rather angry and the truth of the matter was that I just wanted to know.

Ken was sorry once again as he realised what I was saying.

"I'm sorry but it's not you that's locked up."

"I'm sorry too but it's not me that did the burglaries," I replied sharply.

"Fair play," said Ken. "Look, all I can tell you is that I never talked about it in Mrs Goodyear's presence. I always thought she knew but I can't say for definite. I think it's a bit funny that she should disappear though, don't you?"

"Yes, I do Ken, I think it's very odd."

"Well, there you are then."

"And she's not here to help me with bail now."

"But you didn't turn up Ken. You knew you were on bail so why didn't you show?"

"Because they'd gone. I went to the house and it were empty, they'd disappeared. I thought she was just flitting to the hotel but when I went there looking for them they'd gone and left no forwarding address."

"Yes, I'm aware of that," I said nodding thoughtfully.

"So I thought if she doesn't turn up and she's my surety, I'd be turning up at court and getting locked up."

"Well, that's not actually right."

"Well that's what I thought. That's the only reason I didn't go."

"Well you'll be able to tell that to your new solicitor. I'll give him what information I can."

"And you'll not drop me in it?"

"Don't be stupid," I replied, "I'll tell him what I know and give him all your information, then it's up to the court. If I might say so, I think you want to alter your attitude as you don't engender much confidence. If you want people to help you, you've got to stop being so objectionable."

I realised that berating Ken in that way was probably pointless so I curtailed my advice.

"Well, best of luck Ken," I said and turned to leave.

"Mr Smith?"

"Yes."

"Do you think I'll get bail?"

"Your problem is that you've committed an offence on bail and you failed to turn up last time. To be frank with you Ken, I think you will be locked up."

"That's what I thought," he said, "but at least thank you for being straight with me."

I just nodded and closed the cell door as I left. It was not a satisfactory state of affairs. I had so many unanswered questions, the main one being did Mrs Goodyear know or not and why was she wearing a ring which had come from the burglary? Perhaps more importantly, where the hell was she? She had vanished without trace and no one had any information as to where she had gone.

I wondered if she knew that Alan had finished at the college. Could he be the villain of the piece, using that poor old lady as an unwitting dupe or was she a guilty party? And why did the policeman call him the 'so-called vicar? How did he know of him?

I always prefer cases with a happy ending, or if that cannot be achieved, an ending at least. This case had neither and it was to haunt me for a long time.

Three months later Ken appeared before the crown court at Sheffield. His mitigation was that he had been the instrument of one or more persons who had used him for their own ends. In sentencing him, the judge said that it had been advanced on his behalf that there were others who had manipulated him and benefited as a result of the crime. He said that he found no evidence to support that proposition and ordered him to serve two years imprisonment. I never saw him again.

Chapter 19

CHRISTMAS WITHOUT MADGE
AND ALBERT'S PRESENT

The following morning I was in the Magistrates' Court representing a variety of ne'er-do-wells when the magistrates came into court. Fate decreed that it was inevitable that the chairman that day was none other than the Lord Chief who stared at me quite fiercely, as though I was responsible for the previous day's wrong doing. I just bowed respectfully, rather like the Japanese do when they meet someone for the first time.

The day's proceedings were a non-event and I trudged back to the office only to be greeted by a flurry of flakes of snow. I hate snow, especially if I have to drive in it, even at Christmas. The Christmas carols were playing over the tannoy system at the church and I became pre-occupied with feeling of déjà vu.

It would be Jack and Albert's first Christmas without Madge. They were going to feel it quite badly, no matter how they tried to put on a brave face.

It would be Batsoid and Dingleberry's first Christmas in their new home in Derbyshire.

I had met a lot of new characters during the year, some good some bad but whatever their disposition they were going to feature regularly in my working life to come.

There always seemed to be something about Christmas and the end of the year and for me it was always a time of mature reflection, bringing with it its own melancholy. Each year since we'd been in practice as Wilford Smith & Co, I thought back to the events of the previous months and wondered if I could have done things better if I'd tried harder and it always seemed to me to be a rather fragile balance between success and failure. It was one of the perils of being self-employed and whilst there was probably no real need to worry, I always wondered where my next case was coming from.

Wilf Steer QC once told me that you are only as good as your last case and a few bad results in a row would look as though you were past your "sell-by date", so I always had those points in mind. Perhaps if I had relaxed a little more and not taken things quite so seriously it would have been better but then that form of insecurity always seemed to bring out the best in me, such as it was.

I had begun to note a considerable change in the way that we dealt with things. Attendances at the police station became more regular as the criminal fraternity became more aware of their rights and not only that, before the no smoking policy came in, it always meant that they'd got someone who might bring them a cigarette. I continued to get some of the most amazing requests from the people in custody at police stations, usually in the middle of the night. One defendant asked me for "the usual", namely a packet of cigarettes but I have been asked for other things such as sandwiches, pork pies, eye drops and even elastic stockings. I remember that Albert once asked for a dictionary, although quite what he wanted that for I've no idea.

The most unusual request I had was for a boomerang, which I wasn't able to fulfil, despite the possibility of getting it back but when I asked for an explanation I was told by the prisoner that his mother, who had died two years before, was Australian so he thought having some artifact from the outback might bring him closer to her!

I packed my briefcase with a number of files, which I was going to forget to look at over the Christmas holiday and sat back in my armchair in reflection. It was the time when Albert usually descended upon me, if not in person then on the telephone, explaining his problem but the office was empty and all the work and effort which had gone in the previous week's trimming up seemed to have been a waste of time, for no one would see it over the holiday period and that would be it until next year.

"But you like Christmas," I told myself, "you like trimming up and it makes the time in the office building up to Christmas that much more pleasant."

Once again I reassured myself that Christmas was one of the best times of the year and we'd managed to get through to yet another year with my health reasonably intact and with just enough money to pay all the wages and bills. It's true the bank was getting a little hot under the collar about the overdraft but that was a problem for the future, so it could have been much worse. I could have been poor old Eddie at the hospital or even Dingleberry with her stroke. I'd started to get into the age bracket where people close to me were getting near to the drawing up of their stumps, whereas some of them didn't even manage a full innings.

In the quietness of the reception area I thought back to my days in hospital, which had taught me that I should value each day that I had on earth more than I had hitherto. The net result, of course, was that in reality I would do no such thing and by the Monday I would be back at work and in the old routine.

I thought about those who had passed away, not least of whom was Madge, the wife of Jack Heptonstall my favourite client; mother of Albert and the rest of her brood. Her death had left a lasting impression upon them all, particularly Albert, who had kept remarkably clear of offending, apart from a bit of driving whilst disqualified. The influence of Caroline, his sometime girlfriend and the daughter of a Chief Inspector of Police, also played its part. It was an odd relationship, which seemed to have ended when Caroline went to university but she was highly supportive and once a month they would meet at the animal sanctuary and go out together on her visits home. Albert didn't visit Caroline's house because he thought his criminal record would compromise Caroline and her father. I had a sneaking regard for him for that because he thought the world of Caroline and despite no shortage of offers, she refused to see anybody else. I knew he would be at his mother's graveside on Christmas Day and quite frankly I wouldn't have expected anything less.

I switched off the light and as always at these times, the sound of carols coming from the church rang around the crisp night air as I walked to the bus station. I'd been out during the afternoon with Wilf and the gang and knowing we would enter into the spirit of the occasion, I left my car at home.

As I walked through town I was looking in Thorntons chocolate shop when there was a tap on my shoulder.

"Now then, what tha doin' 'ere. Tha should be at 'ome."

Another voice joined in.

"Tha's under arrest for impar...imperc...imprec...for... pretending to be a solicitor."

I recognised the voices and when I turned round I saw Jack and Albert, burdened with plastic bags and boxes of all shapes and sizes. Albert had a large bouquet of flowers with a card dangling from the top corner.

"Now then lads, what are you up to?"

"We've just bin gettin' a few things and me and our Albert was goin' up to your office, cos we've got summit fer thee."

"Something for me?" I said expectantly.

"Ah, tha's alreight with us, tha's gilt-edged, so we've got thee summit for Christmas."

He handed me a beautifully wrapped item with Thorntons chocolate box wrapping paper around it, neatly tied up with Christmas ribbon.

"Ey lads, this is fantastic," I said. "I didn't expect anything; you shouldn't have spent your money."

"Ay, I knew we shouldn't," said Jack, "but there it is, we thought you'd like it, which just goes to show we think about thee tha knows."

I was moved by their kindness and generosity.

"Unfortunately I haven't got you anything," I said reluctantly.

"It dunt matter 'bout that," said Albert, "we dunt expect nowt. Tha's good enough to us as it is."

I couldn't help noticing the large bouquet of flowers and Jack saw me trying to read the card.

"They're for our Madge," said Jack quietly, the usual grin absent from his face. "She loved flowers did Madge...only problem was she never got any...it's a bit late now to make it up but it's all I can do," he said thoughtfully.

"It's a fabulous bouquet. It must have cost a fortune."

"Argh, I suppose it did," said Jack.

"My goodness, if she could only see that now, she'd be so thrilled," I responded, missing the point.

"Ay she would that," said Jack, "but maybe she can see it, wherever she is, yer never know do yer?"

"No you don't Jack, that's true. Maybe she's looking down on all of us."

"I 'ope she weren't looking down last night," said Albert.

"Why was that?" I asked, "but never mind...don't tell me...I don't want to know."

We laughed and shook hands.

"I hope we'll see you after Christmas Jack," I said. "You'll have to come down and I'll show you around the new office." I thought it was the least I could do as his family's activities were helping to pay for it!

"Ey, we'll do that," said Jack, "and we'll take thee out fer a drink for Christmas."

"That's great, I'll look forward to seeing you then."

We shook hands again and off they went. For all their faults Jack thought the world of his family, especially Madge his deceased wife.

I continued on my way and passed DC Chapman, a CID officer who I knew quite well. He was speaking on his mobile radio and I just caught the end of his conversation.

"...message received, I'll go up to the Council offices straightaway."

"I was just on my way home," said DC Chapman reluctantly, "when I got this bloody call. We've no bobbies available so I've got to go on it."

"Something serious?" I asked.

"No, not really," said the bobby. "Some bugger's been into the foyer of the Town Hall and nicked a big bouquet of flowers which was presented to the Lady Mayoress. Who'd want to do that at Christmas," said the officer.

"I couldn't imagine," I replied. "Anyway, all the best for Christmas."

I nodded comtemplatively and continued to the bus station reflecting on what Madge would have thought with flowers across her grave with a greeting card saying "Merry Christmas to the Lady Mayoress". Surely they hadn't taken it? But then they had walked from the direction of the Town Hall.

"Surely not," I said to myself, "they wouldn't have taken them, but then again...."

As I got to the bus station I was unfortunate enough to bump into a number of revellers, some of whom I'd acted for on previous occasions. In fairness, they were pleased to see me and were as courteous as they could be, bearing in mind that the majority of them were drunk. One was busy vomiting in the entrance of a hardware shop and I noticed another lad flat out, asleep on a bench and wearing a Father Christmas hat with a can of Special Brew lager by his side.

One young lad, who was a regular client, caught sight of me and appeared to want to wish me the compliments of the season. He stumbled towards me and shook my hand, making an announcement in what sounded like a Peruvian dialect. The closest I had heard to that sort of speech was in a film I saw about South America. Whatever he said I agreed with him, even though I might have been confirming that he was welcome to share my Christmas dinner or I had agreed to marry his father.

"What do...doo...yu...yer...yoo...yooo...what do yooo want for...Christmas...then?" he said.

The only thing I could think of was, "I'll have a pint of what you've had."

He offered me a drink from his can of Special Brew, which I politely declined, shook hands with him again, returned to him a plastic bag of kippers he'd handed to me earlier and walked to the bus stop for the six o'clock bus to Barnsley.

A rather large lady was standing behind me in the queue, carrying about seventeen plastic bags. She was having difficulty breathing and kept saying,

"Oh dear…never again…oh dear."

I turned and we made eye contact.

"All this bloody fuss," she said complaining.

I just nodded and smiled.

"'old me this bag love, will yer?" she said, handing me a large plastic bag full of what looked like potatoes with a dead rabbit on top.

"Thanks love, you're a gentleman."

I nodded and smiled again, saying that it was a pleasure to help a lady in distress. It was not a smart move because she responded to my courtesy by passing me another bag, full of tins of various cold meats and before I knew it I was carrying all the bags, including one which had an extremely large brassiere, which had come out of its packaging, draped across the top. She saw me looking and immediately pressed it inside. She was laughing when she said, "Keep yer eyes off that, I'll be wearing that bugger tonight."

I smiled and nodded again reassuringly.

"We always go to Elsecar Workingmens' on Christmas Eve," she said taking a packet of Park Drive cigarettes out of her pocket. She coughed repeatedly before she lit it, so I didn't quite know what to expect once it was smoking. She took an enormous gulp of smoke and I watched the cigarette burn down to half its length as she did it. She blew the smoke into my face and of course I was unable to wave it away because I was carrying all her bags.

"Bloody 'ell," she said whilst attempting to pull up her underclothes through the confines of her dress. "Meks yer sweat carryin' all these bags dun't it?"

"Well it's certainly making me sweat holding them," I said sarcastically.

"Ay, tha'll be alreight, tha's a big strapping lad."

Big strapping lad or not, I had all her bags plus my briefcase and quite frankly I didn't want to be a porter on Christmas Eve night.

She went on at great length about her medical history without hesitation, telling me how only the day before she had to endure an endoscopy as the hospital tried to resolve her various medical problems.

"'ave you ever 'ad one of them?" she asked.

"No, I've had the other version, I've had the gastroscopy but I've never had...."

"Not the one up the jacksey then?"

"No, not the one up the jacksey as you put it," I said reluctantly.

"You've never lived," she said shaking her head from side to side.

The bus arrived and we started to walk towards it. I offered her the bags back but she declined, saying,

"No, yer alright with them love, you've dun wonderful."

I struggled onto the bus with all the bags and offered to put them in the luggage rack.

"No don't put 'em in there love, somebody'll 'ave 'em away, they'll nick 'em."

I couldn't imagine anyone big enough to steal and wear her bra but nevertheless I carried the bags down the aisle.

"Where are you sitting love," I asked.

"Anywhere tha likes," she said intent on continuing her conversation.

I moved into a seat nearest the window and to my surprise she sat down beside me, crushing me against the side of the bus. She passed me her cigarette end and asked me to put it into the ashtray, which she couldn't reach and I reluctantly did so. I had all the bags on my knees in pyramid fashion but couldn't manage my briefcase, so she just put it on the floor in the aisle.

"Where are you getting' off love?" she asked me.

"Birdwell," I replied.

"Oh that'll be alright," she said, "I get off just before you at Elsecar."

She treated me to the rest of her history of ailments and after what seemed an eternity, we finally arrived at her stop.

"Anyway," she said, "I'm getting' off 'ere. Do yer want to just carry my bags down?"

It was the least I could do and to be frank I was so delighted to see the back of her, I walked down the aisle with her bags to ensure that she got off. She had a short conversation with the bus driver, explaining that I was her "mate" who had come to help her with her bags and then she stepped onto the causeway. I passed the bags to her individually, dropping the bra out of the first bag onto the floor of the bus. I rammed the item into my pocket to conceal my embarrassment until I had passed each bag, one of which split, spilling its contents onto the floor. The driver handed me a bag from his pocket and we collected the various provisions from the floor.

"It's a shame you're not getting´ off ´ere," she said, distracting my attention.

"Ay, isn't it," I replied.

Her conversation was still going on when the automatic door closed. I returned to my seat and within a quarter of an hour had reached my stop. I left the bus to a round of applause from the appreciative audience.

When I arrived home I emptied my pockets as a matter of course so that I didn't lose such things as car keys etc, only to find that in my right-hand pocket was the largest brassiere I had ever seen. My family looked at me expecting a comment but there was simply nothing I could say.

The following morning I was woken by my daughter who had jumped onto our bed with all the ease and grace of a professional wrestler, shouting "he's been!"

"He's been where?" I asked sarcastically.

"He's been here," she said, confused by my sarcasm as she thrust her Christmas present under my nose.

All I could think of was the prospect of a glass of cold water with an Alka Seltzer in it.

"Open it!" she demanded, thrusting the beautifully wrapped present further towards my nose. I entered into the spirit of the occasion and opened it. It was a beautiful silk tie with an equally beautiful and matching silk handkerchief.

I opened the rest of my gifts, which included a gravel tray for the bottom of a budgerigar's cage, which had been wrapped in newspaper. Despite the embargo placed on Page's presence in my household, somehow he had managed to infiltrate our family unit and leave me an unwanted present.

Rebecca opened her presents and eventually retired to her own room to study her booty more intently, whilst I opened my last package; a beautifully wrapped item, tied neatly with Christmas ribbon. A little card was draped by the side of it which read, 'To Steve. Madge would want you to ´av this.'

I opened the box and looked inside and if I told you what it was, you'd never believe it...

In fact I will tell you...it was the most unusual medallion I'd ever seen, based on the cross of the Knights of St John, highly ornate decorated with a filigree surround. It was attached to a very ornate but beautiful 22-carat gold chain. Apparently it was given to Madge's grandmother by a Maltese gypsy and this time it was the truth. I had admired it on many occasions when Madge had worn it and Jack and Albert had remembered.

I had a lump in my throat and even the most forceful cough couldn't move it.

I've kept the medallion ever since and when I am asked about it I say it was a present from a very special friend...perfectly legit...

THE END

(but never say never...)

Neville-Douglas Publishing Ltd

present

Boozers
Ballcocks
&
Bail

by
Stephen D Smith

Boozers Ballcocks & Bail is a no-holds-barred account of the life of a thriving criminal law practice in an industrial northern town in the early eighties. It opens the door on the law in a totally honest and compelling way, giving an insight into the sometimes tragic, but often hilarious world of law courts, prison cells and solicitors' offices.

   "....Laugh out loud material," – BBC
   "....Steve Smith is the legal James Herriot," – Yorkshire Post

Pages: 256 Size: 216x138 ISBN: 1-871647-33-9
Price: £8.99 including postage & packing from:

Neville-Douglas Publishing Ltd
Clumber Lodge, Hemingfield Road,
Wombwell, Barnsley, Yorkshire S73 OLY
Tel: 01226 753324 Fax: 01226 758462

Neville-Douglas Publishing Ltd

present

Plonkers
Plaintiffs
&
Pleas

by
Stephen D Smith

Plonkers Plaintiffs & Pleas is the sequel to the hilarious Boozers Ballcocks & Bail which was the first book in the comedy series relating what it is really like behind the closed doors of the legal profession. **Plonkers Plaintiffs & Pleas** continues the story with page after page of laugh out loud material.

"…Brilliantly funny book." – Charlie Williams
"…A hilarious book." – Yorkshire Television

Pages: 256 Size: 216x135 ISBN: 1-901853-10-1
Price: £8.99 including postage & packing from:

Neville-Douglas Publishing Ltd
Clumber Lodge, Hemingfield Road,
Wombwell, Barnsley, Yorkshire S73 OLY
Tel: 01226 753324 Fax: 01226 758462

Neville-Douglas Publishing Ltd

present

Junkies
Judges
&
Jail

by
Stephen D Smith

The third in the comedy series sees a return to the brilliant characters and situations that befall them in another riotous comedy in the writer's definitive style.

"...Steve Smith is the legal James Herriot." – Yorkshire Post
"...Humour dances through his books." – Charlie Williams

Pages: 296 Size: 216x135 ISBN: 1-901853-07-1
Price: £8.99 including postage & packing from:

Neville-Douglas Publishing Ltd
Clumber Lodge, Hemingfield Road,
Wombwell, Barnsley, Yorkshire S73 OLY
Tel: 01226 753324 Fax: 01226 758462

Neville-Douglas Publishing Ltd

present

Hell is Not for Angels

by
Stephen D Smith

Subject of two BBC Rough Justice Programmes
On 13 July 1990 John Megson was convicted of murder at Leeds Crown Court. The Judge gave him the mandatory life sentence and recommended that he serve no less than 15 years! John Megson was an innocent man and it was to take five years for justice to be done.

In April 1989, a camper was fatally stabbed after upsetting members of Megson's motorcycle gang, the Druids. Megson alone was convicted of the killing and because he refused to break the bikers' code of silence he went to prison for a crime he did not commit. For two years John's father tried to persuade him to name the real killer. He knew his son was innocent. He then contacted Steve Smith.

A single meeting with John in Wakefield Prison convinced a solicitor with 26 years in the legal profession that an innocent man was serving a life sentence for a murder he had not committed. He realised that "I was stuck with John Megson and he with me whether we liked it or not."

Pages: 264 Size: 216x138 ISBN: 1-901853-00-4
Price: £8.99 including postage & packing from:

Neville-Douglas Publishing Ltd
Clumber Lodge, Hemingfield Road,
Wombwell, Barnsley, Yorkshire S73 OLY
Tel: 01226 753324 Fax: 01226 758462

Neville-Douglas Publishing Ltd

present

Shoebox to Silver Shoes

by
Stephen D Smith

The remarkable story of Trisha, the Medium, telling of her life from the moment she was left as a new-born baby in a shoebox on convent steps, to her adoption into a Chinese family.

Following her adoptive father's tragic death she ended up as a child prostitute on the streets of Kowloon, but then she was visited by spirit and her enlightenment began.

The story follows her life from an involvement in murder to her return to England and eventually, the ability to speak with the dead.

Pages: 192 Size: 216x135 ISBN: 1 902853 51 9
Price: £8.99 including postage & packing from:

Neville-Douglas Publishing Ltd
Clumber Lodge, Hemingfield Road,
Wombwell, Barnsley, Yorkshire S73 OLY
Tel: 01226 753324 Fax: 01226 758462